Praise for *Content Nation*

"Today, most everybody lives in content nation. If you're under 25 or so, you're a native—born into the digital world. The rest of us who have immigrated are lucky to have John Blossom to dissect and explain the wide-reaching ramifications that citizenship entails—how business, education, relationships, information dissemination, and much more are affected. *Content Nation* is a must-read if you want to understand what it means to live online today and how you will be interacting in years to come."

> —David Meerman Scott, bestselling author of *The New Rules of Marketing & PR* and *World Wide Rave*

"If you are into new media, publishing and the Internet this is a book you simply must read. *Content Nation* is not only a great map to the new emerging online publishing territory but also a high-precision scanning electron microscope into the different dimensions that the new global media conversation is bringing about. Internet publishing and social media are changing forever they way we interact, exchange, work together and communicate. John Blossom, reveals the key patterns, strategies, and trends that normal people like you are using to make leap from a spectator seat right into the director's chair. And this is the enthusiastic message John Blossom spreads so pervasively inside *Content Nation:* Become your own media, engage, share, participate, make your voice be heard!"

> —Robin Good, social media pioneer and editor of *Robin Good's MasterNewMedia*

"It's hard to imagine a book that makes a broader and deeper examination of social media than *Content Nation*—or that gives more useful advice."

> —David "Doc" Searles, co-author of *The Cluetrain Manifesto*

Content
Nation

Content Nation

Surviving and Thriving as Social Media Changes Our Work, Our Lives, and Our Future

John Blossom

WILEY

Wiley Publishing, Inc.

Content Nation

Published by
Wiley Publishing, Inc.
10475 Crosspoint Boulevard
Indianapolis, IN 46256
www.wiley.com

Copyright © 2009 by Wiley Publishing, Inc., Indianapolis, Indiana

ISBN: 978-0-470-37921-9

Manufactured in the United States of America

10 9 8 7 6 5 4 3 2 1

Library of Congress Cataloging-in-Publication Data is available from the publisher.

This book is dedicated to you, the citizens of Content Nation, who are creating a better world through your courageous publishing.

I also dedicate this book to David Rivers, former editorial director at Risk Waters Group, who passed away with so many others at the World Trade Center on September 11, 2001. David was a great husband, a great father, a great colleague, and a great friend. We still miss you, David.

About the Author

John Blossom is one of the most widely recognized content-industry analysts, providing thought leadership to executives in search of new approaches to rapidly changing markets for publishing and technology products and services. Mr. Blossom founded Shore Communications, Inc. in 1997, specializing in research and advisory services and strategic marketing consulting for publishers and content service providers in enterprise and media markets. Mr. Blossom's engagements as president of Shore have included strategic marketing consulting for major corporations and startups as well as speaking engagements at major conferences and advisory services for senior industry executives.

Mr. Blossom's career spans more than 20 years of marketing, research, product management, and development in advanced information and media venues, including the researching, marketing, and development of financial information services at global financial publishers and financial services companies (Citicorp; Quotron; Reuters Group PLC, now a division of Thomson Reuters; and Waters Information Services), serving as a vice president and publishing-industry analyst at Outsell, Inc. and with earlier experience in broadcast media, human factors engineering, corporate training, and teaching. Mr. Blossom's ContentBlogger weblog won the Software and Information Industry Association 2007 CODiE award for Best Media Blog.

Mr. Blossom has been interviewed frequently by the business press and has been quoted in many major news and trade publications and media outlets, including *The Wall Street Journal*, *USA Today*, Marketplace radio, ABC Radio National, *CEO Magazine*, Information Today, *EContent Magazine*, *Upgrade Magazine*, BusinessNow television, *Wall Street & Technology*, *Waters Magazine*, and *Securities Industry News*. He speaks regularly at major industry conferences, including BookExpo, the SLA Annual Conference, SIIA Information Industry Summit, Buying and Selling eContent, InfoCommerce Annual Conference, the OCLC Symposium, and other venues.

Mr. Blossom has resided in Westport, Connecticut for more than 17 years.

Credits

Executive Editor
Carol Long

Development Editor
Christopher J. Rivera

Production Editor
Liz Britten

Copy Editor
Kim Cofer

Editorial Manager
Mary Beth Wakefield

Production Manager
Tim Tate

**Vice President and Executive
Group Publisher**
Richard Swadley

Project Coordinator, Cover
Lynsey Stanford

Compositor
Maureen Forys,
Happenstance Type-O-Rama

Proofreader
Heather Dweller

Indexer
Jack Lewis

Acknowledgments

First and foremost I want to thank my wife, Dr. June-Ann Greeley, PhD., an accomplished medieval scholar and an associate professor of religious studies at Sacred Heart University who has shown so much loving patience with her 21st-century husband's interests. I am very proud of her abilities and, through her insights, have come to appreciate deeply how much human values are a constant through the centuries. This book would not have been possible without our many years of sharing our views of the world with one another. In relation to Content Nation, I also want to thank June-Ann for introducing me to a pile of books many Christmas holidays ago that included *The Cluetrain Manifesto*, a book by Chris Locke, Doc Searls, and David Weinberger whose insights were life-changing for me in 2000 and which are still altogether profound today. When I said as much to David Weinberger many years later, I don't think that he got the life-changing part of that equation, but I am sure that he has heard it many times from other people of a more youthful bent. My thanks also go to our wonderful son Christopher, who has shown patience with his father's pursuits and who is now learning to blog himself.

I offer special thanks to my parents, Jill and John K. Blossom, who have demonstrated their own loving patience with their still-growing son through the years and who enabled me in my early years to explore the world and to allow me to explore my sometimes eclectic interests with remarkable patience. My father's knowledge of the English language always challenged me to excel that one step further in my own writing efforts. My father's father, John E. Blossom, was a contributing author to textbooks whose royalties helped put me through college and upon whose typewriter I wrote my college and postgraduate papers. His memory and his inspiration will be special to me always as an author and as a grandson. Thanks also to my wife June-Ann's parents, Fred and Mary Greeley, who have encouraged June-Ann and me as a couple and as parents through the years.

I must also thank the people who have been a part of my company Shore Communications Inc., which has provided consulting and research services to publishers and content-technology companies for many years. To the many people who have served as team members at Shore and for all of our customers who we have helped through the years, my deep thanks for being the springboard for this effort at creating new forms of valuable communication.

David Meerman Scott has been a friend of mine for many years and his guidance and mentorship have been a key component in my professional success. Thanks very much, David, and thanks for convincing me that I should have the courage to take on this project and for offering me such valuable insights and encouragement along the way.

My thanks also to the people at the Software and Information Industry Association and American Business Media, as well as Information Today, Inc., organizations that have introduced me to so many fine colleagues who have contributed to my insights into the content industry and who have helped to foster my career.

Thanks also to Robin Good (also known as Luigi Canali DeRossi), the founder and editor of Robin Good, whose personal and professional support have been an essential part of my outlook and whose global outlook on social media is truly inspiring.

Finally, on a personal and collegial level, my thanks to Reid Conrad of Near-Time, Inc., whose technology, insights, and support inspired me to move forward with this project. My hat's off to all of you, and to everyone else in Content Nation who is working to make the world an exciting place to live in through the fostering of social media.

There are some people who responded to my call for Content Nation contributions, and I wanted to thank them here for their willingness to be a citizen of Content Nation as it has come to life:

- Peter Bihr, online media strategist
- Barry Graubart, vice president, product strategy & business development for Alacra, Inc.
- Michael Levy, a product marketing manager for onesource
- Rand Schulman, chief marketing officer, insideview, inc.

Contents

Preamble:
Chasing the Mammoth

It is 11,000 years ago in central France. At the edge of a grassland stands a small band of humans, clad in skins and holding spears and equipment for camping and cooking. The glaciers of the last great ice age have retreated far to the north, leaving behind a new landscape of plants and animals. Our hardy band of human ancestors are on the hunt, but the abundance of large game such as mammoths, which their own ancestors had been chasing through the ice age for their meals, has given way to a mix of bison, elks, and plants with grains that are becoming the diet of these nomads. They are beginning to favor new techniques and tools for hunting and gathering to adapt to this environment—including the creation of more permanent camps to take advantage of more reliable food sources. If we were to check back with the great-great grandchildren of this tribe, we'd probably see that their nomadic ways had started to give way to small village-like settlements with some permanent structures to store grains and a new concept that was evolving along with those structures—ownership of places and things.

Most anthropologists date the origins of modern human history from such small village encampments that gave rise to ownership societies, societies that gave rise to another new concept—economies. With ownership came the growth of trading goods created through specialized skills, skills that would have been less able to create a sustainable lifestyle in nomadic societies. Construction, woven clothing, jewelry, decorations, and crafts began to become the focus of human activities as agriculture and more convenient sources of meat simplified the basics of survival. Recently, in Syria, a dwelling from 10,000 years ago was unearthed that had walls decorated with colorful and remarkably modern-looking patterns. It didn't take long for people to begin to think creatively about how to add value to their personal living environments once food on the table was more assured.

The concepts of a trade-oriented ownership economy and of adding value to one's personal environment eventually formed the cornerstone of the media industry. Ownership of hand-crafted, inscribed monuments, scrolls, and eventually books became a mark of distinction for the rich and powerful, spawning new industries of craftsmanship and distribution. From the days of the Roman Empire, rich people would have their slaves record events happening in the Forum in Rome to be delivered to their villas in the neighboring hillsides. The first news services, then, were privately owned. With the rise of a merchant middle class and printing-press technologies, ownership of publishing and publications began to benefit great numbers of people, along with other mass-produced goods. Electronic communications via the media of radio, television, and eventually today's Internet also have had growth predicated on a collaboration between high technology owned by content producers, and mass-produced goods owned by content consumers. Media has thrived on ownership, and ownership in turn has used media to promote its growth.

Now, new trends are emerging that are threatening the fundamental premises that underpin society's ability to deliver on previous expectations for ownership. One of the strangest and most fundamental things that's changing is as basic as what is happening outside my home office window every day. It's now November in a Connecticut town outside of New York City, and it's been a downright balmy autumn. Again. Birds that are still in our backyard this time of year used to be native mostly to states hundreds of miles to the south only a couple of decades ago. Elsewhere, record droughts and fires are straining the resources of the western United States while record floods are challenging European cities. Polar ice caps are receding to the point of endangering both animals and native tribes that have relied on their presence for thousands of years. The earth is in a period of major climate change, as major as the changes faced by our roaming band of nomads in a French field 11,000 years ago. Like our ancient friends in that scene, we're just trying to do the best that we can to get from one day to another.

Also, like those nomads who had been chasing the mammoth and having to try something new to get by, getting life to work on a day-to-day basis today, in an environment being shaped by rapid changes, means recognizing that the changes that we're experiencing don't relate in scale very effectively to things that our grandparents or even their grandparents ever experienced. Strangely, though, today's human society seems to be pushing in the opposite direction from that prehistoric society's evolution—away from a sedentary life and toward a much more mobile human society that needs to look at opportunities on the run. Ironically, then, in an era of global climate change we seem to be pushing toward a society that in some ways may resemble those people who were chasing the mammoth at the end of the last great climate change—except that we're more likely moving toward a nomadic existence rather than further away from it. This movement, in turn, challenges the key component of our sedentary society's success—ownership.

The enormous scale of change in our increasingly mobile society is evident very noticeably in the publishing industry. As rapidly evolving electronic technologies such as search engines, mobile phones, weblogs, and wikis have entered the awareness of average people, we are witnessing a huge change in the climate for media production. Where ownership of publishing facilities and the technologies that delivered their output used to enable end-to-end ownership of both the medium and the message, now we are beginning to see that the value found in publishing content is moving away from these relatively fixed economies. Once-unassailable media conglomerates such as TimeWarner, NBC, and Pearson are giving way to publishers such as Google, Wikipedia, and Facebook that enable value from content to be assembled on the fly by both technology and highly collaborative peers. In the past the concept of publishing value could be measured in the "village storehouses" of office buildings in New York City's Rockefeller Center or the thickness of a glossy magazine on a newsstand. Today's content value is as ephemeral as the last edit on Wikipedia a few seconds ago, your last search on Google, or the last comment that you read on Digg or Newsvine. Its lasting value could be gone in about as much time as it takes an audience to consume it.

Already in publishing, then, we are well along the road to a new kind of "chasing the mammoth" nomadic publishing culture—and already we are seeing the impact of those changes on human society in ways that are as fundamental as was the shift from stone-age culture to modern civilization. This concept became clearer to me after I read the book *Wikinomics* by Don Tapscott and Anthony D. Williams. Don and I had both delivered speeches on a program about the future of publishing at the BookExpo USA conference a year before *Wikinomics* came out (I'd like to think that my presentation influenced Don's thinking as much as his book has influenced my current thinking!). *Wikinomics* chronicles how an increasingly collaborative global economy is creating value in business today.

At its furthest extension, though, I saw that the Wikinomics concept is really about returning human society to the pre-historic era of nomadic hunting tribes, which could shift their location and resources as needed to respond to rapidly changing environments without the need to have external hierarchies protecting land and other owned property through wars. Given the issues of our physical environment that are unfolding before our eyes, the timing of the development of Internet-based collaborative and peer-based publishing may turn out to be quite fortuitous. These social media tools now at our disposal may turn out to be as important to our future as the bow and arrow turned out to be to early humans shifting from mammoths to elks as prey. In our new world of social media we are surely chasing value in elusive contexts as our ancestors were chasing the mammoth through the frozen landscapes of the ice ages. This insight led to an important presentation that I delivered at the Buying and Selling eContent conference, entitled "Chasing the Mammoth: Redefining Publishing in a Social Media Ecology," in which I created the outline of how social media's rules for success were not unlike those of our ice-age ancestors' rules.

The world of today's businesses, governments, and other major institutions is certainly not ready, for the most part, to accept the depth of this kind of change in their own structures that's being fomented by social media. We're still in the era of publishers trying to turn the wild animals of content that we chase in the nomadic social media culture into the domesticated animals of an agricultural culture. This is an important goal for the here and now, but it is going to take more imagination than that to keep up with the rapid changes that social media is enabling—much as our change in global climate is going to catch many vested interests by surprise, including political, business, and personal interests. Every one and every thing and every way that we do things is going to change more radically than most can ever imagine, but what does this really mean? What are the real things that need to be done in the rapidly emerging world of nomadic value, and what will it wind up looking like in the end? Most importantly, what do you and I need to do to change in order to make the best of these changes?

In other words, in a world where everyone is a publisher, what does it take to be a productive and effective world citizen?

This question tied into an article on my Web site that I had written six months before *Wikinomics* came out, entitled "Content Nation: A World of Personal Publishers Declares Their Influential Citizenship." In this article I laid out the premise that the number of people who were really serious about publishing via social media had grown so quickly that if you added them up they would be one of the world's more sizable nations. Taken in the context of today's social media environment little more than a year later it's fair to say that this

Content Nation is well on its way to becoming a superpower. Its economic and political influence is becoming enormous and growing so rapidly that even the most starry-eyed entrepreneurs in California's Silicon Valley have a hard time wrapping their minds around the global scale of these changes. I could see that it would take more than just one clever fellow in Connecticut, or even a few smart people, to chronicle the importance of Content Nation and its implications for business, governments, and other key societal functions.

This realization led to the Web site ContentNation.com, on which this book has been developed—and will continue to be developed over time. I realized that the only way to develop a book on the topic of Content Nation properly would be to invite Content Nation to be a key contributor from "day one." The courage to do this came from another fellow who was on that trend-setting program at BookExpo—Chris Anderson, then the editor in chief of *Wired* magazine. Chris was in the process of introducing his book on the Long Tail, a concept that Chris had introduced in an article in *Wired* more than a year before that fateful presentation. Stacked before Chris were massive piles of the pre-release version of his business book, all part of the typical book-publishing publicizing event.

Good stuff, I thought, and it was a good book, but this process was ironic, to say the least: here was the author of the seminal book on how the Web is enabling producers to reach smaller audiences of targeted consumers more effectively, and more profitably, than those who focus on mass goods and experiences for mass audiences, and yet the crowning output was a book that was being rushed to market to take advantage of the latest trend while the publisher could afford to print it in volume. What if, instead, a book didn't start as a one-time volume publishing event but was something that became a publishing event of varying volume over time? What if books could adapt to the "chasing the mammoth" model and reap different kinds of rewards for different people at different times in the concept's lifecycle?

So ContentNation.com was established to start building a community for the Content Nation concept that can be used to create value for different people in different ways at different times. For those who visit ContentNation.com for the first time, it's for now an ad-supported Web site. For those who collaborate on the Web site, it's a social media community. For those who want to know the latest on these trends, it can be a news service. For those who want to keep abreast of how it all fits together, it's a subscription eBook with periodic updates that can be delivered either electronically or via print-on-demand services. For those who want to gather and discuss these concepts, it's an events community. For those who want to share with others the Content Nation insight and experience on a commemorative basis or to build relationships via gift-giving, it will be a traditional book offered by traditional publishers in their traditional editorial and production cycles.

In whatever of these forms and modes you're reading this, welcome to Content Nation. It's a privilege to be a part of a movement that is literally changing human existence beyond all imagining—and a privilege to be developing and sharing that experience with you, fellow citizens of Content Nation.

And now, on to the book!

1

Content Nation:
A World of Influential Publishers Declares its Citizenship

This is a story about you—one of billions of publishers in the world today.

> Sent an email lately?
> > You're a publisher.
> Posted a photo, a video, a comment, or a vote on a Web site?
> > You're a publisher.
> Keyed in a text message to friends on your cell phone?
> > You're a publisher.

If you use technology to create information and experiences that can be shared with others, you're a publisher.

Some of your personal activities may seem to be too small in scope to put under the banner of a word like "publishing." After all, not everything that we publish has a huge audience or seems to be very important, but if others find what you've published to be valuable, then you've achieved what every publisher in the world tries to achieve.

Publishing by individuals is nothing new, of course. Humans have been scratching down notes to one another on cave walls, scraps of broken pottery, paper, and many other types of media for thousands of years. With the advent of the Internet and other advanced communications networks, however, the scale of what one person can do with publishing tools has changed radically. Affordable computers, mobile phones, and many other types of devices connected to communications networks have enabled billions of people to share content with one another globally and locally as never before. Technology now allows any person on the planet to publish things to virtually any number of people in any place at any time at little or no personal cost—without them having to know in any great detail how it happens.

Worldwide publishing, once the pursuit of a handful of wealthy and powerful people, is now a tool in the hands of the world.

Most importantly, the everyday people who are using these tools are discovering what it's like to have an audience for their publishing. Writing an email to one or two friends or leaving a voicemail message is one thing: posting something on a Web site that can be viewed by millions of other people around the world or by anyone in your home town is quite another. When the audience talks back to you, it adds yet another new dimension to personal publishing. Students, farmers, business professionals, teachers, researchers, politicians, homemakers, and anyone else who can access our global communications networks are now engaging with other people who have similar interests and establishing appreciation for one another through their common publishing capabilities.

In the process of becoming publishers who can reach and interact with a potentially global audience whenever they need to or want to, something is changing in the way that everyday people look at themselves and their world. We are creating new and strengthened relationships and allegiances. We are beginning to look upon institutions that we used to rely on for providing us with cohesion and value in our lives as less valuable in the face of publishing technologies that allow us to organize ourselves and our lives more to our suiting. We are creating and participating in new markets for goods and services that do not require traditional suppliers and brokers. We are doing our jobs differently. We are living our lives differently.

As everyday people have been using today's ubiquitous publishing tools, many are looking upon their publishing not as an occasional activity but rather as an essential part of who they are. For these publishing enthusiasts their identity is changing; at first unconsciously, perhaps, but eventually in a conscious way. Their birth certificates haven't changed. Their passports haven't changed. Yet they are ready to change how they view themselves and participate in society as surely as people who have moved to a new country decide to become citizens of that nation when their need to be a part of its culture permanently becomes an overwhelming desire or necessity. There are now millions of people worldwide who are in effect ready to declare themselves citizens of a new global nation of people who have made influencing other people through their own publishing a central and permanent part of their culture and their lives.

You may be one of those people today. If so, I welcome you to Content Nation.

The Birth of Content Nation

I came up with the concept of Content Nation a few years ago, when the tools that enabled online global publishing for everyday people were just beginning to gain in popularity beyond a small pool of technology-oriented enthusiasts—people using weblogs, wikis, social bookmarking Web sites, and other new tools that enabled people to publish easily and conveniently. Content Nation was a useful handle to express that there was a large and significant movement of people using publishing tools to reach the world, but it was also a way to say that there was more than just scale at work: there was also a mindset. Some sports fans may talk about their allegiances to a baseball club, for example, and say that they're part of "Red Sox Nation." In doing so they acknowledge that they're part of something that's bigger than themselves and their own fandom. They're making a statement about their outlook on life, their commitments, their values. So it is with Content Nation. People involved with today's publishing tools seem to enjoy being a part of something that's about who they are and what they're a part of as much as what they do.

Key examples of the power of Content Nation were starting to surface fairly regularly even several years ago. One of the most prominent examples came out of nowhere from a teenager living in the suburbs of Montreal, Canada who became known as "Star Wars Kid." Ghyslain Raza was a high-school student in late 2002 when he decided to record some video footage of himself in his school's video laboratory, acting out some fight scenes from the movie *Star Wars* with an imaginary light saber. Little did he know that a few months later a couple of kids from his school would take his video and post it on Kazaa, an Internet file-sharing service. Within a couple of weeks Ghyslain's little private "shadow play" became an international Web hit as people shared his video with one another, wrote about it on weblogs, and created their own remixed videos of Ghyslain's antics. By mid-May of 2003, well over a million copies of the clip had been downloaded, interviews with Ghyslain had been published, and donations were solicited and sent to Ghyslain to compensate him for the trouble that his friends had brought him. By 19 May mainstream media outlets such as *The New York Times* and *Wired* magazine had started to pick up the scent, but by then the story was already old by the standards of the audience most involved in its unfolding. Today it's estimated that more than 15 million people have downloaded some version of Ghyslain's original video.

It was clear to me at the time that something fairly profound had happened with "Star Wars Kid." In a matter of a few days a worldwide publishing

sensation had been created, distributed, publicized, and monetized via donations with little or no help whatsoever from the world's established publishers. A social network of people who found it to be to their liking packaged it,
recommended it to their peers, amplified its value, and placed it in contexts
where others would find it to be similarly valuable—others who would in turn
continue to amplify its value again and again. These were people who were
publishing Ghyslain's original and remixed images very intentionally and bit
by bit they were creating a phenomenon with enormous impact with very little
effort by any individual.

There have been "sleeper" hits throughout the history of content publishing,
but nothing before had illustrated so graphically just how powerful independent publishing can be through Web-enabled channels. The ultimate content
itself was not terribly profound, but that fact in and of itself should indicate
the importance of this event: if millions of copies of something as simple as
Ghyslain's gyrations could make it around the world in record time to millions of people based on its passing amusement, what would be the impact of
something far more valuable that could be created, adopted, amplified, and
monetized by these networks?

The answers to this question are the foundation of Content Nation. Fun and
frivolous things being published by everyday people have impact, to be sure,
but some events that have surfaced prominently in popular culture have underscored that this new generation of publishing tools is enabling a growing array
of people to influence our work and our lives in a wide variety of ways.

The Kryptonite Evolution 2000 U-Lock was considered to be an excellent
product to keep your bicycle secure back in 2004 but in September of that year,
posts on Internet user forums and weblogs noted that it was amazingly easy to
open this particular lock with the tip of a simple ballpoint pen. A homemade
video demonstrating how to do this was posted on BikeForums.com and from
there it was picked up by the popular Engadget weblog. Within a few days
of the original video being posted it was known widely to people around the
world that this Kryptonite lock was not secure.

The company manufacturing Kryptonite locks was aware of the issue from
the original forum postings almost immediately, but it took them several days
to realize how quickly the awareness of the problem had spread from one person to another publishing the news on the Web and creating hyperlinks to the
emerging news stories from mainstream media outlets. What they had assumed
was an observation among a few bicycle enthusiasts on a fairly obscure user

forum had mushroomed into a major global business story. The result was a major and costly embarrassment to the company caused and severe damage to its reputation—and a radically heightened awareness among major corporations as to how broadly and rapidly the impact of Content Nation had grown.

In 2004, a major investigative news story on a U.S. presidential candidate from a widely respected television news source like *CBS News* was bound to be taken very seriously by the public and by other media outlets. When *CBS News*'s Dan Rather, a veteran reporter and news anchor with more than 30 years of experience, ran a story on candidate George W. Bush's military service record, Content Nation responded with a vengeance to question his authority.

The basis of Rather's claims of Bush's military records having been falsified to project a more favorable impression of his service was a memorandum produced by one of Bush's former commanding officers. The memorandum appeared to Rather's supporting staff to be very authentic, but within a few minutes of the report being broadcast on CBS Television outlets a forum posting on the FreeRepublic.com site had published a critique of several physical and stylistic details in the revealed memorandum that argued against its authenticity.

To: **Howlin**

Howlin, every single one of these memos to file is in a proportionally spaced font, probably Palatino or Times New Roman.

In 1972 people used typewriters for this sort of thing, and typewriters used monospaced fonts.

The use of proportionally spaced fonts did not come into common use for office memos until the introduction of laser printers, word processing software, and personal computers. They were not widespread until the mid to late 90's. Before then, you needed typesetting equipment, and that wasn't used for personal memos to file. Even the Wang systems that were dominant in the mid 80's used monospaced fonts.

I am saying these documents are forgeries, run through a copier for 15 generations to make them look old.

This should be pursued aggressively.

47 posted on **09/08/2004 8:59:43 PM PDT** by **Buckhead**
[**Post Reply** | **Private Reply** | **To 11** | **View Replies**]

Thousands of weblogs and millions of posted links, comments, and video remixes picked up on the initial posting and forced a reconsideration of the evidence by *CBS News*. Within a few weeks of the blog-driven controversy Dan Rather resigned in disgrace from *CBS News*. A pivotal media figure had been eliminated from a powerful position by the ability of Content Nation to create its own authority to match and to best the established media's authority.

If ever there were a figure in public life who was tightly monitored and managed by governments, it was Iraq's former president Saddam Hussein after his capture by U.S. troops in December 2003. Barely able to move out of his solitary-confinement cell for months, except to attend his public trial, Saddam Hussein was a puppet on a string in the hands of his Iraqi and U.S. captors.

This control was extremely important to the U.S. and Iraqi governments once Saddam Hussein had been sentenced to die by a hangman's noose. Neither government wanted Saddam Hussein's execution to be televised, because they feared that the image of his death would make him a martyr to be pitied by people who would otherwise remember the evidence revealed at his televised trial that lead to his conviction and execution.

This tight control was thwarted when a person attending Saddam Hussein's execution in December 2006 recorded on his mobile phone, unnoticed by others, a video of Hussein's last words and his death by hanging. This video was posted on the Web within an hour of the event and picked up by weblogs, major news outlets, and video file sharing services around the world very rapidly. The efforts by the most powerful nation on earth and the nation that its military occupied to control the public message created by the death of the most important figure in modern Iraq had been thwarted by a person who had decided that it was time to join Content Nation.

Some of these events are doubtless familiar to you already: examples of how people communicating with other people through publishing tools without the intervention of established sources of power and authority can change radically the perception of what's interesting, important, and true on a wide basis. As important as these and other key events were in many people's lives, they were just the birth pangs of Content Nation, merely early and influential evidence that publishing by anyone and everyone was starting to influence our economy, our society, and the very way that people live their lives and think about their futures.

The growth of personal publishing from its early phases into a phenomenon that is now becoming the primary communications culture for millions of people worldwide is the real story of Content Nation. In a matter of a few years the publishing of text, Web page links, video, audio, and other materials by everyday people via today's electronic communications networks—what many refer to now as "social media"—has become the dominant focus of audiences using the Internet and related communications networks. According to the Alexa.com service that ranks Web sites based on Internet service provider traffic statistics, six of the global top ten most popular Web sites in February 2008 were sites focused on social media. The ability of these statistics to provide exact rankings may be debatable, but the general picture that they paint is clear: what was once an increasingly powerful but secondary form of communication is becoming a primary form of communication globally.

ALEXA.COM GLOBAL WEB SITE TRAFFIC RANKINGS AS OF FEBRUARY 24, 2008 (SOCIAL MEDIA SITES IN BOLD)

1. Yahoo!
2. **YouTube**
3. Windows Live
4. Google
5. (MSN)
6. **Myspace**
7. **Facebook**
8. **Hi5**
9. **Wikipedia**
10. **Orkut**

It's not just that the world is becoming a nation of influential publishers. The time has come when the world is reading, listening to, and watching Content Nation as a source of authority and trusted insight. Content Nation has achieved scale. Content Nation has achieved depth. Increasingly, Content Nation is redefining what people consider to be quality sources of information, entertainment, and interaction. What's more, Content Nation is not just about what happens in major media markets or developed nations. Content Nation is also creating major changes in how small, medium, and global businesses manage their operations, well out of the sight of typical media outlets.

Content Nation is creating new and better ways for people in developing nations to communicate with one another and with the world, and is accelerating their ability to create economic and political change. Content Nation is establishing a global culture of publishing that is changing our work, our lives, and, inevitably, our futures. In doing so, Content Nation will change fundamentally how people survive and thrive in a rapidly changing world.

How rapidly? How fundamentally?

Read on.

The Scale of Content Nation: Truly a Nation in the Making

Although social media tools are increasingly prevalent, not everyone who makes serious use of them. A 2006 poll by the Pew Internet & American Life Project gathered an interesting picture as to what kinds of people are generating their own content online and why. The study found that the major reason most people (52 percent) use weblogs is to have a creative outlet, with only 7 percent citing making money as a major motivation. In other words, for most people just the joy of publishing is enough to motivate them to give it a try. We're creative beings by design, for the most part, destined to shape our thoughts and feelings into personal publishing artifacts for the world to discover.

The Pew study also shows that many people want to have a platform to influence others as well as to be a creative outlet. Twenty-nine percent of respondents cited motivating other people to action as a major reason for weblogging, with more than 61 percent saying that inciting people to action was either a major or minor reason. A similar 27 percent said the desire to influence other people's thinking was a major motivator. The Pew report played down this factor in saying that "just half say they are trying to influence the way other people think" to highlight the pervasiveness of less public uses. But wait. If, as the report says, there were about 12 million adult bloggers in the U.S. at the time, that means that there were more than 3 million webloggers in the U.S. alone who have tried to persuade the thinking of others on the Web as a prime motivator, including, but not limited to, the 57 million adult Americans who were reading weblogs.

Let's round this up to a global guesstimate for a moment. A survey at about the same time by comScore Networks gives us data showing that the U.S. had only about 22 percent of the world's Internet users at the time. Using that fig-ure as a corollary to scale the Pew data would give us more than 13.6 million adults in the world trying to influence other people via weblogs alone, much less other types of publishing. That's a pretty small group out of 6.5 billion people in the world, but it's significantly more than all of the professional publishers in the world put together. To put it in perspective from another angle using global population data, if this group of influencers were their own country they would be the 65th largest nation in the world in 2006. I updated my calculations from a couple of years ago based on more recent data from similar sources and saw that the community of serious bloggers alone had grown by 2008 to become the 50th largest nation in the world—more than 22.5 million people and growing quickly.

Beyond relatively well-tracked data on blogs there are millions of people using social networking portals like MySpace, Facebook, Orkut, Hi5, and other outlets to create a profile and publish information regularly. A study released by the Pew Internet & American Life Project this year indicates that about 64 million people in the United States, about 22 percent of the U.S. population, use social networking sites. Worldwide the estimate of people using major social networking sites is about 274 million people. Many of these people probably have a weblog as well, so we cannot really add these statistics to statistics on weblogs accurately. Taking just the data from social networking site estimates and applying the same rules on serious influencers from the earlier Pew study on weblogs, we'd wind up with about 73 million people globally who are try-ing to influence others seriously via Internet social-networking services. This would rank serious social media publishers at the 16th largest nation today—comfortably ahead of Iran's population and closing in on Egypt's.

Add in people who key in content from the billion-plus mobile phones and other networked mobile devices now in use, collaboratively edited reference services such as Wikipedia, online classified ad services such as Craigslist, product- and restaurant-review online services, user forums, email newsletters, professionally oriented social media tools, and other key publishing capabili-ties, and before you know it you're likely in the hundreds of millions of people who take publishing seriously—perhaps pushing this group into a population that rivals the 10 most populous nations of the world.

There is truly a Content Nation out there, a growing body of opinion-makers who are influencing individuals and institutions as never before on a wide variety of issues.

This is not to downplay the wider and more playful nature of weblogs, social networking sites, and other outlets revealed in this data. It's very important to recognize that the creative content that entertains us is coming from a vast pool of people who are going to absorb our general attention more and more as people use the Web to find authentic views of the world. It's equally important to recognize that the pool of people who view weblogs and other personal media tools as ways in which they can have a say in all kinds of matters—our personal lives, politics, business, finance—reaches far beyond a handful of well-known webloggers.

Individually, the scope of influence that these publishers have is relatively insignificant—an audience of a couple dozen people at most would be typical for many and far less in many instances. Even if these webloggers averaged only about 24 unique individuals who experience their publishing with some regularity, in sum the nation of people potentially influenced by webloggers seeking influence would be the fourth largest nation in the world—comfortably ahead of the United States of America in population.

The enormous potential of this publishing medium in the hands of people who want to influence others on such a broad scale poses opportunities and challenges to both traditional publishers and society as a whole. For traditional publishers, the influence and attention gained by these millions of micro-audiences has the potential to dilute greatly both the attention and the influence that other sources of opinion and insight offer. Yet the data from the 2006 Pew study reinforces the view that major media outlets are probably benefiting significantly from the presence of webloggers: 72 percent of the polled bloggers look for information about politics online, significantly ahead of the 58 percent of Internet users who do so, according to Pew research. With influential webloggers large and small, media outlets have an opportunity to have their content—and advertisements—drawn into communities driven by the opinion-makers who consume them.

This poses a problem for corporations trying to reach audiences through advertising in media outlets: if people are listening to webloggers as a primary source of content, how much attention and influence is going to be left over to be harvested by traditional advertising in traditional media outlets? The influencing of opinion on many commercial, public, and personal levels is shifting far more rapidly than we may imagine as a result of personal publishing technologies such as weblogs. It requires both publishers and producers to be armed with content that's ready not only for a consuming audience, but for an influencing audience from its first appearance online. In spite of many companies moving aggressively to use social media to reach their markets directly, many marketers and advertisers have not yet adapted to the scale of this challenge.

More ominously, it may in time lead to people taking a new look at why it is that they have been buying many products and services if the artificial demand created by traditional consumer-brand advertising begins to dissipate. The good news is that social media is turning out to be a great way for companies to have a conversation with their markets. The bad news for many companies is that people are free to have a conversation with anyone they'd like in social media. The nation-scaled influence of people in Content Nation is able to take on not only the influence of the world's great nations, but also the world's great corporations.

The nation-sized scale of influence-seeking social media enthusiasts does need to be taken in perspective: only a fraction of total audiences read them as of yet and a relatively small portion of people produce them with any degree of regularity or quality. The Pew data from 2006 suggested 80 percent of webloggers had started publishing only in the previous few years: Content Nation's influence was in its infancy then. As time has passed and the younger generations who have grown up with social media as a mainstay of their everyday lives become professionals, consumers, voters, and decision-makers, Content Nation has matured rapidly into the mainstay of personal and institutional communications.

Much of the power of this movement toward social media is something that doesn't really register with the average person: Content Nation is a nation of publishers whose citizens are only beginning to understand the importance of their role and its collective power.

To those who can understand the importance of their personal publishing, I say: Be a citizen. The time has come for you to accept that being one of those millions of people around the world committed to influencing a vast portion of the world's population means that you have become something new. You have journeyed through a doorway and have found yourself among people who may have been strangers at first but who are now your fellow citizens, united through influential publishing.

To those of you who are publishers and producers of content in the more traditional sense—the major media companies, the advertisers, the marketers, the journals, the newspapers, the television and radio stations, the music producers, the conference producers, the governments, the enterprises—I say as well: Be a citizen of Content Nation. Recognize that while your legacy of professional content production entitles you to an important place in its ranks, you are going to find yourselves increasingly among the publishing citizens of Content Nation as peers.

This is a story about you—one of billions of publishers in the world today whose decision to be influential is changing the world as never before.

To those of you who still discount the influence of Content Nation's citizens: be prepared to have them change your mind. Social media is going to change our work, our lives, and our futures as never before.

A Brief History of Social Media: From Campfires to "Common Sense" to Craigslist

A cynic might look at this data on the growth of social media and shrug it off. After all, what's new about social communication? We've been doing it since the dawn of humankind. You could say that the first stories told around campfires passed along from tribe to tribe were the first forms of social media, allowing people to collaborate over time on tales of important events. Cave paintings from tens of thousands of years ago with shadows of people's hands daubed onto stone walls show that the earliest people liked to communicate with one another in lasting forms. Isn't social media just another way of saying that humans are by their very nature publishing beings?

Well, that's probably true. Perhaps the question might be asked a somewhat different way: did we get sidetracked from being natural publishers and are we just getting back to our roots? Did we have a few relatively brief millennia in which a few people controlled communications to masses of people, and are those of us in more developed nations just beginning to rediscover our natural abilities to create and share content without such a centralized authority? In other words, if what we're seeing with the emergence of Content Nation is not something new at all but rather a return to something very basic in human society—namely, the ability of people to communicate with groups of peers without highly centralized control of publishing technology being a major factor—then perhaps society itself is going to undergo major changes as the result of such capabilities.

If the diversity and decentralization of control found in social media publishing reflects our natural desire and ability to publish in autonomous social units, and such publishing is beginning to overwhelm centralized communications, then we must face the reality that something very profound and fundamental is shifting in our society—something that asks us to look at what we were doing prior to publishing's centralization as much as it asks us what we are facing today and tomorrow.

Let's trace the history of social media for a few moments. Where does the history of publishing begin?

Perhaps the answer to that question can be found in examining briefly our most fundamental human publishing "technology:" language.

Even though our bodies and minds are designed for speech, the ability to speak any particular language is not something innate. Language is, in essence, a communications program, a verbal coding technology invented for a purpose, one that must be "loaded" into each new person who wants to communicate using that language. Once loaded into a group of people's minds and practiced with their bodies, a language can evolve very rapidly in given localities into a wide array of unique communication systems.

We have not only many languages, but dialects and accents that can vary quite a bit within several kilometers of a given location. According to the Census of India conducted in 2001, 29 languages are spoken there by more than a million native speakers, with 122 languages or distinct dialects spoken by 10,000 or more people. A similar study in 1993 of African languages found more than 800 distinct languages and dialects, with about 10 of them spoken by more than a million people and the remaining spoken by groups of 100,000 people or fewer, some including sign language and whistling as their format. Humans have always been inventive communicators and have flourished by communicating in ways unique to very specific societies. We like to "speak the same language"—literally and figuratively—with people who share our view of things.

In looking at current research into how languages evolved in the development of human society, it appears language evolved first as a system that enabled tribes of people to communicate with one another in a form that was not easily understood by possible competitors for food and other resources. This encoding was something that people in a very local region could use to flesh out who was on their side and who wasn't. You might think of language from this perspective as the first form of encrypted communications.

This use of language as a tool to identify sameness and otherness continued to be the case through history. In the biblical book of Judges the warriors from the ancient tribes of Gilead defeated warriors from Ephraim trying to escape from them by testing to see whether they could pronounce the word "shib-boleth" the way a Gileadite would: those who could not were put to death. Language was a technology for war as surely as a sword for these people.

In World War II the most successful encryption of military messages was maintained not by the technology of machinery but by U.S. soldiers from the Navajo tribe of Native Americans. Navajos who were in the U.S. military used their native language over battlefield telephone systems to communicate messages from officers to front-line troops. The opponents of the U.S. were never able to decipher these Navajo messages successfully. Language as a technology defeated all other advanced technologies of that era.

From these perspectives it's clear that language itself can be a very powerful "life or death" technology—perhaps the most powerful one in our command.

Okay, so language is powerful. It helped us to form into thousands of groups well-adapted to living independent of one another in countless unique environments. How does that get us to our current story of social media?

The answer comes from how people adapted to changing technologies that favored more centralized communications.

The key turning point in the rise of people as publishers came with the rise of early human civilizations in the wake of the receding glaciers of the last great ice age about 15,000–20,000 years ago. In his book *Before the Dawn*, author Nicholas Wade argues that the rise of more permanent human settlements, used at first more for the convenience of a still-nomadic hunting society and by about 10,000 years ago for the storage of domesticated grains and livestock, created opportunities for individuals and communities to own food, buildings, and, eventually, land. Ownership created opportunities for trading of surpluses of crops, materials, and hand-crafted goods with other groups and cultures.

With ownership came counting and records. With ownership also came wealth and power, and the ability and the desire to have what others did not have. Put these two together and a new encoding of language was born: the written word. Written language enabled owners and traders to communicate far more effectively over long distances and to large audiences. All of a sudden someone rich and powerful could have their words spread anywhere—if they could afford to pay people to deliver their messages to other people. The richest and most powerful people could afford to communicate their desires and expectations via messengers and stone tablets and monuments to countless people in their own regions and far away. The media had been born—and it worked for the kings, the pharaohs, and the merchants who needed control.

Social media was still an important part of human existence even after the rise of large-scale civilizations. Folk music, ancient stories, travelers with news, and the ability to read what the rulers had written on their monuments and to adapt those languages to their own purposes enabled people to carry on tribe-like communications. As the languages of the powerful kept on driving much of what was published, there were few who had the influence to have their communications shared with many others beyond a small family, local community, or trading partners. There was, if you will, the media of the people and the media of the privileged, living side by side.

As trading grew, though, publishing technologies became out of necessity more widespread and more affordable, and enabled more easily reproduced publications. Writing on clay and stone tablets was replaced by writing on papyrus scrolls, and, eventually, paper. Studying written paper texts was easier and became more common. Anonymous folk stories, religious codes, and other oral traditions could be collected and transmitted further and to more places on paper. Still, the times that people took pen to parchment were fairly few and far between in most instances and it took a fair amount of influence to get your story retold in written form far and wide.

In the age of the Roman Empire the prosperous and powerful people who did business in the Forum at the center of Rome would retreat oftentimes into their villas upon the surrounding hills and have their servants in the city center write to them about the events of the day. These written news accounts, called *diurnae*, or journals, were perhaps the beginning of both regular news publishing and the beginning of the written language as everyday social media. They were more than just personal accounts shared with close family and friends or with trading partners. They were accounts of daily life written for a paying audience who wanted to witness events that were far away—and to respond to those events as they chose. They started out as private communications, but they were shared with others and discussed. The first "newsgroups" had been born, if only for the elites.

Media of all kinds stagnated in their form and influence for many centuries until the invention of the printing press in the 15th century. At first very expensive and experimental, the original books and proclamations coming out of early printing presses were to no surprise tightly under the control of the rich and powerful. But printing technology spread rapidly, scaling down to smaller and more affordable equipment. Printing was the first publishing technology that enabled entrepreneurial efforts to reach mass audiences. By the 18th century local presses were beginning to blanket many nations with newspapers, journals, books, and pamphlets. Pamphlets are especially important to our story, because they were used oftentimes by people who wanted to publish their own opinions on the issues of the day.

One of the most famous pamphleteers of the mid-18th century was an English immigrant to that era's American colonies named Thomas Paine. His 1776 pamphlet *Common Sense* could be called rightfully one of the first hits of social media. An anonymously authored pamphlet, Paine's *Common Sense* laid out the case for American independence and a proposed charter for a new continent-wide government. Paine had thousands of copies of *Common Sense* printed initially at his own expense and donated its copyright to the new American states after independence had been won. It was a publication meant not for building his own power but for building the influence of a powerful idea.

As influential as *Common Sense* was in the hands of people who purchased it, its influence was increased many times over by the people who brought it to the local coffee houses and taverns that were the social and business centers of that era. In discussions across the colonies at these gathering places, *Common Sense* became a publication that was shared and read via open distribution and discussion until it was known well by most people in the colonies. It played, by many accounts, a pivotal role in emboldening the leaders of a fledgling and uncertain rebellion against the greatest global power of their age to reject its governance of them altogether. An anonymous and inexpensively reproduced publication, produced by a person of no great standing or reputation and shared by hundreds of thousands of everyday people in a relatively short period of time, became one of the most influential communications in all of human history.

Paine noted in *Common Sense* a great irony that arose when a people who communicate openly and widely with one another ultimately have more and better insight than those who rule them: "There is something exceedingly ridiculous in the composition of monarchy; it first excludes a man from the means of information, yet empowers him to act in cases where the highest judgment is required." It is an insight that rings loudly through history into our current era. If, as social media author Barry Libert has coined, "We are smarter than me," what does it mean when the "me" is the head of a great nation? Was publishing really the tool of the powerful and wealthy or was it enabling new structures for delivering power and wealth through more democratic communications?

COMMON SENSE

Common Sense exposed not only the ability of everyday people empowered with publishing to influence one another into becoming a political and military force; it also exposed several concepts that are at the heart of social media:

- Leveling communications technologies tend to level power structures. The forces of armies, state, and wealth ultimately proved to be no match for an idea whose time had come that could be spread and built rapidly into a consensus by affordable publishing tools.
- Level power structures in social media tend to enable the formation of new social identities and alliances. The British colonists in America thought of themselves first as citizens of Britain and then of their own colonies; their identity as a nation was ambiguous at best when *Common Sense* was first published in January 1776. Reading and discussing *Common Sense* in public places provided a common literary and social experience that was instrumental in forging a new sense of national identity.
- Although specific authors may gain influence through social media, ultimately the author is less important than the message. Anonymity, when used to conceal the identity of an individual, can enable people to concentrate on the message instead of the person. Who you are isn't as important as what you say and what people think about it.
- Altruism matters. Concentrating less on revenues from the rights to copy a publication and more on maximizing its influence for a greater good can provide enormous payoffs for those who benefit from it and, ultimately, the person who created it.
- Sharing inexpensive or free publications widely and quickly enables the rapid formation of a widespread outlook and, consequently, influence. That influence and its ability to spur widespread action is more valuable oftentimes than the publication itself.
- Don't be afraid to publish diamonds in the rough. A lot of *Common Sense* proved to be not that valuable and insightful, but the parts that were good proved to be exceedingly good. Get it out there. See what people think.

The success of *Common Sense* was replicated in varying degrees by other pamphlets and treatises in the 18th and 19th centuries that led to political change and scientific advances. As the 20th century dawned, the time of the pamphlet as a powerful form of social media was waning. Motion pictures, radio, news-wire services, telephones, and phonographs were new technologies for publishing not only text, but sounds and sights that were easy for average people to absorb and appreciate. An explosion of metropolitan newspapers enabled everyday and influential people to get some opinions out to local communities on a regular basis instead of through occasional pamphlet publishing.

Unlike pamphlets, which were produced oftentimes by hand-operated presses and relied on distribution from one person to another for broad awareness, these newer forms of publishing were based on the scale of production and distribution possible through mass manufacturing. Newspapers, radios, televisions, phonographs, and other mass-produced items enabled these newer forms of media to moderate, filter, and package content that used to be mostly in the hands of their creators and their audience to distribute and share as they pleased.

This powerful centralization of commercial publishing distribution led to controls to prevent competitive outlets from arising. The concept of copyright, used at first to ensure the economic survival of the emerging printing business, became focused more on expanding the wealth of well-established publishers than on ensuring outlets for new information and ideas. Radio broadcasting, initially a free-for-all that enabled amateurs to have as much audience as professional broadcasters, was regulated to keep citizen radio communications limited and segregated from commercial communications. New scientific ideas seeking acceptance were published in expensive journals only by major publishers and universities and only after rigorous and lengthy review.

After a brief hiatus from influential publishing being almost exclusively in the hands of the powerful, the post-ice age norm of centralizing the control and ownership of publishing had reasserted itself.

The rise of mass media might have brought the story of widely influential social media to an end were it not for the Cold War.

After World War II the United States was investing heavily in research to develop advanced computers and communications networks for managing its command and control of the nation's global military forces. In 1963 J.C.R. Licklider was chosen to head the U.S. Department of Defense's Advanced Research Projects Agency (ARPA). Licklider foresaw in those early days of computer technology many of the developments in the computer industry that would unfold in the decades ahead.

One of Licklider's futuristic visions was a universal "intergalactic network" of computers in which any one computer could communicate with any other computer without requiring a separate electronic circuit connecting directly to each other computer or to a central computer that could act as a control point for accessing all other computers. Instead segments of an electronic message could be routed to and from a destination computer through any other computers on the network as conditions allowed—like relay racers passing their batons from one group of runners to another—and then reassembled at the destination computer in complete form.

In October 1969 Licklider's vision of an "intergalactic network" of computers first came to life as the Department of Defense's ARPANET. The communications methods pioneered by the ARPANET eventually became worldwide standards and were improved upon to make it easier for computers to transmit electronic messages to any other computer over a wider variety of computer networks and to improve message routing. On January 1, 1983 the ARPANET was retired and the first computer network using the communications methods employed by today's Internet was born.

This little sideline into computer network architecture underscores one unique aspect of the architecture of the Internet that is very important to social media. By its nature the Internet is a computer network in which any computer can communicate with any other computer in the world that's connected to it, without needing to pass messages through a central control point. But the Internet also allows any number of computers to communicate simultaneously without central control.

This was a first in the history of human communications technologies. A single voice could shout only so far. A newspaper, book, radio station, or any other media relying on mass production had relied on some central publishing authority to distribute its content. A telephone could allow anyone to communicate worldwide, but only to one person or to at most a handful of end points at a time. The Internet enabled one communication to be published and received by any number of people in the world simultaneously—and could allow them all to respond simultaneously as they pleased. The storytelling campfires of the ice age could now be extended in a global circle of communications.

This new communications capability was an innovation that was in many ways as crucial a tool for human communications as language itself. Communications to and from any number of people could be self-organizing on potentially any scale instead of being organized via hierarchies such as governments, religions, tribes, or businesses. It was as if the topography of what was possible for humans to do together through common communications had been wiped as clean as much of the earth's surface was when the world's great glaciers retreated at the end of the last ice age. New ways for society to survive and to thrive were inevitable back then as a radically different environment took form; new ways for society to survive and thrive were certainly inevitable as the Internet enabled a new global environment for human communications to take form.

The huge potential of the Internet to transform human communications might have taken many decades to evolve to the point of worldwide influence through social media were it not for two key developments: the emergence of affordable personal computers (PCs) and the birth of the World Wide Web, today referred to commonly as the Web. Affordable personal computers evolved rapidly in the early 1980s and became reasonably powerful and widespread devices by the early 1990s. By that time the Internet was certainly worldwide but confined mostly to government, university, and business research facilities and major businesses that used it for limited forms of publishing, such as email. But with the introduction of the Web, the marriage of widely available PCs and global publishing via the rapidly expanding Internet began to accelerate the development of social media on the Internet.

The beginnings of today's social media can be found in the very first Web site developed by Tim Berners-Lee at the European Organization for Nuclear Research (CERN) in 1992. Though Web sites contain information created in many different human languages and in many different forms, they all use the same common "language" of programming standards for formatting and accessing information. It is this capability that offers the real common language of the Web. Anyone can build a program to access a Web site and to display information available on it in an easily readable format by following these standards. Many programs built to operate and access Web sites using Web standards were made available for free use, a move that helped not only to encourage the use of the Web but also the sharing of other technologies for advanced Web functionality. No longer was access to information reliant on generally expensive and proprietary special software produced for special purposes. The potential of the Internet to enable anyone, anywhere to publish and read information from anyone else could now be realized in full.

The other critical feature found in Tim Berners-Lee's first Web site was a simple news page—a listing of recent events and announcements relating to early Web development. New items would be added to the top of the page and older items pushed down onto archive pages of earlier items. Items were typically very brief, written in an informal tone that would be easily understood by others who knew the general context of the information being discussed—in other words, a news page written by and for peers in the language of peers.

This was in some ways the first prototypical weblog, a page with small snippets of plain text as well as hyperlinks that enabled quick navigation to related information with a click of a mouse on the colored and underlined hyperlink text. No longer was it necessary to get on a mailing list or acquire a special login to get information from other people on a computer network; anyone could access such a page easily and be informed about current events and new Web content by peers. Anyone could access related information via hyperlinks without having to know arcane Web addresses or to have a special index of related sources. These features are still at the heart of most of today's social media publishing. But this was still a one-way communication and still required a fair amount of expertise to be able to publish the page—however it wasn't far from the traditional publishing model in spite of the potential of its technical underpinnings.

World-Wide Web News November 1992

(As usual, this is distributed in plain text form, but the original hypertext contains lots of links and in software yet, telnet to info.cern.ch (128.141.201.74), and select information about the WorldWide

Client software

Three developments on the clients side. Tony Johnson of Boston University, developer of the Mida
ftp://info.cern.ch/pub/www/src or ftp://freehep.scri.fsu.edu/freehep/networking_news_email/midasv

Here at CERN, Nicola Pellow is back until the end of the year, and has picked up the Mac Brows

The full-screen client (using curses) has been released by Jim Whitescarver of NJIT, see release no

The NeXTStep client has been revised. The 0.13 version generated bad SGML at times, so anyon
ftp://info.cern.ch/pub/www/bin/next/WorldWideWeb_0.14.app.tar.Z

More and more hypertext on line

New W3 servers have appeared at KVI ad at CWI both in the Netherlands, IN2P3 in France, an
information as well as various other goodies.

CWI has a hypertext version of the Gnu documentation and of a guide to Audio formats , and NC
produce online hypertext documentation recently are ADAMO and RD13.

Meanwhile, Cornell Law school have a server with hypertext of US Copyright Law... as law tends

Browse the WAIS servers

It's sometimes been a bit difficult browsing through what there is in the WAIS world. Now, looking
by name of "source" and by internet domain. These lists are generated automatically at CERN from
databases on 88 hosts accesible.

(Previous issue was September 1992)

Tim BL

Another early form of social media on the Web was the newsgroup, a facility that enabled people to post messages and to post replies to those messages. This basic form of community discussion remains in many of today's social media services. Some newsgroups were open for anyone to read and post information, whereas others restricted access for posting or reading information. Newsgroups were the first example of a social media community on the Web, enabling people to share expertise and common ideas and to define topics for discussion.

These early but primitive forms of social media on the Web attracted many specialized enthusiasts from academic and technology communities, but in general the limitations in the design of their basic features didn't allow social media to reach a broad audience for several years. It took three additional developments in technology before social media really began to explode in its scope and impact for typical people using the Web.

The first technology change was the development of software that made it far easier for anyone to publish and read content without a detailed understanding of the technology that makes it possible. Although key technology components such as better browsers and computer networks that could transfer large quantities of data more quickly were important in a shift to more accessible Web information, in general two forms of software were key to the evolution of social media on the Web, in particular wikis and weblogs.

Wikis (a name derived from the Hawaiian word "wiki," meaning "fast") were a new kind of publishing tool that started surfacing in 1995. Unlike previous Web publishing software, wikis enabled anyone to publish entire Web sites with almost no technical knowledge and to allow other people to edit them as well right from the same software they used to view Web site pages. Many people could collaborate on a common Web site pages or a series of pages using freely available wiki software. This was a huge move forward in enabling communities to share their expertise and to build knowledge collectively and collaboratively. Information no longer had to be "perfect" before it was exposed to other people: in fact, by exposing it to other people it could evolve and take on new depth and form over time. This in effect turned the traditional editorial process for publishing inside-out: now anyone could write and edit content together to be viewed and enhanced by global audiences. It was in a sense a return to the ice age tradition of stories and histories being developed collaboratively by many people over time.

Weblogs were another important publishing tool that helped to accelerate social media into a global publishing phenomenon. A handful of technology specialists had maintained personal online diaries since the early days of the Web, using specialized publishing tools to maintain their content. But in 1998 the Open Diary service made its debut on the Web. Open Diary enabled anyone to start their own online diary with almost no technical knowledge required and, most importantly, no need to set up their own Web site to start publishing. A budding online journalist could configure a new personal diary in a matter of seconds, start typing text into a simple online form, click their mouse on a form button, and have their content appear in an online journal format for the world to read.

Thousands of people began to use Open Diary and other similar services, such as Blogger.com, which soon added the ability for people reading these diaries to publish their own comments on a diary entry, enabling discussions like the ones newsgroups had provided earlier but with the journal writer acting as the focus for discussions and an overseeing editorial control. The Roman *diurnae*, personal news journals for specific audiences, and the pamphlets of Thomas Paine's era had been reborn through a tool that let anybody be a source of news and discussion for anyone in the world.

The second key technology development that enabled the rapid explosion of social media was the Web search engine. Search engines look at where content comes from without inherent bias as to the source of who has produced it: if a search engine determined that a personal weblog or a wiki page was a very relevant source of information that matched someone's search-engine query, it would have just as much chance of being chosen as a highly relevant page by a search engine would as a page produced by a professional publisher. Search engines enabled the perceived authority of social media to be escalated in the eyes of readers on the Web—a factor that helped to grow audiences for its content more rapidly.

SEARCH ENGINES

Search-engine software examines information on Web sites and creates a searchable index of each and every word found in computer files that it can access. This enables people to look for content based not only on specific predefined categories or human-built keyword indexes, but on any term that might appear in a document.

The third key technology that enabled the growth of social media from a niche phenomenon to a global phenomenon was peer-to-peer social networking services. Instead of relying on central computers to store and distribute content, early peer-to-peer services took advantage of the inherent peer-to-peer architecture of the Internet and provided software that made it easier for people to connect directly to other people's computers on the Web, in effect turning any computer into a Web site that could share information with others.

Napster and other peer-to-peer file-sharing services enabled people to share digital music stored on other people's computers, and messaging services such as ICQ enabled people to send text messages directly from one person to another on the Web to enable chat-like communications. Though newer styles of social-networking services have supplanted many of these earlier services with Web sites that no longer rely on peer-to-peer software, the earlier services established the value of connecting millions of people around the world with valuable content and discussions provided by like-minded people.

The availability of peer-to-peer networks that could connect like-minded people eventually inspired other types of peer-oriented social-networking services. Newer services include Craigslist.org, which enables anyone to post free online advertisements for goods and services, personal ads, and events; eBay, which matches peer-to-peer buyers and sellers; and newer types of social-networking services, such as MySpace, Facebook, YouTube, Digg, and LinkedIn, are all direct descendants of early peer-to-peer services that encouraged people to provide just a little content to connect with a lot of people.

Here we are in the world of today's social media. We've come a long way since those early cave paintings and campfire stories, but in many ways we have indeed come full circle back to the beginning of our social media history, technology uniting groups of people through mutual communication capabilities, people connecting with people the way that they like to connect with them. Collaborative storytelling and knowledge generation. Voices shouting into the air and being heard as far as they can carry—which now, thanks to the Web, can travel to the ends of the earth and beyond. And through the scale, influence, and power of Content Nation, social media is becoming one of the most transformative forces in human history.

Why Social Media Matters to Our Work, Our Lives, and Our Futures

What does the emergence of Content Nation, a nation of influential publishers, really mean to our everyday lives? It means first and foremost that the patterns of our lives that we've taken for granted for centuries, perhaps even millennia, have the potential to shift as never before. It will be a shift that affects not only what entertains us but also how we survive and thrive in our work, our lives, and our futures. Already social media tools are helping large and small businesses alike to become more productive and to change the way that they do business with their customers and how they organize themselves. Already people are using social media to change how they manage the most fundamental questions in their lives—How will I find people who really enrich my life? Who should I support in politics? How will I find my next job or customer?—and in the process they're changing our everyday decisions in profound ways.

Already we can begin to see the potential outlines of how social media may impact our future. Will it be a future dominated by large organizations trying to create mass-produced goods for mass markets using mass-marketing techniques? Or has social media begun to introduce elements of a new way to organize local and global economies that will change the fundamental patterns that have dominated human commerce since the dawn of civilization? In a world in which human economics are running up against potential limits of sustainable human consumption on a planet with limited resources, will social media point to new ways to create rewarding lifestyles in an era of modern technologies?

Perhaps most profoundly, as social media introduces changes to some of these fundamental ways in which people manage their lives, will social media change some of the fundamental ways in which we organize human society? When there is possibly more potential for ensuring humans surviving and thriving on a global scale in a system that enables loose confederations of people to solve problems and share solutions, is it likely that institutions such as governments, local communities, and even families will begin to change?

Where Social Media Is Taking Us: How Something So Simple Can Change So Much

The preceding questions may seem to be way too broad in scope for a book on something as contemporary as social media. Yet as you work through the chapters of this book that focus on the more here-and-now aspects of social media, I think that you'll begin to see the outlines of where social media is already pointing toward some of these potentially profound shifts in human society. We're already well past the infancy of this phenomenon, past the "oohs" and "aahs" of a new technology as a rudimentary plaything, past the initial glimpses of how it can improve productivity, and influence markets and human relationships.

In the 2000 book *The Cluetrain Manifesto* the phrase "markets are conversations" captured the idea that the Web was bringing us back to our roots as a society that learns from one another directly our needs and how best to fulfill them. Those direct online conversations are now more than a decade old, yielding rich insights into not only how existing markets will unfold anew with social media, but also how new markets are forming that will take us far beyond industrial-era marketing paradigms and toward new and revived interchanges that add value to our human experience.

Like that key phrase from *The Cluetrain Manifesto*, the impact of social media's influence can be deceptively simple depending on the scale that you use to apply it, just like the changes that a piece of ice can make may be deceptively simple based on scale. Let a small cube of ice melt on a table, and something simple is changed: put a mile of ice over a continent, and life is changed forever. So it will be with the scale and depth of Content Nation's influential impact as it begins to reach into the lives of every person on the planet. When the fundamental power of any one person to exert an influence over almost any other person on the planet changes, a tool with great scalability emerges that will exert a change on the future of what makes us human as surely as language itself changed our humanness.

This book's mission is not to tell you yet again that social media is important, but rather to help you get a better understanding of how today's global influence from social media is setting the stage for things far greater than we may be able to imagine easily today. The pieces for a new kind of future are falling into place rapidly—so rapidly that many people really aren't capturing just how different that future will look when it's complete. We see the changes in our everyday lives already, but what is it about Content Nation that will amaze us beyond even today's far-reaching visions?

In the process of detailing how Content Nation is emerging and transforming our lives, we'll take a look at the "what" of social media, the "secret sauce" of what makes it work and where it works best; the "who" of social media, the people who use it for themselves, for their enterprises, and for enhancing existing media outlets; the "how" of social media, looking at specific arenas in which social media is having its greatest impact; and the "where" of social media, a look into where these profound changes are likely to take us in the not-too-distant future and the distant future. This book is just the beginning of our own conversation on social media, of course: if you've made your own decision to be an influential publisher, ContentNation.com will stage additional insights into how social media is changing our work, our lives, and our futures.

2

What Makes Social Media Tick:

Seven Secrets of Social Media

I've used the term "social media" as a handle for the types of publishing that everyday people are using to be influential publishers in Content Nation. What really is social media and how does it work? Let's take a look at what makes social media "tick" and what has really changed when people use today's technologies to change the dynamics of how people create and find value through influential publishing.

Social Media Defined: Anything that Helps Individuals to Publish Influentially

Often, the terminology used to define how individuals are using today's publishing tools to influence other people can be quite confusing. People refer to Web 2.0, user-generated content, social networking, and other terms to try to encompass the movement toward people becoming influential publishers on the Web and beyond. All of these terms and others have their place in describing useful tools for people to publish to the world. I find, though, that the term "social media" serves as a good umbrella for encompassing all of the available technologies that will not be limited to a specific application of publishing or a particular era of publishing. As discussed earlier, social media has been with us from the first human utterances and will be with us long after the Internet has been supplanted by other forms of global communications that empower individuals to be influential publishers.

For the purposes of Content Nation, let me offer this definition of social media: *Any highly scalable and accessible communications technology or technique that enables any individual to influence groups of other individuals easily.*

You might find this to be a pretty simple definition. Well, it is, in the sense that it describes a pretty broad range of activities and technologies. Because it is a fairly broad definition, however, it covers a lot of possible methods of communicating via publishing. The need for such a broad definition becomes more apparent when you look at some of the other terms that are used commonly to describe various aspects of social media publishing tools and techniques.

The term "Web 2.0" is used typically to describe technologies such as wikis, weblogs, and other collaborative tools. These are certainly important tools in the history of social media that have led to its becoming influential on a global scale through Content Nation. There were earlier publishing technologies that also had a widespread influence based on them being scalable and accessible to fairly typical people. There are also technologies such as those found in telephone networks that may have very little to do with the Web but that provide very similar benefits to people wanting to influence others. Web 2.0 is important in that it has accelerated the growth of social media's power as never before, but is too limited to encompass everything that Content Nation can do to generate social media.

The term "user-generated content" is used often to refer to a lot of the same activities as referred to by "social media," but the term "user" implies a relationship with a computer and a role that is generally not as authoritative as someone who controls some other source of content, like professionally produced news, as if they were just some sort of secondary input channel for central computer processing. Social media is about people influencing other people in a social situation through technology. Often some sort of computer is there to help that situation result in one person influencing a group of others, but social media is about what people do to influence other people at least as much as the technology that they use to do those things.

The term "social networking" is certainly a part of what is produced as "social media," but it does not cover every form of social media. As more and more publishing products offer functions that enable people to keep in touch with one another and have conversations, I think that we'll see the term "social networking" being used to address a commonly available feature in a number of different types of technologies.

By contrast I think that the suggested definition for social media fits well as an overarching term from a number of angles.

- *Social media uses highly scalable and accessible technologies.* The scale and access may vary with the technology and audiences being addressed through social media, but the need for it to be scalable to whatever size audience a person needs to reach and the ease of accessing it remain constant. Thomas Paine's pamphlets took advantage of affordable printing that enabled him to print thousands of copies of his pamphlet and get them out into the hands of other people. It was pretty easy to get it published and it scaled well for his then-huge audience of about a million people. Today's Web 2.0 technologies are even more scalable— you can have a publishing service that drives an audience of a handful of people or hundreds of millions off of the same kind of publishing platform—and they are accessible, meaning that anyone can use these technologies to start their publishing very easily and affordably, often for free. Certainly other technologies will emerge that will extend the scalability and accessibility of social media even further.

- *Social media enables individual people to communicate with groups of other individuals.* Social media is a peer-to-peer medium, as some people might say, meaning that the audience for social media publications tends to relate to one another as equals for the purposes of communicating and sharing information. Authorities on a topic may communicate with people who are less authoritative, but, in general, the authority of someone in social media is not based on their control of the communications technology or some particular position that they hold in an organization, but rather on the basis of what they share being authoritative in the eyes of the peer audience.

  These communications tend to be one-to-many, meaning that a person creates something that can be shared with many other people; or many-to-many, meaning that any number of people can share information with any other number of people simultaneously. The Web's technology facilitates this, but it's an attribute that is available even when Web technologies are not present. Social media is more about a circle of equals that expresses leadership fluidly amongst peers than a pyramid-like hierarchy of pre-ordained people in superior roles who control the distribution of information to others via technology.

- *Social media enables influence.* Because it's delivered on highly scalable technology, the exact scope of social media's influence can be unpredictable. Like many people using social media, Ghyslain's friends who posted his "Star Wars Kid" on a file-sharing service discovered that the scalability of social media can allow something that was meant for a limited audience to all of a sudden influence a worldwide audience. The same can be true of any type of socially conveyed content: some stories told around a campfire in the ice sge probably stayed around that campfire and went no further, limiting their influence, just like some weblog entries may not be read that widely or attract that many comments, but some of those ice sge stories were shared at other campfires as well; over time, some of those shared stories became powerful legends and myths that would be handed down from generation to generation.

SOCIAL MEDIA SECRET #1: *It's all about the ability of people to scale their influence independently.*

Demystifying Today's Social Media Tools: Accelerating Access, Influence, and Audience

Although the definition of what constitutes social media is short and simple, the publishing tools that facilitate today's social media are diverse and continuing to expand at a dizzying rate. It is in some ways not unlike what happened with our ice age ancestors tens of thousands of years ago as the last major period of continent-covered glaciers faded away: faced with new kinds of ways to hunt and gather food in a climate changed by the receding ices, they went from having a handful of different types of stone tools to dozens of different kinds of tools, objects, and designs. Today's explosion of social media publishing tools may not last as long as stone axes, statues, and hand tools that survived the ages, but they may yet prove to be as influential.

The wide array of publishing tools used to produce social media can lead to some confusion as to what types of publishing can be considered as a part of social media. Though the boundaries can be gray at times, there is a solid core of types of publishing that line up with our definition of social media. The following is a list of types of publishing that can be considered social media, the goals of each type of publishing, and the social aspects of each type of publishing.

- **Personal publishing:** Weblogs, commonly referred to as blogs, are the most prevalent Web-based personal publishing tools today. Whereas

weblog publishing tools can enable a wide number of people to publish items to a common weblog, typically each item on that weblog is
authored by a single person. Earlier electronic publishing tools, such
as email, enable people to distribute newsletters or to copy people on
messages that may not have started out as content meant to influence
large groups of peoplea capability that still plays a very powerful role
in personal publishing. Messaging tools such as Twitter also enable
personal messages to be distributed in a highly scalable form, enabling
any number of people to tune into very short text messages from mobile
devices or PCs.

- *Publishing goal:* Enable one person or several individuals to tell
  their own story to many people.
- *Social aspects:* Personal publishing accelerates the ability of individuals to communicate their personal point of view to others,
  often building up their perceived value to others based on their
  knowledge, their insight, or their personality.

- **Collaborative publishing**: Wikis are the most common form of Web-
  based collaborative publishing, which enables groups of people to collaborate on common documents and to build complete Web sites over
  time. Wikis enable changes to a page from any contributor to be displayed to their audience immediately, with corrections being applied as
  needed. Wikis and similar tools can be used for any publishing purpose,
  including developing news. Though the online encyclopedia Wikipedia
  is perhaps best known for its millions of articles on various long-lived
  topics, its current-events and news pages help people to edit today's
  news and headlines very effectively also. Wikipedia has also demonstrated that collaborative publishing can enable teams of authors to
  correct mistakes rapidly and update long-standing articles to reflect
  current events almost as quickly as they occur. The implications for
  building timely, well-edited sources of knowledge using collaborative
  publishing technologies are enormous.
  - *Publishing goal:* Enable multiple people to collaborate on com-
    mon documents for use by themselves or for both themselves
    and for many other people.
  - *Social aspects:* Discussions and comments relating to common
    articles, building collaborative skills, usually membership-driven
    or private communities of authors who may share their publica-
    tions with the public or a broader private community.

- **Social-network publishing:** Social-network publishing enables people to build and use relationships with other people—social networks—using tools that let people share information about their personal and professional needs and interests. Social-network publishing is one of the fastest-growing kinds of social media today, encompassing a wide array of publishing technologies. Most social-network publishing services include a few key features: a self-edited personal profile, which includes facts and categories that relate to a person and other personalized content; the ability to create networks of friends and associates through designating people as members of your personal circle of contacts; and the ability to communicate with personal contacts easily. Common examples of today's social-network publishing include MySpace, Facebook, LinkedIn, Orkut, and Hi5.
    - *Publishing goal:* Enable people to find other people with affinities and to share those affinities with those people and with others through publishing.
    - *Social aspects:* Linking to profiles, sharing content, and building knowledge through discussion topics and providing references to experts.
- **Feedback and discussions:** Many publishing services enable people to provide various forms of published feedback and discussions to help other people get additional insight to a topic or a product. Often these services are embedded as features in Web sites that are generally not oriented toward social media. A key example of this would be a Web site such as Amazon.com, which provides the ability for its members to write reviews and to provide ratings of books and other products that they sell. Sometimes reviews and ratings such as these may be collected initially on one Web site and licensed for other Web sites to embed in their own Web pages. Although reviews and ratings are seen often in the context of other content, they are sometimes packaged as a source of social media for others to use to enhance their own Web content. Discussion publishing services appear in many different forms, including the ability to provide comments on weblog entries and online news articles, newsgroups and user groups, forums, and online bulletin boards.
    - *Publishing goal:* To share information and opinions on a specific topic or item that can be exposed easily to others looking for insights and opinions, some of whom may choose to share their own insights and opinions.

- *Social aspects:* Provide an opportunity to share insights and opinions with others, sometimes resulting in others engaging in online "conversations," other times helping them to gain knowledge through reviewing the knowledge and experiences of peers.
- **Aggregation and filtering:** Often social media enables the assembly of content aggregated from a publisher's own sources and other sources that are of interest to an individual or group. Aggregation is the process of assembling collections of content that come from a wide variety of sources. Categories and "tags" (personally defined topic words) give social media content organization that makes it easier for people to filter out what is of most interest to people in key topic areas. Social bookmarking services such as Digg and del.icio.us that enable people to build and share lists of links to Web pages, and photo- and video-sharing sites such as YouTube and Flickr are examples of popular aggregation and filtering services in social media.
  - *Publishing goal:* Enable people to aggregate collections of content from various sources that can be shared with others publicly or privately.
  - *Social aspects:* Build an appreciation of a person's ability to provide valuable insights through choosing other people's content.
- **Widgets and mashups:** Programs known as "widgets" that package content from other sources or generate new content automatically can be added easily by anyone to their Web pages in many social media products, enabling them to aggregate content from other sources for themselves and for others. Sometimes more technology-oriented people use application programming interfaces (APIs) from suppliers such as Google and Yahoo! to create new programs known as "mashups" that aggregate both social media content and content from other sources. Sometimes mashups are whole Web sites unto themselves; other times they may be delivered as widgets that can be embedded in other Web site content. Though the content in a widget or mashup may not always be from individual publishers, their use by individuals to aggregate content that's of interest to them or to contribute content to them extends their ability to create useful context for content through their own publishing efforts.
  - *Publishing goal:* To add value to social media through providing additional content that complements and enhances one's own content.

- *Social aspects:* Enable social media to provide a context for other content that enhances its value, and in doing so give people more reasons to engage on a personal level.
- **Personal markets and marketing:** One of the most important aspects of social media is that it enables people with something of value to reach other people who need something of value to them easily and affordably. In the instance of weblogs, the value provided is the content itself. In other instances, people are looking not just for content but to get goods and services from other people. Services like eBay and Craigslist. org enable individuals to market goods and services to other people through their Web sites without having to rely on established forms of media to moderate the process of marketing or executing a deal for what's being offered. Almost anyone can set up a page on eBay and sell anything that they have to offer to anyone looking for those things— and many people do. Craigslist is a simpler service than eBay, focusing primarily on free classified ad listings, but it is a broader service in that it enables people to advertise jobs, events, and interests in dating and other social contact.
  - *Publishing goal:* To enable anyone to discover people who have interest in something that they have to offer and to create a market for those things.
  - *Social aspects:* Markets can be created directly between any person making an offer and willing to accept an offer, instead of having to rely on intermediaries to match supplies with demand.

Although these categories of social media publishing tools often represent many distinct types of social media publishing in and of themselves, many social media services combine these capabilities to create unique services. It's very common to find comments as a standard part of weblogs, for example, even though they're not required and not always used frequently by people reading a particular weblog entry. The Content Nation Web site, ContentNation. com, uses technology from Near-Time, Inc., which combines the capabilities of wikis, weblogs, widgets, aggregation, and social-network publishing in a single platform. It's not so important to categorize each and every social media publishing service as one type or another as it is to appreciate that the willingness of people to participate in social media tends to make a broad array of features attractive and useful to them. To give you an idea of how these categories of tools match up with some of the more well-known social media services,

Table 2-1 illustrates how any number of social media services may incorporate tools from any number of social media publishing categories:

Table 2-1: Social Media Services

Social Media Categories	Social Media Services				
	Blogger.com	Wikipedia	Facebook	eBay	Newsvine
Personal Publishing	Yes		Yes	Yes	Yes
Collaborative Publishing		Yes			
Social Network Publishing			Yes	Yes	Yes
Feedback and Discussion	Yes	Yes	Yes	Yes	Yes
Aggregation and Filtering	Yes	Yes	Yes		Yes
Widgets and Mashups	Yes		Yes	Yes	Yes
Personal Markets and Marketing			Yes	Yes	

Whatever the combination of capabilities on whatever platform, all social media publishing tools have one common goal: to increase access, influence, and audience for the individuals using them. It may be through their own publications, through publications that integrate their content into others, or through publications developed collaboratively, but the end result of social media is that more people have more influence over more other people as easily as possible.

SOCIAL MEDIA SECRET #2: *Technology matters in social media, but not as much as understanding what people are looking for: to influence others and to be influenced by them.*

Collaboration and Competition:
Building Social Order in Social Media

Looking at all of these social media tools and the egalitarian content that they help to create, you'd think that we were creating a new utopian society through it, as if all human conflicts will melt away and people will line up to discuss ideas and develop new content with their own concerns and objectives put to the side. Nothing could be further from the truth. Unfortunately, social media does not mean that we're headed back to the Garden of Eden. Instead, as we look back at our ice age ancestors, we have to acknowledge that wars between tribes were fairly common and conflict a way of life that balanced and in some ways facilitated the need for collaboration. Social media does not eliminate human nature; it only gives it new ways to express human nature that may have an impact on how we can survive and thrive.

Though one of the more important aspects of social media is its ability to enable people to collaborate at a peer level far more effectively, collaboration is not the same thing as putting all differences aside. When you think of the ulti-mate goal of social media—to have influence over others—it's no surprise that managing conflict and conflicting interests is something that is an important part of its success. Social media enables ideas to compete with one another more effectively in venues that offer more open expression to more people than ever before. Just like the coffee houses and taverns in which Thomas Paine's pamphlets were discussed were often lively places filled with heated discussions, conflict and confrontation is expected in social media and is in fact encouraged often.

Look into the discussion section of many Wikipedia articles and you'll see very active divisions and often daily efforts by people of opposing views to shape the collaborative content on controversial topics. There are also ongoing struggles between people who would like to have their content be the most popular content, either to further their own personal objectives or because they are trying to manipulate social media to further the economic or politi-cal goals of others. Sometimes language can be abusive as insults are traded back and forth in comment threads. Social media may offer many benefits from lacking hierarchy and encouraging collaboration and networking, but it also exposes that, left to their own devices, people still need ways to enforce order and fairness.

Yet this very need for order underscores one of the key advantages of social media: order can come from people who collaborate to enforce mutually accepted standards of behavior. Many successful social media Web sites have both implied and explicit rules of behavior that are enforced by both the community as a whole and select members of that community. On Wikipedia, for example, volunteers police new and changed articles and determine whether there has been content added that is inaccurate, misleading, or otherwise not meeting the expressed standards for publishing on Wikipedia. They act as editors in some respects and as "spam" filterers in others, but also as collaborators to help the content of an article to improve. Many social media publishing tools that enable comments also enable people to cast a positive or negative vote for comments that people have posted.

The opinions of peers are perhaps the most powerful control for managing conflict and encouraging collaboration and quality in social media. Nevertheless, sometimes there needs to be a more explicit hand provided by the owners of a Web site to eliminate content that is libelous or abusive. How can this be done while still ensuring a sense of a community "owning" its own democratic authority? The answer seems to be that there needs to be an explicit commitment to ethical standards by people involved in a social media Web site.

On the Newsvinesocial media Web site, for example, there is a "Code of Honor," five key points that outline acceptable content and acceptable behavior expressed through that content. People who do not abide by these standards are subject to having their content and membership in Newsvine moderated or eliminated. Newsvine also enables articles and comments to be flagged as abusive or inaccurate, controls that may trigger automatic action by the Web site's software—collapsing the display of comments, for example, so that they can only be read by clicking a link instead of viewing them along with other comments automatically—or the flagging may trigger action and comments by Newsvine staff monitoring the Web site.

By contrast, weblogs and other personal publishing tools are much more like traditional media outlets in that each author seems to have their own standards for what is considered acceptable and unacceptable content. The popularity of such content generally grows only when it is exposed to the comments of others, both within the comments section of a typical weblog and the more open and diverse comments that might be found when a weblog entry is discussed in another social media Web site.

Corporations, public-relations specialists, and political campaigns are also eager to try to exert influence as if they were individuals when in fact they are representing the interests of others on a professional basis. This is sometimes called "astroturfing," a person pretending to be a "grass roots" person in social media just speaking for themselves. Social media communities adopt a number of strategies to deal with astroturfing, some of which we'll discuss later.

Although anyone is free to say what they'd like in social media, if people want influence, they need to be able to gain the respect of a community, regardless of what tools they are using to express themselves. In social media we may start out like a lone voice in the desert, but successful social media rarely stays that way.

SOCIAL MEDIA SECRET #3:　*Social media is not about the law of the jungle but the law of the campfire: values matter and having people who are willing to enforce values matters.*

Content in Context: Understanding the Value of Social Media

You've heard a lot about this thing called "content" in this book so far. What really is content, anyway? In a sense we know what content in publishing is about in a fairly intuitive way. We know that when we go to a store that the content of a product is what we use inside its packaging. In publishing we could say similarly that content is "the stuff," the thing that we use in a publication as opposed to what is used to bring it to us.

Though there is certainly a distinction in content between what we use and the technology that delivers it, there is another key factor that is required for something to be content: people. If there's not a market for a product inside a package, it's just something inside a package that will stay there forever or be thrown out eventually. In a similar way content requires an audience that values content. No audience, no content. An old philosophical brain teaser goes, "If a tree falls in the forest and no one is around, does it make a sound?" So it is with content: its value comes from having people who are able to use it.

An example that illustrates this point can be found in a recent breakthrough by scientists in deciphering the first known sound recording. The first sound recording was not made by phonograph inventor Thomas Edison, but in fact by a Frenchman named Edouard-Leon Scott de Martinville in 1860, 17 years before the debut of Edison's famous invention. Scott developed a device called a phonautogram that was able to etch patterns on a piece of paper in response to sounds. Unfortunately he did not have any technology to transform these etchings into sounds, so his recordings were seen but not heard.

Then, in 2008, audio historian David Giovannoni worked with scientists at California's Lawrence Berkeley National Laboratory to devise a method to translate Scott de Martinville's etchings into audible sounds. For more than 140 years Scott's etchings were merely patterns on pieces of paper: it wasn't until the scientists in Berkeley came up with technology to make those etchings valuable in a new way that they became audible content. From this standpoint, Scott's invention was important and interesting, though Thomas Edison is still recognized rightfully as the inventor of the first system that could both record and reproduce sounds—the first audio recordings with an audience.

Content is by its nature defined by the presence of social values, something that requires people to define and validate its value. The value that people find in content is therefore *contextual*—that is, its value depends on both the audience and the means by which they experience something. As Scott's etchings sat in storage for decades they were not content with context at all, just etched paper in a container. Looking at the etchings may have allowed someone to appreciate them as designs on a piece of paper—a visual context, perhaps even an artistic context if they were to be displayed in a museum. It was not until the etchings were translated into sound that they had the potential to have an audible context as content.

With these examples in mind I would suggest that in the arena of publishing and media *content is information and experiences in contexts that may provide value to audiences.* Is something a scribble on a piece paper, a work of art, or an audio recording? It could be all three, depending on the context in which it can provide value to an audience. Then again, someone's piece of art could be another person's piece of junk, or vice versa. Content *may* provide value to an audience—but it may not be the value that the producer of the content expected. Certainly the kids who put Ghyslain's "Star Wars Kid" video online could not have expected the worldwide value that it attained.

This definition of content is crucial to understanding the value of social media and why it tends to perplex many people, especially people who produce and sell traditional forms of media and information. For these people content is all about selling the "water" of content inside the "pipes" of technology that deliver it. Control the technology that delivers the content and you control your ability to benefit from people receiving its value. From this perspective most publishers tend to think of themselves as the ones who control the faucet at the end of the pipe. People will come to the faucet when they need water, and turn it on.

This "faucet" has had many different incarnations through the years: paying for a newspaper or book, turning on a television or radio with a limited number of channels, putting a CD into a playback device, purchasing a ticket at a theatre for a play or a movie, subscribing for access to a Web site. These kinds of services made sense when the limited ability of people to publish and deliver information required the most advanced services possible to make content available on a large scale. The model still makes sense even today, when the most advanced insights and technologies can distinguish a publishing service enough to provide a very high level of value to specific audiences, especially in the context of professionals trying to do their job.

In Content Nation, a world dominated by the ability of influencers to publish almost anything to virtually anyone at any scale with ease, the "where" and the "how" of content no longer fits the faucet model neatly. Content is everywhere, like rain falling from the skies, accelerated by the enormous growth in social media. Distribution in this era of hyper-abundant content is no longer as valuable as collecting the right content in the right place at the right time for the right people. Value in publishing is produced today by getting what is easily distributed in the right contexts.

This is where the full value of social media comes into play. Social media is one of the most powerful tools today for enabling content to find its most valuable contexts. A travel Web site may list pretty much the same information on a hotel as any other travel Web site, but offering it in the context of reviews written by thousands of people who have experienced that hotel first-hand can offer insights that can influence a decision to book a reservation as much as or more than the price of the accommodation or the features that the hotel has to offer. Someone can look at news headlines on a newspaper Web site chosen by a handful of editors from a handful of news sources or click a link to a news story from any number of possible sources on millions of social media Web sites. Someone can choose between a handful of columnists at a major newspaper for their opinions on major news events or they can choose from millions of weblogs offering their own opinions on that columnist's opinions—and, increasingly, original and timely news coverage. Someone can hope to find a person in their home town who will buy some spare items in their home or they can post an entry on Craigslist or eBay and have the whole world looking at things available for sale in their home—and perhaps finding just the thing that they've been trying to find for years.

In all of these examples the key is not so much the core information or experience, but the value it receives when people who can influence other people are available to provide valued context to the content. The mass distribution enabled by modern technology allows more people than ever to access content. When there are billions of content factories on the planet, all with near-zero distribution costs, the real advantage of social media is that it has vastly outproduced the ability of traditional publishers to create contexts for content. In Content Nation, millions of influential publishers have the attention of highly focused audiences, creating high value in millions of unique contexts.

While publishers were focusing on trying to build huge audiences for a handful of contexts, social media enabled a huge number of contexts for equally huge audiences. The potential for creating value in social media is therefore ultimately much higher than in traditional publishing, though realized often in contexts that most traditional publishers aren't equipped to manage. You might say that social media's ability to provide more valuable contexts is like combining the power of the printing presses on which Thomas Paine's pamphlets were produced with the power of the discussions about them held in that era's coffee houses and taverns. Traditional publishers understood how to be editors, producers, and distributors of content, but they had no idea how to be tavern-keepers or barroom orators.

SOCIAL MEDIA SECRET #4: *Social media gets its value from its ability to create millions of influential and highly scalable contexts for content, far more than provided by conventional media.*

Social Media and the New Aggregation: When the Product Never Leaves the Factory ▬

Aggregating content is one of the most powerful tools for creating value in publishing. The ability to assemble content from multiple sources and to add value to it has been one of the cornerstones of publishing profits for centuries. In the traditional aggregation model, one publisher performs or acquires all the functions of content aggregation to provide an audience with a finished product based on content provided from numerous publishers, authors, and other content sources, including sometimes their own unique "in-house" content. Be it a publishing company, a social media service, a newspaper, a news- and journals-retrieval service, or an enterprise-based publishing plat- form, the value of aggregation services has been premised on having all the components of aggregation under its command. What is changing through Web-based social media publishing tools, though, is the fundamental model in which content is aggregated.

The traditional model for producing aggregated content is illustrated in the pyramid-like structure found in Figure 2-1, in which one content-production capability provides a base for the next capability. It is similar to the model of manufacturing automobiles introduced by Henry Ford and others when massive quantities of standardized components from internal and exter- nal suppliers were assembled in a central facility to ensure the economies of scale, trained labor, and product quality required to produce a product affordably.

When printing presses were the primary focus of the publishing industry the correlation between the factory model and the publishing and aggrega- tion process was exact: publishers were manufacturers and distributors of content from centralized plants. In the more recent era of computers the "fac- tory" became a computer center, with the relational database as the primary production engine, a software method for organizing content for efficient aggregation. Databases allowed for efficient content collection, normaliza- tion, indexing, storage, retrieval, and access control, capabilities around which content aggregators developed commercial supplier agreements and distribu- tion channels.

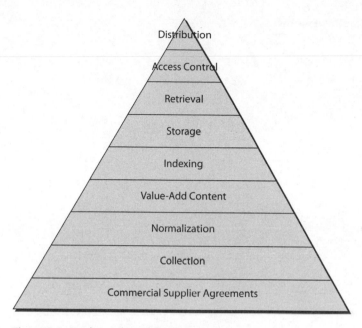

Figure 2-1: Traditional production model

Why did this model succeed so well for so long? In large part it's because it had no viable competition. As illustrated in Figure 2-2, the efficiency of centralized production control is based on the assumption that the producer has strong technology to produce a product and that the client for a product has comparatively weak technology to produce and consume the same product. With this technology dominance publishers could charge premium prices easily based on the real or artificial limits imposed on production and could also limit the emergence of competitive producers.

In this representation of the traditional aggregation model, the production pyramid results in a "faucet"—the point of value control—at the top of the production pyramid through which the value of an aggregator's products and services can be easily established and maintained prior to fanning it out for distribution to clients who have no choice but to accept the control that the vendor has over accessing the content product. Once the product escapes the control of the producer, it is in the hands of the purchaser to use as they please.

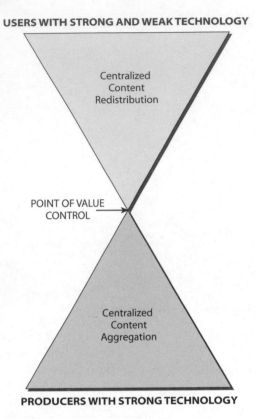

USERS WITH STRONG AND WEAK TECHNOLOGY

Centralized
Content
Redistribution

POINT OF VALUE
CONTROL

Centralized
Content
Aggregation

PRODUCERS WITH STRONG TECHNOLOGY

Figure 2-2: Producers with strong technology; users with weak technology

Social media distributed via the Web and in major enterprises exacerbates the problem of profitable content production in the factory model significantly. The Web effectively eliminates distribution as a competitive barrier, a factor that reduces costs not only for traditional content "factories," but virtually any computer on the Web that can produce content for anyone in the world. As illustrated in Figure 2-3, the point of strongest value control—the "faucet"— is no longer at the traditional aggregator's "factory," but on the Web pages, PCs, and mobile devices of individual publishers and the computer rooms of institutions where most content aggregation now occurs through social media and other publishing tools. These new choke points can create their own pyramids of aggregation from content sourced from the Web and local sources and distribution pyramids locally and within the greater distribution funnel of global content.

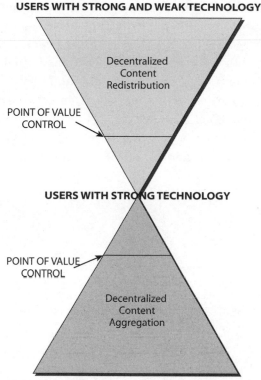

USERS WITH STRONG AND WEAK TECHNOLOGY

Decentralized
Content
Redistribution

POINT OF VALUE
CONTROL

USERS WITH STRONG TECHNOLOGY

POINT OF VALUE
CONTROL

Decentralized
Content
Aggregation

PRODUCERS WITH STRONG AND WEAK TECHNOLOGY

Figure 2-3: Shift of control in the content-production model

Does this mean that aggregation is dead as a business model because of social media? Far from it: aggregation is thriving in social media. Social media enables aggregation to move away from the "all-singing, all-dancing" factory model servicing mass audiences and to provide highly focused aggregation of content for very specific audiences very effectively, selecting only those components of aggregation that are needed to serve a particular audience at a particular point in time—and who in turn can provide their own value to others via aggregation. I have termed this emerging model "The New Aggregation." The New Aggregation focuses content product and service development on the attributes of content aggregation best suited to serve specific audiences who can themselves participate aggressively in the production, aggregation, and distribution of content.

In the traditional aggregation model, content is production-centric, building a monolithic, mass-produced service similar to our earlier pyramid diagram. By contrast, as illustrated in Figure 2-4, The New Aggregation topples that pyramid and turns it on its side, with individual publishers and institutions being able to select specific attributes of aggregation products and services from multiple suppliers and other agents, as well as without any intermediaries, via network connections. At the top of the value chain, individuals and institutions may in turn feed content to others to amplify its personal and professional value and in turn gain value from one another via business or personal transactions.

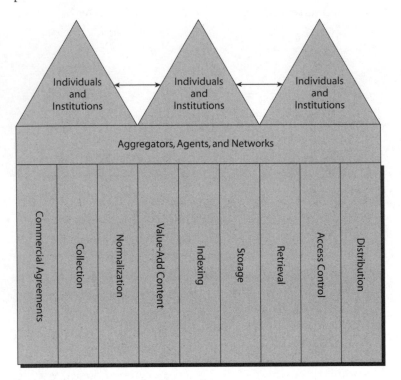

Figure 2-4: The new production model

Viewing individual and institutional participants in social media as key components of the aggregation model is a crucial factor in developing a services-driven aggregation model. Social media publishing tools enable them to combine sources of content in innovative ways to create content value more efficiently than traditional publishers and aggregators. For example, if a Web search engine can locate content on a social media site easily, why bother with elaborate indexing or a separate search engine? If another publisher has stored an article on their own Web site, why go through the legal and technical trouble to be able to store it yourself if you can just provide a link to it?

In enabling content to be easily consumed through social media publishing tools, traditional publishers increase the likelihood that their audiences will see their services as weaker and essentially redundant in comparison to those offered via social media. Clever marketing and implementation techniques can overcome these redundancies to some degree but they cannot eliminate the inevitable pressure on the profit margins of traditional publishers as they try to sustain their self-contained aggregation model. Traditional publishers are challenged to position themselves not only against other similar companies via aggregation, but also on an attribute-by-attribute basis against social media publishers who are not wedded to the traditional model and can focus on those attributes of aggregation that offer the most influence over very specific target audiences.

The decentralized model of content aggregation also encourages content to be aggregated and disseminated before it is ready for mass distribution as a "finished product." Insights are aggregated more rapidly and fluidly in the social media model as content is collected, indexed, given additional value, distributed, and them amplified anew into new forms of aggregation by others using social media publishing tools. Instead of relying on very rigid forms of indexing content, for example, social media encourages people to develop their own indexing via tags and to enable others to add their own tags as content is aggregated and re-aggregated.

In the social media model we may never get to a definitive indexing of content—and we may never have to: the product of social media never has to leave the factory. Its value is found in its ability to be reinvented anew again and again in the hands of people who discover content anew, make it their own, and then collaborate with others to make it something new yet again. Each point in this process creates its own points of value: it's rare that there's a need for a "faucet." In fact, a faucet would often slow down the process of creating and aggregating content effectively in the social media model. Once you've entered the social media factory, via a Web site registration or some membership-based access model, you may never have to leave it to get its full value.

SOCIAL MEDIA SECRET #5: *Social media has a production model, but its goal is not mass production from a handful of huge factories, but mass contextualization in millions of small factories to create and aggregate content again and again in constantly renewable and useful contexts.*

Social Media and Marketable Relationships: The Value of Brands, Affinity, and Endorsement

If in creating and using social media we are always in the factory modifying the product, then it is rare that we'll create finished products. If this is the case, how does social media ever make money? With social media it becomes important to take a different view as to when and how its value is transformed into something that can allow people to benefit from their participation in social media.

Going back to Ghyslain's experience with "Star Wars Kid," we can see that the creator and publishers of social media were not asking for money—yet somehow it came. The content was produced and published, people engaged the content, remixed it in many instances, and then eventually some unsolicited donations came in. So it is in general with social media: the benefits of publishing, no longer tied to the factory model, are free to be controlled and compensated in any number of ways, some of which can be planned and controlled, others of which cannot but can add up to an expected benefit.

One of the keys for creating value in social media is to recognize that *social media creates value through marketable relationships as much as through marketable content.* On the one hand a lot of content generated by social media may look to be purely altruistic, something given up for free just for the love of it. Sometimes it is just for fun, just the way what sometimes you can hear a musician playing music on a street corner mostly for the love of it—and maybe a few tips out of kindness. For Content Nation, the people who really use social media to influence others, altruism doesn't have to go unrewarded.

A key example of this can be seen in how people who write popular weblogs make their living. There is certainly a growing number of weblogs created by professional writers, including many now published by journalists through their newpapers' Web sites, that make money in a very traditional way. Writers are paid, they post articles, they have advertisements that bring in revenues. In these instances the content in the weblog is distinguished from traditional publications only in the sense that it provides aggregation of comments, links, and other features that increase the engagement of an audience for that publication. This is how many media companies approach social media: they see it as a new technology that can support their usual way of doing business, with the social aspects held at arms' length.

Most people who write weblogs don't work on this model. Most write weblogs for free, or, through ads on their site, get a modest stream of revenue that rarely matches the efforts that they apply to the publication. More to the point, many of the more popular weblogs are written for free. Robert Scoble, co-author of the book *Naked Conversations* and a widely recognized expert on Web 2.0 technologies, has a popular weblog that has no ads or other noise— just his thoughts, your comments, and a link to his book. The purpose of the weblog is not to make money but to help people around the world to get to know what he's thinking on most any day. The weblog is ultimately his own advertisement for himself, a person who has marketable value as an expert in his field. Though altruistic in a general sense, weblogs like Robert's are more about enlightened self-interest, creating awareness in much the same way that a quote in a magazine article, an appearance at a conference, or a personal meeting might help a person build relationships.

February 14, 2008

Microsoft researchers make me cry

It's not often that I see software that really changes my world. It's even rarer that I see software that I know will change the world my sons live in. I can count those times pretty easily. The first time I saw an Apple II in 1977. When Richard Cameron showed me Apple's Hypercard. Microsoft's Excel. Aldus' Pagemaker. And something called Photoshop, all in his West Valley Community College classroom. Later when I saw Marc Andreessen's Netscape running the WWW. ICQ and Netmeeting which laid the ground for Skype.

Like I said, these things don't happen often.

Yesterday was one of those days. Curtis Wong and Jonathan Fay, researchers at Microsoft, fired up their machines and showed me something that I can't tell you about until February 27th. I'm sure you'll read about his work in the New York Times or TechCrunch, among other places. It's too inspiring to stay a secret for long.

While watching the demo I realized the way I look at the world was about to change. While listening to Wong I noticed a tear running down my face. It's been a long while since Microsoft did something that had an emotional impact on me like that.

Why torment you with a post like this? Because it's my way of making sure that stuff that really is extraordinary gets paid attention to. And because I wanted to get down the emotional impact of what I saw before that feeling totally wears off. I also wanted to get down some lessons that others at Microsoft might learn from so that they can have this kind of impact in their own work. Imagine if Microsoft did 10 things a year like what Curtis and Jonathan showed me yesterday? If the innovation engine at Microsoft were working that well there wouldn't be any pressure to buy Yahoo. Heck, and if there were a constant stream of stuff like what I saw yesterday Yahoo wouldn't be resisting going to Microsoft. They'd +want+ to go to Microsoft. Yesterday is the first time since leaving that I wish I were back working at Microsoft.

Now, I can hear Christopher Coulter in my head. The thing these two guys did won't have a business impact the way, say, Microsoft Office did. There isn't a business model here. But does every damn thing need a business model? Does a scientific paper that changes the world need a business model? Does it need more audience than just the other 50 scientists in the world who care about that topic? No.

In Robert's case, as with others, those relationships can turn into discussions that result in consulting contracts, speaking engagements, or offers to write books. By creating and participating in social media, people build up themselves as a marketable brand in much the same way that high-profile media figures such as movie stars or recording artists build up their personal brands through personal appearances on television talk shows. In this case, though, the branding is highly scalable and is applied to a very specific cross-section of people who are interested in Robert's thoughts.

Through search engines, links to his articles from weblogs and other social media outlets, and from mentions in traditional press outlets, Robert's writings help him to find a powerful context within his global "tribe" of like-minded people without having to promote himself through a press agent or other traditional channels. This tribe in turn builds a sense of affinity through this and other social media outlets: we know Robert because of his weblog, but we also get to know him because of his active presence on Twitter and other social media platforms as well as through his appearances at conferences.

On Robert's weblog, like most others, he writes about specific topics that talk about specific people, products, or companies. Sometimes his comments about them will be positive, sometimes negative. When it's a positive comment he is providing an explicit or implicit *endorsement* for them. This type of endorsement can be very powerful: it's provided by something that he wrote for free, presumably, so you assume that it's a freely given endorsement; it's usually a very targeted endorsement for a specific person or thing at a specific point in time, so it's highly actionable fairly immediately by very specific people who want to be influenced by it; and it can be amplified by others linking to it or writing about it, providing more free endorsement power.

Recently the Facebook social networking service tried to introduce its "SocialAds" program to match up ads for commercial services inside the content posted by Facebook members. There was a strong rejection of SocialAds at first because the ads appeared in a way that made it seem as if a member had endorsed the advertiser's products and services when in fact they had been matched to the member's content automatically. People understood intuitively when their power of endorsement through their own social media was being abused, and objected. People will be willing to endorse people and products when they can do so willingly, but most are hesitant to apply their personal endorsement to anyone or anything haphazardly.

Multiply this power of personal endorsement millions of times across all of the social media outlets that create content every day and we're no longer looking at world-famous personalities offering the most powerful endorsements via paid contracts, but instead at worldwide tribes of people with affinities who are influenced by millions of others in Content Nation, with the most influential of these people building powerful personal brands—and for some, very lucrative careers as people well connected to others well attuned to their insights and abilities. We don't have to have our content leave the factory of Content Nation because we can make a pretty good living staying there.

SOCIAL MEDIA SECRET #6: *Social media enables individuals to create content in contexts that put them in direct contact with other people who value their insights and in doing so give them many options as to how to translate that value into ways to survive and thrive.*

Social Media and the Timing of Value: Long Tails, Long Snouts, Many Peaks

There are plenty of people who are interested in making the enormous value of social media publishing translate into making money, be it directly or indirectly. While there appears to be tremendous potential to make money from social media, people publishing social media need to adopt strategies notably different from those used by many traditional publishers. Most importantly, perhaps, it requires thinking differently about the "when" and the "how" of making money through publishing.

Much of the content in this book was published on the ContentNation Web site before it was published in book form. We did this to get feedback on the book as it developed and to attract news, articles, and discussions from social media enthusiasts. We continue to add information, modify the book, and to build interest in the topic via Content Nation even today. This is counterintuitive for most traditional book publishers, so I thank the publishers at John Wiley & Sons who went along with this.

Opening up the content in this book to people on the Web was done not just to be trendy, but to demonstrate that social media encourages a new kind of economic cycle that is transforming both publishing and other elements of our global economy. Social media shows us that value can be gained from the ability of people to access insights from people when they want and need them on a very personal scale.

If you're reading this in a book format you're reading something that was produced through a mass manufacturing business model, but much of the value that I got from writing about this topic was on my weblog and in other social media outlets long before the opportunity to write a book ever came along. People got to know me, much in the same way that Robert Scoble became known, people got to know the book, the book was produced, and then the cycle started again. Content from the book is discovered anew, leads to new discussions, and, possibly, new mass-manufactured content.

At each point in this cycle there's an opportunity to cash in on the value of content that scales to the audience available at that time. This cycle works differently for different kinds of social media models. In the instance of O'Reilly Media, Inc.'s Safari Books Online bookstore, for example, it can mean using a social media model to build up subscription revenues. The Rough Cuts program from Safari Books Online allows technology-oriented subscribers who need the very latest insights on fast-moving technology topics to get access to early drafts of technology books as they're being written. Chapters of the book are made available as they're being written and subscribers can comment on them and help to shape the materials as these books progress. The book then is finalized, published in printed form, and then passes into the Safari Online Books online service that allows people to access entire libraries of published books online for a subscription fee.

In each of these three phases—pre-print electronic version, printed version, post-print electronic version—the same content provided value, but in a different form at a different time and quite possibly with different audiences. In the pre-release form the book's content attracts the leading thinkers and designers who needed the book's content and the community of people commenting on it to stay at the very forefront of technology. It was more like a piece of customized training in this mode than a traditional book. The printed version drew people who were more likely middle-of-the-pack technologists who needed to keep up with new trends, but who didn't have to be on the very leading edge of knowledge in a subject. The post-print online version helps people who are in most instances trying to address specific problems with specific pieces of content from the book, much as they would any other piece of content on the Web.

In other words, although social media lives largely inside the content factory, it's okay to let things out of the factory now and again if there's a reason to produce a mass media product. Unlike typical mass media products, the products that escape from social media into mass production and then back into evolving social media forms use mass media more as a transient form than as a final goal. If there's a mass market for something, then fine, build it. Over time more value is released from social media in its pre– and post–mass media forms than in its brief life as a "hit" for mass audiences. Mass production and distribution becomes the exception rather than the rule while highly focused audiences create and consume content on an ongoing basis for highly scalable audiences.

In 2004 Chris Anderson, then Editor-in-Chief of *Wired* magazine, wrote an article on a phenomenon he called "The Long Tail." He noted in the article and in a subsequent book by the same name that through the power of Web search engines people were able to find things to buy—such as books and music CDs that were not big hits just as easily as the latest big hits. His premise was that there was at least as much money to be made in selling the "long tail" of less popular items through millions of small markets for them on the Web as there was to be had in focusing on selling millions of a small number of items to the mass market for a short period of time.

Chris Anderson's idea was rather a hit itself, but it focused largely on things that were mass-manufactured in the first place. In social media, where often finished products never leave the factory but instead gain value through people finding them and interacting with them, the question is rarely "how do I sell more of less" but more "how do I realize the most value out of anything at any time?" From this perspective social media does not focus so much on the "long tail" of opportunities to realize its value long after something's been published for a mass audience, or even the tall peaks of momentary high value in mass markets. Instead social media tends to focus on what people at O'Reilly Media call "the long snout" of content value that can be realized prior to its ever being ready for use in a mass market. When content does reach a peak value in this environment it tends to be for very brief moments of intense value for very specific audiences.

From this perspective the value of social media is not too unlike what I used to experience in my days with financial content vendors such as Reuters Group PLC. Powerful banks and investment firms would invest countless millions in the most advanced computer and communications technology to get information on stock markets and other traded investments to take advantage of fleeting moments when they could have better insights into the financial marketplace than other people making trades. Be it on a trading floor in a major investment bank, a major exchange, or countless other locations, financial markets created what was in many ways the first electronic social media, though only for a handful of elite financial traders.

Often traders at these institutions would execute their trades over large banks of interconnected telephone lines or computer-based messaging systems, communicating directly with the potential buyers and sellers of financial securities and executing trades as soon as they saw from their available information that the conditions for executing them were right. As trades were executed over time this information would make it into more public channels—first on electronic displays, then on television and radio networks, and eventually in daily newspapers and in electronic databases used for analyzing historical trends to initiate new trading opportunities. So it is with social media in many ways: content from social media outlets may be valuable only to a few people at a time, but it can have great impact before most other people even know that it exists. You have to be in the factory—or in this instance, in the trading room—to be in on its most valuable opportunities.

SOCIAL MEDIA SECRET #7: *Social media's influence may be broad or narrow, long or short, but its value almost always benefits more from people who want to be ahead of other people than from those who are trying to catch up with others.*

The secrets of social media lead us to an interesting place in our story. If you look at our key examples of social media successes so far, it turns out that lots of different types of people—people in the traditional media business, people who work in their own businesses and in major enterprises, as well as people who make social media just for themselves—are able to create value through the highly scalable and accessible communications of social media. Who are these people? How does social media help them to survive and thrive? Most importantly, who's winning and who's losing as social media gains influential strength?

3

Social Structure in Content Nation:
Changing Tribes, New Leaders

So far we've seen that Content Nation is big, that its power scales very rapidly, and that its influence can take on many different shapes, but who is really creating social media? How do they organize themselves, and how do they manage to create structure that's meaningful using little more than wired and wireless connections to one another? In some ways social media provides certain common denominators of structure and behavior that are impacting society as a whole and providing new social structure and new leaders within that structure. In other ways, though, social media impacts society's existing social structure and institutions and changes how they organize themselves.

Some of these changes are likely to have a very positive effect on society as a whole, but not all of them will be positive for all organizations and individuals equally. In some instances the changes that social media is stimulating are threatening, especially for those who are afraid of losing their existing power, wealth, and influence. Though there is much that will be changing in society through social media, it is in reality a far less threatening force than some may imagine.

Democracy, Not Marxism: Room for the Powerful and for Everyday People in Social Media

Because social media is about having influence over others via publishing, it is by its very nature something that affects the structure of power in human groups. In any group there is a power structure, one or more people who have more influence over others in specific situations for specific purposes. Who controls what and how via a power structure is at the core of most conflicts, be it among humans or other animals. So it should not be surprising that social media is viewed with suspicion or even fear sometimes by those in positions of power.

Andrew Keene, a popular author who has dubbed himself "the Anti-Christ of Silicon Valley," writes in his book *The Cult of the Amateur* about how much of what has been considered valuable in modern culture is being threatened by social media, painting a picture of starving artists, scientists, and bankrupt media companies brought to their knees by everyday people tapping away on social media Web sites. Rhetoric from Keene and others unsure about the ultimate impact of social media seems to parallel talk about the "Red Scare," when communism was feared by many as a force that would overtake Western nations after World War II.

Certainly social media provides a democratizing force for publishing that is already changing the balance of power in the publishing world, and, as we've seen already, in ways that are changing society as a whole. Because all social systems have power structures, I think that it's a myth to say that social media will result in a system in which there will be no power structure or a rule by the mob only. Some fear a fulfillment of the 19th century philosopher Karl Marx's vision of communism as a system in which all people would be equal because "the workers own the means of production." Notably, nations that tried to implement this communism to its fullest extent wound up with dictatorship governments. As the British author George Orwell noted in *Animal Farm*, a spoof of communism set in a community of barnyard animals, "Some animals are more equal than others."

It is not so different in social media, where the rhetoric of absolute equality does not match what actually happens. The reference Web site Wikipedia, for example, allows anyone to create and edit pages on the site, but there is a standing committee of largely volunteer administrators and others who monitor and edit these pages when there is content. Digg, a popular social bookmarking site that allows anyone to submit links to Web pages for voting and discussions, quietly implemented a network of people to monitor submissions and comments for quality and ethics violations. Inevitably, social media publishing services, as with any other organized human activity, will require people who will have influence over what others do.

The question isn't whether people will have influence over what others do in social media, but rather who will have that influence and how they will exert it. In most instances social media thrives when that influence is based on what participants in a social media community choose to have as influence over their participation. What this means is that most social media communities enable the community as a whole to determine who has power within the community among its peers—including organizations that in traditional publishing models had definitive control.

A good example of this can be found in the Facebook social networking community. The Facebook publishing platform enables individual people to set up a page that can attract friends, but it also allows people to set up a page for an organization, a brand, a product, or a fan page for a person in the public eye. Facebook members can declare themselves "fans" of a particular company, product, or public personality, in much the same way that they can declare themselves to be friends of everyday people who are Facebook members. Overall the mechanisms, page design, and relationships between people and these other entities are equivalent: a page for an iPod, shown below, is about the same as a page for a Facebook member, shown just below it. Apple gains influence through Facebook, but because it must build its influence in the same manner as a Facebook member, its ability to influence that community from a position of authority is only as strong as its ability to have its authority accepted by other members.

So it is not that powerful organizations and people will not have power in Content Nation; it is rather that their power will have a different context and a different level of influence through different channels. When some people speak of the "democratization of content" through today's online publishing, this is probably the most significant aspect of that democratization. Content Nation enables people and organizations from all perspectives to establish relationships on a collaborative peer basis. It is not about "the people" controlling the powerful, but rather the powerful recognizing that nobody can determine with whom they want relationships but people themselves. In other words, in social media influence does not mix well with coercion. It's a big world of publishers out there and people will move on to another community of publishers if they're not comfortable with the direction of a particular publishing community.

The good news for major corporations and media companies is that people seem to use social media to build relationships with brands, with colleagues, and with customers in ways that are sure to help them become more profitable and effective organizations—if they adapt the right strategies for social media.

The Three Tribes of Content Nation: Personal, Media, and Enterprise Publishers

From the examples that we've looked at already, you should begin to see the outlines of three specific groups of social media users, each with their own goals and each with their own tools and methods:

- **Personal publishers:** People publishing via social media to meet their personal needs, either on a social or a professional basis or, very frequently, both.
- **Media publishers:** People or organizations using social media tools to create marketable content and online services.
- **Enterprise publishers:** Organizations working to improve their communications inside and outside their organizations for reasons related to their core mission.

All of these major groups overlap in some ways, which is a key aspect of social media's power. Modern social media tools are coming into a world already formed in large part by the economic forces that have driven both media companies and businesses through the rise of the industrial era. Each of these groups has an important role to play in Content Nation. Everyday people are the focus of much of social media, but as it changes how people engage the world economically and politically each of these three groups— tribes, if you will, sometimes cooperating and sometimes belligerent in their efforts to survive and to thrive—have to learn how to manage new and evolving boundaries as they create valuable communications through social media. Moreover, in many instances social media is changing how or whether people join one of these tribes to start with—and how they act once they join them. Inevitably, all three of these tribes are changing as a result.

Personal Publishers: The Heart of Content Nation

The power of social media is driven largely by individuals of all ages from all walks of life who enjoy being publishers and sharing content with one another. "Enjoy" is probably the key word to consider here. Though sometimes people get compensated directly or indirectly for publishing via social media tools, most people using social media tools do so because it's something that's personally fulfilling and that is, ultimately, a natural human function. Whereas technology has been the focus of much of publishing's power in recent centuries, social media focuses on the fundamental value of human interactions that are captured more naturally through social media technology.

The "Hole in the Wall" Experiment: We Are Publishers Who Influence and Lead By Nature

The essential nature of people to express themselves through electronic publishing was proven fundamentally by a very interesting experiment in New Delhi, India in 2000. NIIT, a company focused on using technology to promote learning, decided to see how people completely unexposed to computer technology would interact with a computer and the Web without any input from anyone else. Researchers at NIIT decided to embed a PC with a high-speed Internet connection in a concrete wall of their building next to a vacant lot in the middle of a very poor New Delhi neighborhood and monitored its use via remote cameras. Without any instruction from anyone as to what this device might be or how to use it, the children of this poor neighborhood would come up to the "hole in the wall" computer and start to discover how to use it to draw pictures and to browse the Web, often leading one another in learning how to use it and influencing one another by working together. It would appear from this experiment that by our very nature people want to publish, want to learn to do so collaboratively, and want to find what their peers have published.

Content Nation Around the World: Social Media Has Universal Appeal

The universal appeal of communicating via social media is underscored by a 2007 study by IBM (see Figure 3-1) on global social media use. Though the U.S. leads clearly in the use of social networking sites, with about 45 percent of respondents having used social media and 25 percent having contributed content, most surveyed nations showed relatively similar patterns in their overall use and creation of "user-generated content" such as weblogs and wikis. Although English-speaking nations have benefited more from social networking services to date than nations more focused on other forms of social media, there appears to be substantial and universal interest in social media. The relatively low levels of use for user-generated content in the U.S. and Australia and the relatively high levels of use in those nations for social networking services reflects the rise of social networking tools as primary points of social media publishing. Not everyone needs to write a blog to experience success in social media.

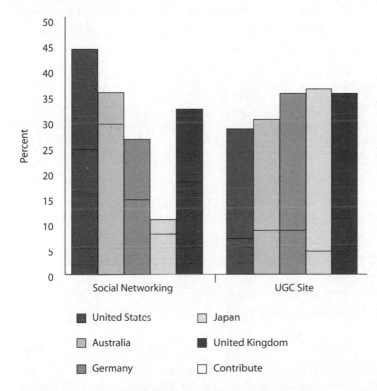

Figure 3-1: Percentage of global respondents who visit or contribute to social networking or user-generated content (UGC) sites

The Generations of Content Nation: Digital Natives Lead but Are Not Alone in Creating Influence

These social media pioneers are not just young people; people of all ages have discovered its value. A 2007 Forrester Research study indicates that it is not just young people who are creating social media. While the report indicated that 37 percent of U.S. Internet users aged 18 to 21 are publishing content actively via blogs, uploads to video sharing sites, comments, ratings, and reviews, the study also indicated that people aged 27 to 40 were also very active publishers of social media. Nineteen percent of U.S. Internet users in the study aged 27 to 40 were publishing to blogs and upload sites, while 25 percent were posting comments, ratings, and reviews. Even in the younger end of the "baby boom" generation of people aged 41 to 50, there were 12 percent who published content directly and 18 percent were adding on content via comments, ratings, and reviews. Social media has a strong appeal even for the generations of people who did not grow up with the Web as a key presence in their lives when they were as young as the children in the New Delhi "hole-in-the-wall" neighborhood.

Although adults are beginning to make strong use of social media, clearly the generations that have grown up with the Web, mobile phones, and social media from their youngest days are painting the picture of how Content Nation is changing the nature of human communications. A 2007 Pew Internet & American Life study on teens using social media services found that of the 93 percent of people aged 12 to 17 in the U.S. who used the Web, 64 percent of them created some form of content online. Publishing electronic content is becoming a default behavior for the generation that is preparing to enter our universities and work force.

Interestingly, there are gender differences in how these so-called "Digital Natives" view themselves as publishers. While 35 percent of online teen girls in the U.S. were publishing their own weblogs, only 20 percent of teen boys were bloggers; however, 19 percent of teen boys were publishing videos online while only 10 percent of teen girls were publishing video materials. Though both sexes are using social media actively, the tendency of males to focus on visual communication and females to focus on verbal communication does not seem to change in social media.

Will the abundance of outlets for publishing in social media mean that we will see a generation of women or other specific groups of people becoming more influential in society, business, and politics through social media as digital natives mature? Not necessarily; in some ways, the statistics on U.S. teen girls' use of social media parallel other studies on how girls in the U.S. today are stronger readers than boys and may reflect the generally higher verbal skills of women and the generally more visual skills of men. There's no doubt that changes in society have been accelerated by other technology changes, such as the introduction of the telephone, that enabled new patterns in our political, personal, and work lives. In thinking of how the telephone replaced the telegraph as a primary electronic communications method more than a century ago, though, it is clear that social media is likely to have a more rapid dominance and replacement of other forms of media—possibly within one or two generations at most rather than several.

Content Nation Leads in Getting Attention: YouTube versus Major Television Networks

A few clues as to how rapid the shift from traditional outlets to social media outlets may be for young audiences can be found in looking at who is looking at what. In Figure 3-2 you can see that in a one-year period visits to YouTube, the leading social media portal for video uploads, grew its leading position by nearly 50 percent, relatively unimpeded by the presence of major media outlets, including Hulu, a recently launched Web site providing access to full-length television shows and clips from U.S. commercial television outlets. Hulu's growth was relatively strong for about a month after its launch, but it leveled off rapidly, well below YouTube and also well below the growing traffic for NHL.com, a Web site for fans of the National Hockey League that's equipped with social media features to help grow its following among the "tribe" of ice hockey enthusiasts. This doesn't bode well for other sources of commercial content keeping pace with digital natives who are discovering one another's voices as publishers online.

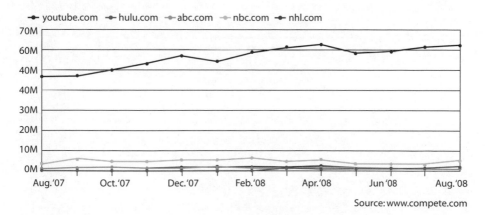

Source: www.compete.com

Figure 3-2: Number of unique visitors to various Web sites

That Canadian Girl: Gaining Professional and Personal Influence and Leadership through Blogging

Who are the leaders of this wave of personal publishers? Although there are some names in social media who are generally high-profile individuals independent of social media, the stars of personal publishing in social media are noteworthy for what to many would be their un-noteworthiness. You might call "That Canadian Girl" a typical example of someone who uses social media for a variety of purposes. "That Canadian Girl" is a weblog that recounts the exploits of Véro, a French-Canadian woman living in the United Kingdom who says of herself "described as cheeky and irreverent, I write about technology, gadgets, marketing, often trying to scratch the slick surface of someone's latest glitzy campaign like one might scratch their iPod by putting it in the same pocket as a set of keys."

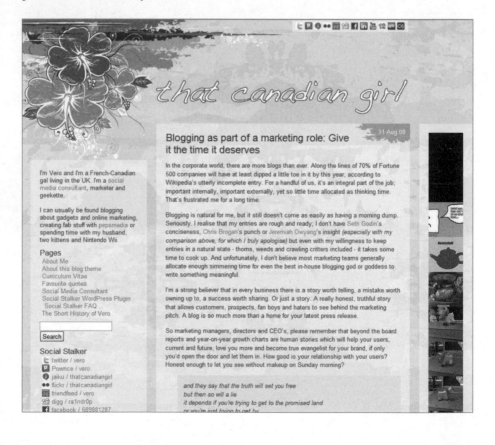

Véro's weblog is a mix of analyses of online marketing, recipes, video clips that amuse her, photos of her cat—and an acknowledgment that she's one of the more influential technology bloggers in the U.K. Dozens of people comment both on her personal content and her more business-like content, interacting with her both on a social level and a business level. A "serious" marketer would have recommended mass-mailing campaigns, a corporate Web site, and other techniques to promote her business, and those certainly have their own place. Instead, Véro has spent a few minutes each day for the past five years just being herself on a personal and professional level—and growing a healthy business while having fun. Two to four thousand people visit her weblog every month and it's linked to by more than a hundred other weblogs. That's a great amount of influence for just a little bit of publishing, influence that many professionally produced publications would like to have.

Agropedia: Using Social Media to Improve Indian Farming

The leaders in social media aren't necessarily people who are well versed in online technologies. India's Jayanta Chatterjee, PhD, a professor at the Industrial and Management Engineering Department of IIT Kanpur, is leading a team developing a service called Agropedia, which provides a wide range of information on farming in India. With a tremendous variance in climates, conditions, and other variables, not the least of which being India's dozens of languages and dialects used by farmers who don't have access to the Internet, creating a cohesive information resource can be difficult. Agropedia helps to address some of these concerns by enabling farmers to use the telephone to share their expertise on specific farming methods and issues—they simply have to speak their knowledge into the phone in their own language and Agropedia will organize their sharings for retrieval by other farmers with the same language, interests, and needs both via the phone and via the Web. Social media doesn't have to be just for the cutting-edge leaders of technology—the technology concepts that power social media can be adapted to technologies that can be used by anyone to make even everyday family farmers influential leaders in sharing knowledge and insights with their peers.

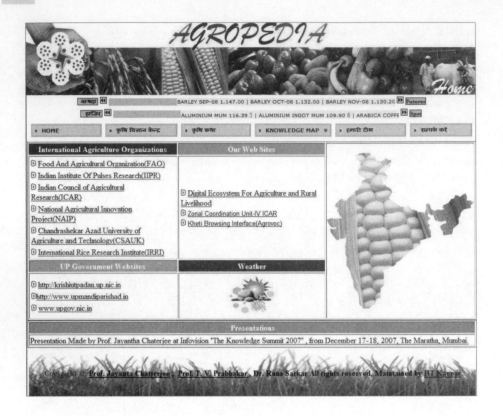

Newsvine: Anyone Can Become a Reporter at Any Time

Leaders and influencers can come from unlikely places in the realm of journalism as well. Chris Thomas, a Virginia technology worker who goes by the online handle "Killfile," received calls and messages from his wife and friends on the campus of Virginia Tech in April, 2007 moments after a mentally deranged gunman opened fire on people on the VT college campus. Killfile was the first to break the news of this traumatic incident on Newsvine, an online social media news community where he was the top contributor of news reports. Killfile filed 35 updated reports in his Newsvine article in the course of the day of the shootings, as well as an aftermath summary, including up-to-the-moment reports from people on the scene via cell phone calls, instant messaging, and police radio reports, providing in many instances key breaking details of the event that traditional news outlets took far longer to compile, using key details often from Killfile's reports. Although Thomas received special recognition for his efforts as Killfile on Newsvine from its administrators and was interviewed on MSNBC, a cable television news company that eventually purchased Newsvine, he continues for the most part to be a leader and influencer in the Newsvine online community as he has all along—an amateur who loves breaking news but who lives his own life apart from the world of media as well.

Twitter: Personal Instant Messages
Turn into World-Changing Headlines

Social media also creates leaders and influencers when major catastrophic events hit a nation. Blogs, downloaded videos, and quickly developed information-sharing services helped people to show the world what happened and to organize in the wake of 2004's earthquake-induced tsunamis in Southeast Asia and 2005's Hurricane Katrina devastation of New Orleans and southern Mississippi, but more recently the speed of social media as a leading force for propagating news was felt even more intensely. When a massive earthquake hit China's Sichuan province in May 2008, the Twitter social media messaging service enabled people with mobile phones to spread the word globally to people following their short text messages while the tremors were still underway—including people publishing prominent blogs who were being tracked by mainstream news organizations. Twitter messages formed a global stream of breaking headlines that started major media coverage and activated responses from world organizations. Countless messages, photos, and videos followed from social media services that provided the basis for both information and responses—responses that included social media enthusiasts who set up a missing persons registration bureau at a crossroads around which rural refugees had gathered in the absence of governmental support services. Although major media organizations and governmental services played a key role in responding to this disaster, social media enabled everyday and largely anonymous people to be leaders and influencers in their own right.

So who are the leaders and influencers in personal publishing via social media? Anyone. Everyone. Some have extraordinary and enduring talents and passions for publishing content; others dabble for a while and then move on to other things. In some instances leadership in social media will be fairly constant, as in Killfile's consistent efforts to be at the top of Newsvine's rankings of contributors, but in most instances leadership and influence could come from anyone at any time in any place that meets the needs of the moment, just as leaders and influencers in ice age hunting parties were those most able to address the challenges of the moment with tools that were pretty much the same as anyone else's. Like the farmers in India using Agropedia, leadership and influence may be very localized and specialized, affecting people in a relatively small community with their own communication methods and survival skills, or, like Véro or Killfile or the thousands of people in China's Sichuan province, the community in social media in which they have influence may be a nationwide or global network of people who appreciate them for who they are in the moment, providing structure to their efforts through the structure of how content is organized in social media services.

The ability of social media to provide highly scalable leadership and influence from any quarter of the globe on any issue from any perspective at any moment is the key factor that is shaping how it is influencing social structure in our world today. Other forms of mass-scalable communications can be effective as well, but the power of millions of people from any walk of life with any form of reward system in place, including altruism or just plain old fun, enables social structure to form spontaneously around any idea, concept, cause, objective, need, or want that suits them at the time. For centuries, societies have been developing and forming social structure based on large, fixed organizations such as national governments, corporations, financial institutions, and other institutions whose power has emanated largely from their ability to communicate with the world on a scale that individuals could not achieve on their own. The emergence of social media and its enthusiastic adoption as a default method of communication by a generation now coming into adulthood challenges us to recognize that its implications for social organization are far wider than we may have thought.

Media Publishers: The Old Media Becomes the New, the New Media Becomes the Old

When does social media become just plain media? That's not an easy question to answer given the rapid scalability of social media and its ability to generate income on a par with many established media outlets through advertising and other methods of monetization. In general, though, there are some people who decided to use social media tools with the express purpose of making a living off of their publishing directly, and some who make a living through established media outlets who come to use social media to expand and shift their influence and to find new sources of revenue for themselves and their operations.

Whether it's those who came into publishing through the new tools of social media or those who came into publishing using older tools and discovering social media tools, there comes a point at which social media publishers are in it for their personal living more than for other social motivations.

TechCrunch: Pure Media, Pure Blog

A prominent example of a social media property that's a media property in its own right is TechCrunch, a weblog covering new products and breaking events in media and technology. Developed by Silicon Valley entrepreneur Michael Arrington, TechCrunch has made its way to the top of the most popular weblogs and commands an online audience focused on the business of technology as large or larger than many prominent technology magazines and journals. Arrington's favorable opinions and reviews of new products are sought after by press relations specialists as avidly as those of any reporter for a major media outlet. The TechCrunch blog itself is written not only by Arrington but by several other staff writers, and is one of a series of media properties developed under the TechCrunch brand. Ads about 250mm square with a two-month run on TechCrunch can go for about $10,000 or more. In many ways there is little to distinguish TechCrunch from any other major media company's online publishing property—it's a strong ongoing publishing business that reaches more than a million people visiting the Web site monthly and more than 780,000 people subscribing to its email news feed. This is influential and successful mass media by any measure.

While TechCrunch carries the profile of mass media in many ways, it's also at its heart a social media product. TechCrunch started off as and remains a weblog, with features such as the ability to enter comments, the ability to subscribe to a free feed of articles posted on the blog, and the ability to create a link to an article posted on TechCrunch via social bookmarking services such as Digg, del.icio.us, and Reddit. These are features that can be found on the humblest of weblogs anywhere, and yet they are used very effectively to help TechCrunch scale its publishing very cost-effectively. The content in TechCrunch, while newsworthy and written with a journalistic outlook in mind, is just as often opinionated, off-the-cuff, and written with a personal tone that is not what one would expect from a typical news article. TechCrunch uses both the technology and the outlook of social media to be a leader and an influencer on a mass media scale, but is still a social media publication.

The Huffington Post: Building Influential News Outlets through Social Media Curation

The Drudge Report was a relatively small Web site in the mid 1990s known for its links to key breaking news stories on the Web and its own occasional original reporting of political events based on founder Matt Drudge's connections to leading political figures. The Drudge Report was thrust into the major media spotlight in 1998 when it decided to break the story of President Bill Clinton's relationship with White House intern Monica Lewinsky, a story developed by the *Newsweek* national news magazine but held from publication. The rise of politically opinionated Web news outlets such as the Drudge Report inspired political activist and news commentator Arianna Huffington to create a new mass media Web site in 2005 based on social media technology and techniques.

Like the Drudge Report, The Huffington Post features links to news stories at other major news Web sites selected and headlined often for maximum political impact, but unlike earlier efforts at political journalism The Huffington Post developed its own network of bloggers who would contribute to the publication their own opinions on major news and political events. Huffington herself writes the lead column at The Huffington Post, an editorial board of one shepherding a variety of opinion-makers who come and go as both regular and guest bloggers to round out the political discussions. As The Huffington Post has grown it has increased its own production of news journalism as well, enabling it to have more content engaging audiences through comments and other weblog features, while continuing to link to other Web sites directly when important news breaks elsewhere. Three years after its launch The Huffington Post now exceeds the Drudge Report in monthly audience, with more than two million people viewing it monthly, and is considered this year to be the top weblog by many site-measurement methods.

Is The Huffington Post really a social media Web site? Certainly it was never meant to be anything other than a Web site with a mass audience, and the independently wealthy Arianna Huffington could never be mistaken for an everyday person starting up a weblog. Yet within her own domain Huffington used the same general social media techniques and technology that anyone could use to start a weblog and managed to use them to scale her operation into a major news and opinion outlet. The site is powerful not only because of its timely coverage of breaking news and the wide variety of prominent opinion-makers who contribute to its blogs, but also because of the large community of everyday people who comment on its blogs and news stories. In other words, just as you don't have to be a famous and influential person to be a leader in social media, you don't have to avoid being famous and influential, either.

In some ways social media outlets like The Huffington Post are bringing journalism back to the early flourishing of newspapers in the 18th and 19th centuries, when newly affordable printing technologies enabled a wide variety of people to put out local journals with news and opinion. It was only in the late 20th century, when competition from electronic outlets and rising production costs forced newspapers to consolidate, that people became used to news coming from just a handful of powerful outlets. The ability of The Huffington Post to scale rapidly into a major media outlet is a reminder that any social media outlet has the potential to become an influential publication on a mass scale through the common technologies that enable the creation and distribution of social media globally.

Xu Jinglei: A Star Becomes a Blogger and Becomes a New Kind of Influential Star

Movie stars are often the subjects of mainstream media, but through social media actresses, actors, and other celebrities are creating media for the masses in a new way. In 2005 the Chinese movie star Xu Jinglei began writing a weblog about her daily life, generally avoiding topics related to her career and focusing on her personal ups and downs. The blog is well written and generally unremarkable in its content, but perhaps for that very reason the relative humility of this high-profile personality winds up appealing to average people in China and beyond. For a brief period in 2006, Xu Jinglei's weblog was the top blog in the world, according to the Technorati blog search and ranking service, and continues to rank among Technorati's top 50 blogs. Xu Jinglei's posted articles attract typically a thousand or more comments from her avid followers, creating a rich array of people contributing to the site as part of a community experience.

Different cultures express influence and leadership somewhat differently from other cultures, so it's no surprise that in a rapidly changing nation such as China, a well-known person such as Xu Jinglei inspires everyday people to express themselves so emphatically as individuals in the comments of her blog posts when they may be used to limiting themselves to more private and personal expressions of their opinions. She is among a growing number of people in China and other nations leading the development of a culture of more open discourse using social media tools. Though her blog in and of itself may be fairly unremarkable, the impact of people gaining the confidence to express themselves through her blog may be an important part of people not used to such open expression beginning to view themselves as capable of being influential publishers in their own right.

Digg: Turning Social Bookmarkers into Editors of a Major Media Outlet

Many social media Web sites use social bookmarking features to assemble content from around the Web, but none has succeeded like Digg. Social bookmarking is a feature that enables someone looking at a page on a Web site to save its address, its title, categorization information, and a brief summary of its content to another Web site where this information and links can be shared with others. It's a good way to share knowledge and to build highly personalized streams of information, not unlike editing your own personal news ticker for friends and colleagues to read.

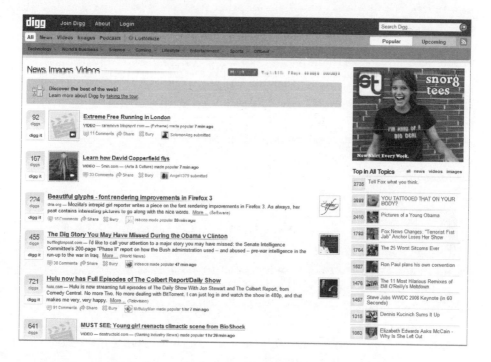

Unlike many other social bookmarking services, however, Digg was one of the first to see that social bookmarking could enable people to build a consensus as to what was the most relevant content on the Web at any given point in time. A voting system was integrated into the technology driving Digg that allowed people to drive up the popularity of a page or to "bury" it if it wasn't liked. People using Digg with a member account can comment on items that have been "dugg" by other Digg members, have their own comments voted up or down, question the accuracy of content, build a network of friends who can share bookmarks, or blog about a bookmarked item on their personal weblog.

In doing these things, Digg members build influence within the Digg member community that enables their content selections to get top rankings more often through the site's programming logic. Though perhaps only hundreds of members may have influence strong enough to determine what might appear on the front page of Digg, it's anyone's guess as to who those people might be at a given moment in time. Certainly, mainstream newspaper outlets don't have hundreds of people determining what goes onto their front pages. Peer into narrower topic areas on Digg and other people are likely to have broad topic-specific leadership and influence.

The result after several years of very careful and continual engineering and re-engineering of a fairly simple concept is a social media Web site that is one of the most influential sites for people looking for the latest news and interesting content on a wide variety of topics. With millions of members acting as enthusiastic filterers and discoverers of content worth sharing, a breaking news story or the latest video, photo, or audio podcast from any source can find exposure, popularity, and an instant community of people discussing it within minutes or moments of it being posted to the Web. Through Digg, any Web content, from the latest news story in a major newspaper to the latest amateur video on YouTube to the most interesting photo on Flickr or any other content, can become the center of social media through its inclusion into Digg.

Though the tastes of people using Digg are likely to be as diverse as those found in any large group of people, the millions of people using it and the programmed logic controlling the ranking and sorting of content—along with an occasional nudge from people monitoring the system—help Digg members to create a well-founded consensus as to what is interesting and important. In the process of filtering, Digg members become both highly influential and leaders in determining what people will look at and discuss on the Web.

Editors for major newspapers used to be the elite leaders who chose almost exclusively what was important for masses of people to read and to determine what was breaking news worth people's attention. With Digg, the consensus of everyday people has become one of the leading editorial powers that influences what gets people's attention. People trust and respect Digg's collaborative curating of content so much that Digg, now gets consistently about 50 percent more people visiting it each month than the Web sites of *The New York Times* or

USA Today. Social bookmarking services like Digg create potent media for the masses assembled purely by millions of enthusiastic people and the computer programmers who build them great social media publishing tools.

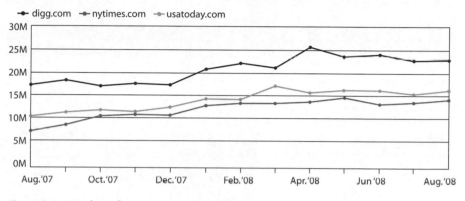

Figure 3-3: Number of unique visitors to various Web sites

Robin Good: Mastering Social Media for Profit and Passion Becomes a Publishing Career

Robin Good, the online persona of Luigi Canali De Rossi, is one of Europe's most enthusiastic proponents of all things relating to social media and personal electronic publishing. He turned his passion for his interests into the Robin Good Web site, which since 2001 has highlighted breaking news and insights from around the world into the latest online publishing tools that can be used by everyday people to publish content on the Web.

Starting out with a fairly simple ad-supported Web site with a few premium reports for sale, Robin Good has shaped his focus and his content over time into a much broader vision of how social media publishing can build into a career that generates enough income to sustain his lifestyle and his interests, but small enough to be manageable by himself and a very small core of supporting staff. Robin Good "walks the talk" of social media in his use of many of the leading-edge social media technologies for blogging, video, and electronic subscription services.

One of the keys to success for Robin Good is his ability to edit content appearing on his Web site to match the ability of online advertising services to deliver advertisements automatically that match up closely to key words appearing in his content. By choosing the right words for headlines and story text Robin can enable these advertising services to put ads on his Web site that will pay him more than other ads. With higher-paying ads served up automatically Robin Good avoids the overhead of an ad sales department while getting more revenue than the typical blogger might have producing similar content.

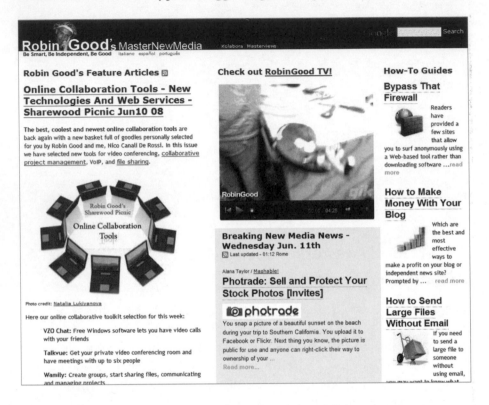

Another important factor driving Robin Good's revenues is his ability to find capable people such as industry analysts who willingly volunteer blog and video content to be used on his Web site—including, at times, postings from my own weblog. Robin Good repackages these offerings into more attractive and well-packaged content optimized for search engines. The contributors of free content benefit from the attention they gain from the relatively large and well-focused audience that views Robin Good content and the improved search engine placement of their own content from links provided from Robin Good's version of their content. Robin Good benefits from having more content to drive advertising revenues with less effort and cost and the social benefits of knowing and supporting thought leaders in his area of interest. This is in some ways social media in its purest form: people collaborating to create more value in their lives through publishing. In other ways, it's a much more traditional media model for a small publisher: get free or cheap talent to make more money from more content.

The other addition to Robin Good content that helps to drive his success is the inclusion of headlines from other news sources along with brief summaries—social bookmarking on a very small scale by someone very expert in his particular field. This steady supply of news from other sources enables the Robin Good Web site to have regular sources of fresh content that can engage site visitors throughout the day with minimal effort.

All of this combines to make Robin Good both a person who enjoys having turned his passion into a profession on a daily basis, often from the comfort of his home office in Rome, Italy, and a person who has a thriving publishing business that enables him to become an influential figure in his industry who can sell his thought leadership in training sessions and other face-to-face events. Although his Web site does not have the larger audience of some other media outlets, with more than 100,000 people visiting it each month, Robin Good has an audience that can help him to meet his goals as a publisher working with social media tools where he pleases.

BakeSpace: Turning a Traditional Passion into a Niche Social Media Publication

Cooking and baking cakes and cookies from family recipes handed down from generation to generation were always a part of the life of Babette Pepaj, a Los Angeles-based producer, writer, and director of television shows who got a hankering to come up with a way to make a social media publication that centered on her passions. The result of pursuing her desires was BakeSpace, an online community of cooking and baking enthusiasts who share recipes and chatter about their lives with other recipe-swapping enthusiasts.

BakeSpace manages a community of contributors that generates most all of the content on the Web site, which in turn generates ad revenues. Though the recipes, comments, and forum discussions posted at BakeSpace by its members certainly form the core of its marketable content, BakeSpace also provides an online chat facility open only to BakeSpace members, enabling them to build deeper personal relationships around food the way that people often would build relationships in the slower-paced home kitchens of a simpler time and place.

BakeSpace combines the ability to build valuable and unique content with a loyal community of enthusiasts who love generating both content and relationships—a media success story built very rapidly on a relatively small scale for a minimal amount of development and marketing effort that has yielded a growing publishing business for Babette Pepaj. Like many relatively small publishers in the media business, she may choose to keep the BakeSpace community going on her own or sell it to a major media company looking to augment its ability to deliver more engaging content for its own online publications covering this niche of consumer enthusiasts. Whichever her choice, BakeSpace is a good example of what happens when an entrepreneur with a passion and a talent for social media decides that they have the will and the way to be an influential leader in their domain of expertise through publishing.

The New York Times and the *Houston Chronicle*: Turning to Weblogs to Drive Growth and Audiences

Although there are bright spots in the newspaper industry, the past several years have produced a long roster of lost profits and readership as well as many papers selling out to larger owners. The problems felt even by major newspapers were underscored in August 2007 when *The New York Times* decided to make news articles and key opinion columns available on its Web site without a subscription fee. *The Times* had decided that it just couldn't generate enough Web content to provide advertisers enough places to put their ads for the non-subscribing audience that was the largest and fastest-growing portion of its readership. At the same time, going to free access enabled its content to be viewed and shared more easily by people highlighting it in social bookmarking services, such as Digg, as well as search engines.

Though opening its existing pages to the public, search engines, and social media services was one solution, the real problem was that, like Robin Good, *The Times* needed more pages in its Web site on which to place more ads and get more ad revenues. Part of the solution for *The New York Times* has been to expand extensively the number of weblogs on its Web site to cover a wide variety of topics and viewpoints. With more than 50 weblogs on topics that parallel all of their major newspaper sections, *The New York Times* weblogs are gaining viewership quickly and building content that keeps people reading more from both staff journalists and people who comment abundantly on many of the weblogs.

The *Houston Chronicle* had similar problems with declining print readership and sluggish online growth and decided to take a different approach to growing more content. Instead of adding weblogs just from its journalists, the *Chronicle* enabled its readers to set up their own blogs on the Chronicle Web site. Unedited by the *Chronicle* staff, dozens of Houston-area residents pump out their thoughts on their Chron blogs—building more pages for more ads and more comments from readers that keep them engaged on the pages of the *Chronicle*'s Web site longer. Through its readers becoming publishers on their own Web site, the *Chronicle* also gains a new kind of influence and leadership under its brand that enables a community to see their own friends and neighbors as part of that brand. Readership is up strongly at the Chron.com Web site over the past year, thanks in part to the growing popularity of social media content that leads the way to more a more personal approach to journalism.

When the Masses Can Be the Media, What Is Mass Media?

Although mass media still has many of the same traits and business goals as ever, the arrival of social media as a major force in electronic publishing is changing the social structure that determines how major media outlets are started, grow, and influence their audiences. Like Michael Arrington, anyone with a few good industry connections can start a fairly successful commercial blog overnight. Like Arianna Huffington, anyone with some visibility in their field and a bit of cash can start a highly influential news organization with little more than a list of influential contacts who know how to write a bit. Like Xu Jinglei, a well-known person can become their own media outlet, showing the world who they are in real life rather than relying on media organizations to shape the image of their lives. Like Kevin Rose and the other founders of Digg, any good programmer and a few associates can come up with an idea to empower people through social media good enough to build an audience larger than a traditional major media outlet. Like Robin Good or Babette Pepaj, anyone can make a fulfilling independent living out of pursuing their passions through using social media tools to make a successful online publishing business that scales to a niche audience. Like *The New York Times* and the *Houston Chronicle*, any existing mass-media outlet can change the long-term prospects for the value of their publishing brand by empowering people to use social media through their Web sites.

If all of these publishers and more can service mass markets through social media with efforts relatively miniscule compared to those required to build the media empires of past generations, and so many people are doing so regularly around the world, then it's fair to say that the social structures required to create mass media have shifted fundamentally. We are at a point in the development of human communications at which having a social structure that empowers any and all people to be leaders and influencers through publishing on a potentially massive scale is now more effective and more important to our future than relying on social structure that empowers a tiny group of central leaders and influencers to succeed through publishing to the masses. Large traditional media companies will continue to have success, of course, because of the resources at their disposal and the strength of their brands and the availability of unique channels for their content, but in a world in which mass media is now more about enabling the masses to create media for everyone or just the right people, traditional mass-media companies are no longer driving the fundamental social structure of publishing.

Enterprise Publishers: Productivity and Public Relations through Personal Publishing

Although the use of modern social media publishing tools in the work lives of people is only beginning to receive broad attention, it should be no surprise that today's social media publishing tools are becoming highly popular in many of today's enterprises, and that they are becoming a key factor in helping to shape today's workplace. Long before computers began to become household appliances, they were helping people in major businesses, governments, and academic institutions to solve problems and to improve communications. Unlike earlier generations of technology used in enterprises, the Web-enabled technologies of social media have been adopted by people in their personal lives often before they were adopted in their work lives. Through their use of home PCs and laptop PCs, mobile phones, and other electronic devices that serve a role in both work and personal environments, the enthusiasm for social media is working its way into the workplace rapidly.

Social Media: Helping Enterprise Workers to Cut through Information Clutter

As with earlier generations of technology, concerns abounded that some social media technologies would hamper productivity. In most instances, though, enterprises are learning rapidly that social media can provide a great boost to productivity, often far more than the boost received from traditional workplace information technologies.

A recent study done by researchers at the Ohio State University and the University of California underscores the productivity benefits of social media in the workplace. In the study, entitled "IM = Interruption Management? Instant Messaging and Disruption in the Workplace," researchers asked both people who used instant messaging services and those who did not to say how much they had to deal with interruptions in the workplace. The study found that those who used instant messaging to communicate with their peers thought that they were able stay on task without interruptions far more so than peers not using instant messaging.

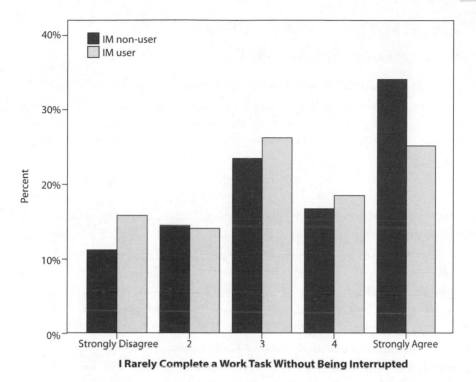

Figure 3-4: Disruptions in the workplace as rated by IM users and non-IM users

This study of instant messaging underscores one of the key advantages that social media technologies offer people in the workplace over traditional information technologies: an enhanced ability to collaborate with the right people at the right time with the right information with as little interference from others as possible. The need for this improved productivity in today's enterprises is striking. A 2005 study by Outsell, Inc. found that professionals were spending 53 percent of their time seeking out information. Importantly, the same study found that 67 percent of professionals were using the open Web as a source of information required to perform their jobs. In spite of decades of corporate investment in information technologies, the information resources inside today's enterprises have failed to become the obvious choice for people seeking information more than two-thirds of the time.

Content Nation as a Promise and a Threat to Enterprise Structure

Just as mass-media publishers held back in embracing social media because of the threat that it represented to their way of doing business, so have information technology managers been slow to bring the productivity benefits of social media into the enterprise. Though social media technologies that can help productivity inside the enterprise are beginning to be more prevalent, they are still far from universal. A 2008 poll by *CIO Magazine* of more than 300 information technology decision makers found that only 30 percent offered wikis as a corporate application, 23 percent offered blogs, and only 10 percent of respondents brought social networks from the Web into the enterprise. Social network services on the Web are key to the lives of younger workers, so much so that a recent survey of workers found 39 percent of 18-to-24-year-olds would consider leaving their job if they could not access social networking services, such as Facebook, to communicate with their peers.

The social structure of many enterprises seems to be in conflict with the emerging social structure that social media helps to accelerate in both people's personal and professional lives. Today's younger worker in many countries using Web-based technologies is someone who has learned how to blend the tools that help them with their personal life with the tools that help them with their professional life. Portable PCs, mobile devices that help people read and send emails and text messages, the wide availability of wireless Internet connections in popular locations and increasingly everywhere—all of these and more are the underpinnings of a movement toward individual publishing as a part of a lifestyle that supports both personal and professional needs.

Michael Idinopulos, vice president of professional services at Socialtext, a leading supplier of wikis and other social media software for enterprises, touches on one of the key reasons behind the conflict between enterprise technology specialists and people used to personal publishing: a struggle for the means by which enterprises succeed. Michael Idinopulos notes that social media technologies like Socialtext's wikis are a type of technology that may not fit in well with the motivations and goals of most information technology managers, who are interested in the standardization of information through their established infrastructure in a way that will scale effectively. This is not too different from the general goals of many major corporations: increase the efficiency of producing lots of standardized products and services so as to maximize revenues.

Interestingly, though, social media tools are reaping large benefits in many instances that do improve standardization and efficiency. A case study of Socialtext's installation at investment bank Dresdner Kleinwort Wasserstein demonstrated that Socialtext's wiki services were being used by more of that institution's 6,000-plus employees than any other internal electronic information service—though it took the efforts of a few pioneers to get the project started. Michael Idinopulos notes that in many instances social media technologies in use in enterprises have come into place initially outside of the efforts of information technology managers, often at a localized level within an organization and often initially outside of an information technology manager's budgets.

You might say that in some instances social media is a citizen's revolt against centralized technology within today's enterprises by people using social media services that are often totally free, relatively inexpensive, simple to deploy, or readily available on the Internet. With these publishing services, many workers in today's enterprises are able to assemble and share information that's crucial to their success as professionals without having to wait for others in a central role to dictate when and how to do it. When almost anyone in an organization can establish a successful information service, new leaders and influencers are bound to emerge.

Jigsaw: Content Nation Creating Enterprise-Class Business Information Outside of the Enterprise

Social media also encourages enterprise workers to create more content that's available to people outside of their enterprise, which can help them with their business goals. One of the more interesting examples of this is a service called Jigsaw, the brainchild of Silicon Valley entrepreneur Jim Fowler. People use Jigsaw to publish and to receive contact information on people in businesses, the sort of information that people collect from the business cards that they get from people they meet. People pay to get access to individual contact information on Jigsaw generally, but for each complete set of a person's contact information that someone provides on Jigsaw the contributor gets points toward downloading contact information for free. Other Jigsaw members can challenge the quality of the information that someone has contributed and take back some of those awarded points toward their own free downloads of contact information. Jigsaw allows people to download the company name and address information that they collect through this process for free, a valuable service that encourages people to contribute to Jigsaw, which in turn improves the frequency of updates to its information. With more than 8 million contacts from more than a million companies in its database—many of them people who aren't normally found through other business information services—Jigsaw has created a highly valuable, enterprise-class business information service driven by individuals collaborating to build quality information. Jigsaw sells its contact information in bulk to enterprises, as well, so that they can update their internally maintained contact information. This puts Jigsaw sometimes in direct competition with other business information services that collect information through more standard data-collection methods. Not only can individuals as publishers enable more value for enterprises when they publish outside the enterprise, but they can challenge the suppliers to enterprises to perform more effectively. The information that everyday people in business collect and share can help to influence the ability of people everywhere to do business effectively, and in the process of doing so create new leaders and influencers in business information services.

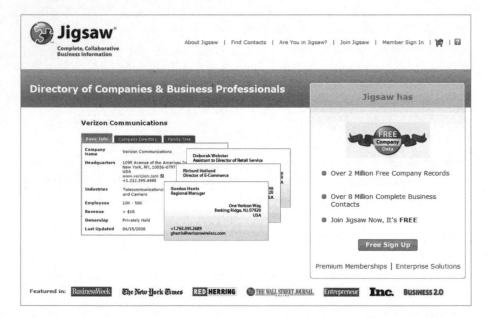

Executive Blogs: Talking with Your Markets...Whenever

Social media also enables enterprises to be publishers to the world at large, most especially to their existing and prospective customers. Just as in the world of mass media, social media doesn't always empower just everyday people; when enterprises want to speak to the world through social media, social media can often put a major enterprise's own executives out in front of the world. Executives publishing weblogs are very common now among CEOs of major technology companies, but they are also increasingly common outlets for companies of all kinds. Auto and truck manufacturer General Motors has put its vice chairman, Bob Lutz, to very good use as a key contributor to its FastLane Blog. Well known in the auto industry for his enthusiasm for innovative and fun-to-drive vehicles, Bob Lutz's contributions draw many comments from consumers passionate about cars and trucks themselves, and in doing so creates a dialogue with the marketplace that GM serves. That's industry leadership and influence that a corporation cannot attain easily through normal media channels.

GM FastLane Blog   **GM** Blogs

Chevy Cobalt SS

« Behind the J.D. Power & Associates Initial Quality Study | Main | A Note from HUMMER: Let the Speculating Begin »

At Last: Behind the Wheel of Volt Test Mule

By Bob Lutz
GM Vice Chairman

This week we announced that the GM Board has approved the Chevrolet Volt program. Yes, development work has been going on in earnest, but now it's official. In fact, recently, at GM's Milford Proving Ground, I drove an official "engineering development vehicle" with the 16-kwh lithium-ion battery pack we've been testing for our E-Flex System and I have to say – pun half-intended – it was electrifying.

The first impression of the day, however, was made before I even got into the vehicle. It hit me on the drive out to Milford, as I passed gas station after gas station with prices for regular unleaded hugging the $4 mark: This makes the importance and potential of our all-electric glide through our proving ground roads even clearer.

Now, don't run to the Chevy dealer and order your Volt yet: The "test mule" I drove – a previous-generation Malibu – wasn't calibrated

Syndicate this site (RSS 2.0)

Syndicate this site (Atom)

MY YAHOO!

SUB BLOGLINES

newsgator

what am I doing...

Newest podcast episode is up; Talking hybrids with Chevy's general mgr. Interested in hearing your thoughts http://tinyurl.com/4vg2uy – Adam

1 day ago

follow GMblogs at http://twitter.com

Archives

Select a Month...

Recent Comments

Brian on At Last: Behind the Wheel of Volt Test Mule: Ok....Make a Volt that people CAN buy and the people will line up around th...

Rum Doodle on At Last: Behind the Wheel of Volt Test Mule: MEMO TO GM'S VOLT TEAM: Don't look back. As the

ITtoolbox: Building Expertise and Knowledge through Online Publishing

It's certainly not just CEOs and leading executives who are helping their enterprises through social media publishing on the Web. In social media sites like ITtoolbox, an online community for technology professionals, people in enterprises that use and sell computer technologies write blogs, maintain reference information in a wiki, post downloadable reports on how to solve technology problems, share ideas through comments and online forum discussions, and build relationships through a social networking community built into the ITtoolbox Web site.

Instead of waiting for a major publisher to write a book or an article on a critical technical topic that affects people on the front lines of enterprises—and having to wait for your enterprise to purchase it—ITtoolbox allows anyone from any enterprise to share their knowledge with one another in an environment dedicated to their profession. At the same time, the companies that sell technology services get to participate in the ITtoolbox community and build relationships with their customers and prospective customers. Not only do everyday people working in enterprises get to become leaders and influencers with their peers around the globe, their suppliers also get an opportunity to be leaders and influencers through their ability to participate effectively in the ITtoolbox community as problem solvers and a good communicators.

Although in some ways enterprises are late to the new dance of social media, as many were late to recognize and adapt to the Web itself, they are also becoming some of its brightest stars, leveraging its ability to build a new generation of publishing-savvy leadership and to influence thinking and productivity inside and outside of their organizations using a new set of tools that are highly cost-effective alternatives to many of the computer technology solutions that they've used to date. Publishing technologies such as email, telephones, databases, and printed documents remain an important part of life in today's enterprises, but increasingly Content Nation's entry into the workplace is changing fundamentally in many ways how people earn their livings.

How we make a living is a large part of what social media is all about, one way or another. Be it someone who publishes on a personal basis, someone who turns to independent publishing as a career, or someone who publishes inside and outside their enterprise to help their organization succeed, we are all trying to survive and thrive in the world somehow. In the age of centralized publishing many came to rely on large organizations to help them get the resources they needed to live well, a factor that determined in many instances who would be our leaders and how people would influence one another. Now with the advent of global social media, Content Nation challenges people of all nations and all walks of life to reconsider how it is that they are going to form new tribes and find new leaders to help them work together and live together effectively. In doing so, many fundamental aspects of our lives are going to change far more than we may be able to imagine.

Let's try to imagine. Let's take a look now in more detail at where some of these fundamental changes created by social media are already impacting how people create value in marketplaces, how they manage their workplaces, and how they manage their personal and public lives—and how these changes are taking us to a far, far different kind of society from what many of us experience today.

The New Media:
Content Nation Challenges the Fundamentals of Marketing

In my first marketing class years ago our professor had a simple definition of marketing that still seems to work today: "Find a need and fill it." The development of all products and services and their presentation to people who could be a market for them is based around understanding who needs what and getting it to them. How do you find needs through social media and how do you fill them? On one level social media may not appear to change the fundamentals of marketing in any significant way. If you visit a popular social networking site or look at a popular weblog you're likely to see advertising and other features that would seem to indicate that social media is not much more than an extension of traditional marketing methods via mass media, but social media is also offering the tools of marketing to millions of people worldwide who never before had access to tools that would help them to play a role in local and global markets, and in the process of doing so they are transforming how goods and services are being sold in both local and global markets.

Social Media as a Marketplace: Matching Supply and Demand

A market is a mechanism that enables someone offering a supply of goods and services to discover and act upon the demand for them, a concept that though simple has not always been easy to manage. Restricting access to abundant supplies can drive higher demand, and not being able to access abundant demand can hold down the value of goods and services. Electronic and print communications have enabled the supplies of goods and services to be matched to the demand for them as never before in the past few centuries. Because, historically, only a handful of media organizations have controlled access to market information, the availability of information about markets did not necessarily change fundamentally how markets would work. Markets benefiting from publishing still relied on a handful of publishers and agents managing the flow of information about those markets, which in turn enabled the wealthiest organizations to be the prime influencers of supply and demand in those markets.

A Fisherman's Tale and a Search for Cheap Gas: Content Nation Empowering Economies

A simple example of how social media can change the balance of markets was highlighted by *The Washington Post* in a story on fishermen making their living off the coast of India. Traditionally, a small fishing boat in India would take its catch to the nearest port and have to accept whatever prices were offered by fish wholesalers for their catch; they had no easy way to know what the demand for their catch might be in a port before heading toward land. With the advent of mobile phones, a fishing-boat captain could contact other fishing boats or wholesalers in multiple ports to determine where the best demand might be for a catch before deciding to head for a specific port, or check prices elsewhere via mobile Web connections. With the mobile phone Indian fishermen have changed the balance of power in their markets from the middlemen with control of local supply and demand to fishing-boat captains who are able to move from one market to another with ease based on the ability to collect their own information about those markets. In the process of doing so, they have become members of Content Nation, using the power of highly affordable communications technologies to define a marketplace for themselves rather than having others define it for them.

As much as a real-world market can benefit from sellers using social media, so can buyers benefit from social media in the real world. GasBuddy.com is a Web site that enables members in the U.S. and Canada to learn about up-to-date prices for gasoline and diesel fuels at local filling stations that have been contributed by GasBuddy members. Using information from GasBuddy, buyers can learn about markets in much the same way as the Indian fishermen can learn about them from a seller's perspective, and in doing so have the information to help them change how they act in their local markets. Sellers can also monitor GasBuddy, of course, and keep their prices in line with competitors, creating more efficient markets for both buyers and sellers, using information provided by people in the marketplace empowered by influential social media.

Not logged in [Log In] [Sign Up] [Points Leaders] [My Profile]   Thursday, September 11, 2008 5:48:49 PM

by GasBuddy.com
ConnecticutGasPrices.com   Add gas prices to your web site.
Click here to find out how!

Home | Message Forum | Price Charts | Map Gas Prices | Gas Price Temperature Map | Fuel Logbook | Wireless | More
Master Station List | Photo Albums | Link To Us | What's New | Helpful Tips | FAQ | Contact Us | Connecticut Classifieds

Connecticut Classified ads
Report a Price Here
☑ Reg   ☐ Mid   ☐ Prem   ☐ Diesel
$
Station (Other)   Area (Other)

Station Address

Comments

Time Spotted
5:48 PM   ☐ Add to my Favorite Stations
Submit   Prices removed after 48 hours

Earn 3 miles per dollar spent on travel and gas
purchases with the Capital One Card

Looking for more prices in Connecticut ? Try:
Bridgeport Hartford New Haven Waterbury

Quick Search for Gas Prices
Find the lowest gas prices in these areas:
Danbury Danielson Groton Meriden New London
Newtown Norwalk Norwich Stamford Torrington
[More Cities]

Search For Gas Prices
⊙ Regular   ○ Mid   ○ Premium   ○ Diesel
⊙ Connecticut Site Only   ○ All of Connecticut
Area   Station
All Areas   All Stations
Beacon Falls   7-Eleven
Bethel   BJ's
Blue Hills   BP
Broad Brook   Chevron
(Hold Ctrl to select multiple areas/stations)
Other Area   Prices in the last
                    48 hours
Search Now! [Top Low & High Prices]

Auto Insurance News
Average Auto Insurance Cost: $69/Mo*
Think you pay too much for your auto
insurance? The sad news is, you probably do.
In fact, you may be paying more than your
neighbors even though you have a clean
driving record, your commute is the same,
and their car looks identical to yours. Why
should you pay more?
Find out what your lowest monthly payment
could be. Click here to get your new payment
today or select your vehicle make below.
Select Vehicle Make: Acura ▼

Become A Member
Join Now to become a
GasBuddy member, and help
everyone save on fuel
purchases. As always,
membership is entirely free.
Local Price Snapshot
Today   3.789
Yesterday   3.780
One Week Ago   3.805
One Month Ago 3.988
One Year Ago   2.905
               Trend
               Prices
               Stable
               [Points Leaders]

Urgent - Gas Price Spotters Needed. Help Fight High Gas Prices

Regular Gas	Midgrade	Premium	Diesel Fuel

Lowest Regular Gas Prices in the Last 48 Hours

Price	Station	Area	Time	Thanks
3.47	fuel depot 644 Putnam Pike	greenville	Wed 1:14 AM	patriots10523
3.59	Sunoco Danbury Rd	New Milford	Thu 10:27 AM	Ahsfc
3.59	Citgo Danbury Rd	New Milford	Thu 10:27 AM	Ahsfc
3.59	Getty Danbury Rd	New Milford	Thu 10:27 AM	Ahsfc
3.59	Hess Danbury Rd	New Milford	Thu 10:27 AM	Ahsfc
3.59	Valero Danbury Rd	New Milford	Thu 10:27 AM	Ahsfc
3.59	Xtra Fuel 497 Jonathan Trumbull Hwy near Lake Rd	Andover	Thu 6:45 AM	mmann
3.59	gator gas rt 1 ($3.64 for credit)	Clinton	Wed 6:51 PM	ctnotbolly
3.59	Citgo 129 Merrow Rd & I-84 (I-84 at Exit 68)	Tolland	Wed 10:20 AM	Pyrrhuloxia
3.59	zoz gasoline first 68 north Tpke rd	wallingford	Tue	johnnyCT

CONTENT NATION MARKETING RULE #1: *Empowering anyone to understand supply and demand builds efficient economies that benefit the most people.*

eBay: Creating a Global Market for Anything through Social Media

Affordable voice and Web-based communications make it possible for anyone almost anyplace on the planet to determine what a fair market price might be anywhere for many goods and services. The eBay network of ecommerce Web sites is a good example of how these basic concepts of marketing, media, and online technology can be adapted to social media tools to accelerate the growth of markets more effectively. Founded in 1995, eBay grew rapidly to become the largest online marketplace for buyers and sellers, now serving in the neighborhood of 84 million people worldwide. eBay enables most anyone to post an item for sale on its site and either to sell it for a fixed price indefinitely or to auction it off to the highest bidder. eBay can take a fee for the sale of an item, but the ability to set up a storefront for, in essence, no money and to have built-in processing of transactions if desired was an attractive proposition to many people.

Millions of people soon flocked to eBay to sell used goods and collectibles from their homes, creating a global marketplace to realize values that would be difficult to obtain through selling items to people passing by one's home. Buyers get to rate the quality of a transaction with a seller, enabling sellers to establish their reputation as trustworthy merchants to the world through the community's "word of mouth" endorsements. Services and books sprouted up to help everyday people become "eBay millionaires" by learning how to maximize the use of its services.

In many instances the claims of being able to make a living on eBay are hardly an illusion. There are numerous examples of people who really did start up successful businesses via eBay that made a million dollars or more. One of the keys to people making that kind of money has been the information made available from eBay's service to merchants that helps these merchants to analyze trends in both searching and purchasing. Services such as HammerTap make it easier for eBay merchants to analyze the trends found in eBay's information and to adjust their merchandise and pricing to take advantage of those trends. These are the kinds of sophisticated analysis tools that were formerly used only by major retail chains to adjust their marketing. Instead of those marketing tools being in the hands of just a few companies, now they're available to any person with an inclination can become their own marketing "guru" instead of being just a good salesperson in a local store.

THE INTERNET MARKETING CENTER

The Insider Secrets to Selling on eBay

Home | "Earnings Disclaimer

IMPORTANT NOTE: If you've been struggling to start or grow an Internet business, this may be the most important letter you ever read...

"Because on the following page,
I'm about to reveal EXACTLY how YOU can
start your own Internet business potentially
worth $50,000... $300,000.... even $1 Million
(or more!) per year...

• WITHOUT a website,
• WITHOUT a ton of start-up capital,
• WITHOUT being a computer techie, and
• WITHOUT any business experience!

PLUS, if you have an existing business, I'll show you
how to *EXPLODE* your sales by expanding into eBay's
giant online auction place of 2 Million shoppers and
growing...

... Spending over $86,000,000 every day!"

Today small auctions and sales represent a declining percentage of eBay sales as established retailers and entrepreneurs trying to become "power sellers" move eBay toward larger merchants selling mass merchandise goods to mass markets. It's interesting to note that as eBay moves toward these mass markets it is finding that fewer people are visiting its Web site. To put it simply, it's hard to be both Wal-Mart and the town-square marketplace, but the eBay model has established that anyone could make a market with any kind of goods in a global marketplace powered by Content Nation. Through social media anyone can build their own personal brand in an online marketplace that places all comers on an equal footing in reaching a world that can purchase their merchandise. Most importantly, just about anything can become highly marketable merchandise through eBay, including items such as used or hand-crafted goods that many traditional retail outlets would be reluctant to sell. The traditional idea of a public market for anyone's potentially valuable goods has been revived and made accessible to anyone who demanded them in Content Nation.

CONTENT NATION MARKETING RULE #2: *Maximize the ability to discover supply and demand, and anyone can make a market for any goods and services.*

Craigslist: Classifieds for Anyone, Everywhere, Creates a New Marketplace for Local Economies

The Craigslist community bulletin board service brought the concept of a global public marketplace driven by social media to a broader range of goods and services, and to a community focus. In 1995 founder Craig Newmark set out to make Craigslist a community bulletin board for the tech-savvy people of the San Francisco area. Since then Craig Newmark and his small group of programmers and support staff, which still includes Newmark, have expanded their service to support people in communities across hundreds of U.S. cities and in communities across 35 nations around the world who want to share classified ads, events listings, and discussions on Craigslist's simple Web site. Ads on Craigslist are free for most people, except for companies posting jobs and for real-estate sellers in major markets. Like traditional newspaper classified ads, Craigslist does not get involved in any transaction and enables sellers to remain anonymous; the service is there as a forum for public communication.

Wall Art: Alaskan landscape at sunset - $40 (Norwalk)

Reply to: sale-723175325@craigslist.org
Date: 2008-06-17, 3:10PM EDT

Alaskan landscape at sunset. 37.5" (L) x 25.5" (W)

- Location: Norwalk
- it's NOT ok to contact this poster with services or other commercial interests

PostingID: 723175325

The pages on Craigslist are very simple in design, almost anti-commercial, you might say. You'd think that such a facility would not have much commercial appeal at first glance, but Craigslist is one of the most popular Web sites today, with about 40 million visitors monthly looking at more than 10 billion page views and having doubled its audience in about a year for the more than 30 million new classified ads appearing on Craigslist each month. There is something about the homely Craigslist that people find to be very attractive. In large part that attractiveness is the concept that its listings are for the most part completely free and unfiltered content; it's just people reaching out to other people like themselves to sell goods and services, to meet one another, or to announce things happening in their local communities or across any of the communities that Craigslist serves. Like the humble town squares that in some places still host market days when farmers and merchants bring goods to sell to their communities, the looks of Craigslist aren't as important as the opportunity to meet up with other people in their community to exchange goods, services, and chitchat. In fact, the homely and neutral nature of Craigslist helps people to have a sense that there are no considerations in using the service other than those of the people using it.

Because Craigslist does not take a part in any transaction for goods and services advertised on its site, an economic exchange between a buyer and a seller can take on any form, including bartering. In May of 2008 Craigslist had received listings for more than 130,000 bartering offers, creating a broader marketplace for transactions not requiring money. Because Craigslist can take advantage of the virtually limitless ability of the Web to store content, the marketplace conversations on Craigslist can scale to any size of community easily, and can scale across communities using search engines to locate goods and services. This can allow commerce of many kinds to scale accordingly.

Not surprisingly, Craigslist has been a real headache for newspaper publishers wanting to capitalize on classified-ad services. At some major newspaper chains classified advertising fell 14 to 20 percent during 2007, while Craigslist, the top-ranked online classified-ad site, doubled its audience and grew its annual revenues by some estimates now approaching $100 million. This is still fairly small compared to the estimated total online market of $3.1 billion for online classified ads, but given that Craigslist charges for only a fraction of the listings that are posted to its site while newspapers and other large online ad services charge for most of their listings, it's fair to say that the financial impact of Craigslist on the marketplace for classified ads goes far beyond its own revenues.

More importantly, Craigslist has succeeded in part by recognizing that, like the traditional town-square marketplace, an online marketplace is a social function that brings together peers in a community as much as it is a commercial function that brings together merchants with consumers. People build personal relationships with one another via social media, relationships that sometimes turn into commercial relationships, but which remain first and foremost personal, part of the fabric of a community. With more and more commerce in local communities being driven by large retail chain stores and more local newspapers owned by large newspaper chains, Craigslist is a reminder that communities acting on their own behalf can be their own very efficient drivers of commerce, when they have ready access to publishing tools.

CONTENT NATION MARKETING RULE #3: *Sometimes the most effective marketplace is a community that communicates with its constituents effectively.*

Social Media as Research:
Building Market Knowledge through
Publishing-Driven Relationships

A marketplace of peers using social media is enabling more people than ever to be independent buyers and sellers in Content Nation. For many buyers and sellers, though, the question of what to buy and sell is one that takes research. In modern society, traditionally driven by mass-manufactured goods advertised through mass media, often buying decisions were influenced by brand advertising. Research is showing, though, that today's buyers heavily trust the opinions of peers in making buying decisions.

An eMarketer study of U.S. adults using the Web found that 91 percent of adults sought the advice of others before purchasing a product or service and that 58 percent of adults named recommendations from friends as their top influencer in buying decisions. Other eMarketer research showed that about 18 percent of today's Web users are influencing others by word-of-mouth recommendations, many of whom are people using social media. Though traditional sources of research such as magazines with product reviews and online Web sites are still important to many people for learning about products and services, increasingly it's everyday people empowered with social media tools who are helping them to understand what's worth buying.

Consumer Product Reviews and Ratings:
On-Demand Word-of-Mouth

It's hard to imagine that anyone would care enough about a cat-litter scoop to share their thoughts about it with the world, but apparently there were 26 people using Amazon.com who cared enough about the ScoopWell Litter Scoop to write a product review about it. Millions of product reviews and ratings from consumers are on Amazon and other Web sites that enable people to examine other people's opinions about household goods, restaurants, hotels, and luxury items. This is social media in the context of a purchasing decision; in this instance, in a very valuable and influential context. Do I spend four dollars or eight dollars on a litter scoop? Twenty-six people writing about the eight-dollar scoop can make all the difference in my purchasing decision. Something like a cat-litter scoop is not something that people would likely see advertised outside of a very small set of publications, yet, thanks to the social media features of Amazon, this particular product can receive strong endorsements right at the point of purchase that advertising would be hard-pressed to generate in the mind of a consumer.

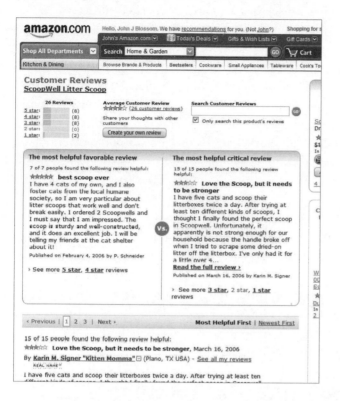

The eMarketer study on word-of-mouth advertising found that such product reviews and ratings were considered by consumers to be more valuable than the influence of radio advertising, Web search engine ads, billboard advertising, and Web site banner ads. Thinking of the billions of dollars spent on such attempts to influence buyers, the free influence offered by product reviews and ratings is valuable indeed. Most importantly, consumer reviews and ratings play a role at the point of purchase that friends, television ads, and other powerful purchase influencers cannot offer. Consumer reviewers are friends of necessity, able to offer a personal touch that focuses a buyer on a community of like-minded people. Few of us could probably think of 26 people we know who could give us an informed opinion about litter scoops or other everyday items that we might be thinking about buying, much less be available when we were considering such a purchase. A 2008 study by the Edelman public-relations firm found that 58 percent of people trusted "a person like me" as the most credible source of information about a company, ahead of a financial or industry expert, an academic professional, a doctor, or a healthcare professional. In other words, when there's a community of like-minded people available to help someone form an opinion on a commercial venture, they are the most trusted source.

Quite a bit of marketing research has been built up around how a person's emotions influence a purchasing decision, much of which focuses on the idea of creating an allure about a product or service that will seduce a buyer into making a purchase. Author and researcher Vance Packard wrote in his 1957 book *The Hidden Persuaders* (Pocket, 1984) about how the "hidden needs" of a consumer—their inner desires and fears—can be manipulated through well-designed advertising and marketing techniques to persuade a person that they should purchase a product. Though many emotions certainly factor into buying decisions, there is one inner emotion that social media seems to bring to the fore: trust.

The world of advertising is one in which marketers struggle endlessly to second-guess where and how they might be able to influence a purchaser in the few moments that they may have via an unsolicited message, appealing to extreme emotions to gain a person's attention as they pass by or endure a message on the way to getting to what they really wanted or needed to do. In social media such appeals are not respected by and large. Instead, the emotion of personal trust, of being able to assess the thoughts and feelings of like-minded people in an environment free of pressure or over-engineered allure, seems to drive decision making for purchasers using social media. That trust is extremely hard for sellers to engineer via traditional marketing methods, and the alternative methods are enormously expensive.

SOCIAL MEDIA MARKETING RULE #4: *Trusted peers are the most powerful tool for people researching sellers.*

Everyday Enthusiasts: Add Them Up and Buzz Starts to Happen

Greg and Kat Baker are a couple of no particular fame who blog together on topics relating to their lives in North Carolina and elsewhere. Their posts are probably of personal interest to just a few people, but if you're interested in a Motorola RAZR mobile phone, you may have found in a search of weblogs Greg's opinions that he posted recently on why he may be trading in his RAZR phone sometime soon and what his thoughts are about which model to get next. Because Greg has posted his opinions without any thought as to their commercial value, you're likely to treat them as honest, unvarnished views of what life with a RAZR is about. If you know Greg personally, chances are his opinions will carry a fair amount of weight, if researchers are correct.

If you're Motorola and you're wondering what people think of your products, Greg's opinions in and of themselves may not be that valuable, but add Greg's opinions to the opinions of all of the other people using social media to talk about their products, and Greg's outlook on the Motorola RAZR becomes input for Motorola's research into consumer-sentiment analysis and product planning. Traditionally, companies would research market opinion by conducting polls or persuading people to participate in a focus-group meeting in which a professional interviewer would tease out their opinions on a company's products and services. The process of gathering and analyzing such information is expensive, time-consuming, and does not always yield information that companies can act upon easily. Moreover, if market conditions change—a competitor introduces a new product or a problem with a product becomes known in the news—the careful work put into traditional market research may no longer reflect what people in the marketplace are thinking.

Greg and Kat's blog
Tales from Greg and Kat, in NC and elsewhere.

Posts by...
- Greg
- Kat

Categories
- Food
- General Life
- Links
- Meta
- Moving
- North Carolina
- Photos
- Science
- Teaching
- Tech
- Work

Archives
- June 2008
- May 2008
- April 2008
- March 2008
- February 2008
- January 2008
- December 2007
- November 2007

Phone Help Wanted
June 17th, 2008, 2:25 pm PDT by Greg

Yay! Kat's back!

But that's not really what I want to write about. Since Kat's back in Vancouver, she needs to get a Canadian cell phone. My RAZR is starting to slowly degrade, so I'm thinking about replacing it before it falls apart totally. So, we're both in the market for phones.

There are two issues here: the phone and the service plan. As much as the mobile industry would like to confound those two decisions, I'm going to treat them separately.

I would appreciate any thoughts people have on how to satisfy these requirements...

Phone

For the phone, our needs are relatively modest. It should be able to... (in approximate priority order)

1. make calls.
2. send/receive text messages with a decent interface.
3. be small and easily back-pocketable.
4. sync its addressbook and calendar with a computer with open/free/common technologies. For me, that means Google Calendar (or an iCalendar file) and Linux. For Kat, it's Apple iCal and a Mac. This is a dealbreaker for me, possibly not for Kat.
5. send/receive emails in some suitably rudimentary way.
6. take pictures, I suppose.
7. maybe access the web, but I don't hold out a lot of hope for mobile browsers not sucking.
8. things that might be nice, but I don't really care: speaker phone, GPS, wi-fi.

I have been playing with a phone finder, but don't have much to report.

Motorola phones are totally out for me: the RAZR was a nice enough phone, but the software sucks hard. The browser is unusable (e.g. no way that I can find to enter a URL: I had to email a link to Google to myself so I could get there), the calendar won't sync with anything as far as I can tell, and it generally won't talk to anything computer-wise.

The worst example of its usability are the outside buttons. On the left of the phone, there is a rocker switch, and a single pushbutton (which you can see in this picture). The rocker switch is used to toggle ring setting/do nothing modes, and the pushbutton is used to scroll through ring settings. Let me say that again: the up/down buttons are used to toggle, and the toggle button is used to scroll. Dead to me.

To make the most of opinions like Greg's on weblogs, forums, and other social media Web sites, powerful search services have been created that harvest the influential insights that publishers have created to analyze the patterns found in their content to define patterns in the marketplace. Services such as Dow Jones Insight, Attentio, and BuzzLogic comb through hundreds of millions of pages of content from millions of social media enthusiasts who mention products and services offered by major companies. These services are able to surface key trends as to what companies, products, and brands are being written about the most online, which of these has positive or negative sentiment associated with them, what key words or concepts are being associated with them, and which people using social media are the most influential on a particular product or topic. Because the search engines used for these kinds of services are able to visit millions of Web sites each day, these insights from the patterns found in social media and other online sources help these companies to understand market sentiment clearly and to act upon it strongly.

The search for sentiment and influence in social media through tools such as these can have an enormous potential payoff. Research promoted by Attentio indicates that 1 in 3 auto buyers use social media to help them make their purchasing decision. Fifty-one percent use it to help narrow their choice, 23 percent to confirm a choice, and 15 percent to select a top choice. Understanding the marketplace, not just as a group of potential buyers but as a group of people who are the ones influencing buying decisions, takes researching markets out of the realm of looking at samples of a population and into the world of looking at a census of a population. It is, if you will, democratic input for product planning.

CONTENT NATION MARKETING RULE #5: *When the buyers talk more loudly than the sellers, it's time to listen to them.*

Building Conversations with Markets: Getting and Giving One-to-One Insight and Feedback

The suggestion box is a time-honored method to collect ideas, but rarely has it resulted in a meaningful amount of feedback from customers about the problems that they really want solved in their products and services. Social media works to change that by enabling institutions to hear directly from their customers and to interact with them as peers. One interesting example of how this can scale dramatically is Dell's IdeaStorm portal, with which Dell has collected more than 9,000 product- and service-improvement ideas in little over a year, with more than 630,000 vote-ups for good ideas and more than 70,000 comments. Dell's staff interacts with members of IdeaStorm by adding their own comments to suggestions and providing feedback as to what Dell is considering doing with them. In blog recaps that come out every week or so, Dell keeps the conversation with clients going by providing updates on how the feedback is being applied to its products and services. Many ideas and their feedback are used to make critical product decisions. In one recent week seven "Ideas in Action" were announced as being in the process of being implemented. Using the tools of social media—community feedback, voting contributions up or down, engaging actively in community discussions, forums, providing regular feedback and updates in a very person-to-person conversational style—Dell both gets powerful market research at a fraction of the price of traditional methods and builds up product enthusiasm among its most vocal and influential front-line customers.

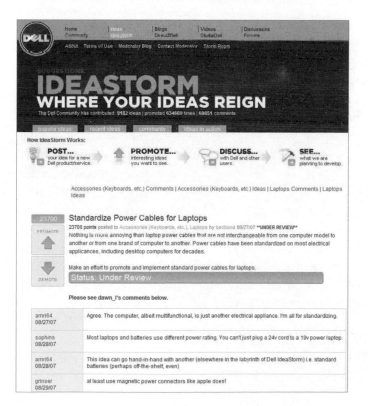

CONTENT NATION MARKETING RULE #6: *If you say that you want to hear from your customers, be prepared to have a conversation with them—a lot of them.*

Turning Product Testing into Product Evangelism: Johnson & Johnson Goes Toe-to-Toe with Customers at CafeMom

CafeMom, a social media portal that was one of the 10 fastest-growing Web sites in 2007 according to Web-analytics site Compete, is a very active social network of mothers who share photos, personal stories, and discussions on everything from diapers to dentists to getting jobs in and out of the home. With a claimed six million monthly visitors CafeMom's fast growth is attracting both advertisers and marketers who want to get feedback from people who are both prime targets for their products and able to express themselves with openness and enthusiasm.

One of the companies attracted to CafeMom is health-products giant Johnson & Johnson, which has seen CafeMom's audience grow quickly past the audience for its own Baby.com portal of expert information and ads. Johnson & Johnson formed a topic group on CafeMom focused on people volunteering to test its Aveeno line of skin products. Two hundred invited CafeMom members were sent samples of Aveeno products and asked to provide feedback on them via CafeMom in a members-only group. Many members responded enthusiastically with comments, before-and-after-photos, and enthusiastic endorsements, such as, "Aveeno products are fabulous…the best diaper rash cream ever is the aveeno brand…clears up a diaper rash in like two applications…love it !" This is not only good product feedback but is using product testing as a way to build up an enthusiastic core group of online publishers who can be strong evangelists for a product and a brand in a community of influencers that will listen intently to their peers' recommendations. You could spend millions on television advertising to influence mothers, or you could start an online conversation with mothers who other mothers trust to be your influencers for you.

CONTENT NATION MARKETING RULE #7: *If you're introducing a product that needs both testing and evangelists, use social media to build relationships with testers who can become evangelists.*

The Big Sombrero: Social Media as an Equalizer for Mass and Niche Market Power

You've seen how social media helps millions of people to discover and create markets, how to build research from millions of personal publishers with opinions, and how to tap them to get feedback on new and existing products and brands that companies bring to market. In ways both subtle and powerful, using social media in the early stages of preparing a product for the marketplace challenges the fundamental idea of how many organizations have thought of marketing in the highly centralized organizations that have been the foundation of major companies in modern societies.

Henry Ford once said of the Model T, his first mass-manufactured automobile, "The customer can have any color he wants so long as it's black." He held on to this conviction long after other manufacturers had begun to mass-produce more style-conscious cars, and in doing so almost brought his company to ruin.

With social media Henry Ford wouldn't have had to make that decision by the power of his will or his intuition: he could have gotten confirmation that people would accept a black Model T as long as it was affordable and did the job right—until they changed their minds—as much as people accepted white Apple iPods as long as they were affordable and did the job right. Intuition, personality, and ego don't have to be the drivers of great products anymore; instead, great products can be created by great listeners and collaborators, people who are willing and able to put the buyer in control of specifying what is creating demand in the moment.

If the markets are becoming empowered through social media to identify, interpret, and respond to demand from buyers rapidly and responsively, then perhaps there is a fundamental shift in how buyers and sellers experience success in the marketplace. If demand is shifting very rapidly for goods and services, and people can respond to those demands quickly enough through social media to catch rapidly shifting demand profitably, then some of the traditional benefits and profits of mass marketing and mass manufacturing are going to be challenged by those who can satisfy demands before they ever reach the scale of mass markets.

A few years ago *Wired* magazine's editor-in-chief Chris Anderson popularized the concept of "The Long Tail," based on the premise that the Web is able to create markets for mass-produced goods—long after they were first mass-produced—by finding new markets for them through search engines and buyer recommendations. The obvious question raised by the "long tail" model in light of social media's power to create responses to the market's demands rapidly is why the ability to find powerful niche markets should be limited to recycled mass-market goods and services.

The Web in general, and social media in particular, enables people to exploit highly profitable market opportunities long before they have been recognized and responded to by mass marketers. Some of the niche markets may go on to be developed into mass markets, but many of them will be quite profitable and well-defended throughout their life without resorting to mass marketing, in part because social media enables a high level of personal communication among market participants that mass marketers will be hard-pressed to challenge. Brand and product loyalty is one thing: when the brand is the consensus of well-networked people with a wealth of information at their disposal, then new concepts of barriers to entry will emerge to challenge mass-marketing techniques. These strongly defensible niche markets can be thought of like the turned-up edges of a big sombrero, creating a larger market "shadow" beneath it than the mass market's crown in its middle. The strengths of niche markets supported by social media, unlike the "long tail" model, may in fact provide a strength that supports certain standard mass-market products and services, but which for the most part lives independent of those mass markets, and increasingly may drive mass markets.

CONTENT NATION MARKETING RULE #8: *The ability of buyers and sellers to collaborate in the development of highly defensible market niches through social media may create more market value than mass markets.*

Social Media as the Message: Marketing as Influencing a Conversation

The Big Sombrero market model offers enormous opportunities for all market participants, but it may be a tricky model to master if you're a company focused on traditional mass marketing. In some instances mass-marketing techniques for communicating with social media participants work pretty well in social media: YouTube's advertising revenues are powered primarily by ads placed on the pages on which videos are displayed, revenues that are expected to climb up to $200 to $500 million by 2009 according to some financial analysts. Viral marketing techniques, long used on the Web to spread enthusiasm for products and services via email and other online communications, have been mastered by many marketing professionals to accelerate the sales of mass-market goods and services. Spreading the word efficiently is the key to mass-media marketing techniques, and in some ways social media accommodates that model well, but a problem arises when you have to confront markets that are already communicating well with one another on any number of topics and on any number of levels. When social media has created its own conversation, how do marketers get invited to that conversation effectively without alienating its participants or threatening a brand product's reputation?

From Diet Coke and Mentos to Facebook: When Your Brand Misses a Worldwide Conversation

The year 2005 marked the beginning of the "Diet Coke and Mentos" online video craze, a phenomenon triggered by Steve Spangler, a popularizer of science who loves to use everyday materials to demonstrate scientific principles in books, live appearances, and television shows. One of Spangler's most popular tricks was to show how Mentos mint candies, when dropped into a soft-drink bottle, could release huge foamy fountains of carbon dioxide. The beverage of choice became Diet Coke, in part because its lack of sugar would make cleanup after his experiments less sticky, and because its ingredients seemed to result in a particularly foamy and spectacular display.

A demo by Spangler of a Mentos fountain on KUSA-TV in June of 2005 happened to coincide with the growing popularity of online social media services that collected videos created and uploaded mostly by everyday people. Homemade videos of people's own experiments with Diet Coke-and-Mentos fountains began to flourish online soon afterwards, with new experiments and new techniques bringing the phenomenon to an ever-higher level of drama and complexity. Thousands of personal publishers—more than 12,000 on YouTube alone—have tried their own hands at online videos of Mentos-and-soda experiments, the most popular of which has been viewed by more than 8 million people.

As people made these videos the logos of Mentos mints and Diet Coke were shoved into close-up focus for millions of viewers, yet it was more than a year before the manufacturers of Diet Coke and Mentos began to take interest in a phenomenon not of their own making that had enormous viral marketing value. It was only after seeing a Mentos fountain spectacular by online video producers EepyBird featured on the *Late Show with David Letterman* television talk show that Mentos provided support for Diet Coke-and-Mentos displays. The marketing support from Mentos began to grow, with prominent sponsorship in live events in which hundreds of people attempted to set world records for simultaneous Mentos-fountains (as of this writing the largest attempt to date was in Riga, Latvia, which involved 1,900 participants). Today the Web site for Mentos displays prominent links to Mentos fountain videos by EepyBird and how-tos for Mentos-fountain enthusiasts, and has played an enthusiastic, active role in record-setting events long after their mass-media exposure has died out. Coca-Cola was more aloof from the start of the phenomenon, refraining from direct endorsements or support. Coca-Cola tried to create its own Mentos-fountain videos on its own Web site as part of "The Coke Show." They flopped. Eventually, diet soda from rival Pepsi began to support live Mentos-fountain events: The Diet Coke-and-Mentos meme was dead. The world's leading brand walked away completely from the phenomenon and since has had tepid marketing and branding efforts via social media.

Photo courtesy of EepyBird.com

The power of the Mentos-fountain phenomenon to provide endorsement value was confirmed in 2007, when an online popularity poll sponsored by *Time* magazine rated Steve Spangler the 18th most influential person of 2007, placing just ahead of Brad Pitt and Barack Obama. Though the Time 100 was an unscientific poll that compiled popularity votes from more than a million people, this was an overwhelming endorsement not only for Spangler personally, but as well for the citizen publishers of Content Nation who were inspired by Spangler. To have more influence in a popular barometer of cultural influence than one of Hollywood's most focused-upon media figures and a prominent candidate for President of The United States of America is an indication of how important it is for people who feel empowered by publishing to be a part of a global cultural phenomenon. More significantly, though, it's an indication of how powerful the potential is for Content Nation to confer or withhold its endorsement in an era in which social media is becoming the primary focus of so many people in a global marketplace.

The importance of the lessons that come out of the influence of this event cannot be underestimated:

- Three highly visible brand-name products gained enormous global viral marketing endorsements that they never asked for and never initiated.
- The phenomenon was completely self-sustaining for the better part of two years. Marketing support was minimal—mostly only for EepyBird-produced videos and live events—and never influenced in a major way what people decided to do on their own.
- People did with these brand-name products as they pleased, sometimes doing things that would make a typical corporate lawyer cringe if it were to be something that might have legal repercussions. Yet nothing untoward happened, and a powerful folk endorsement continued to spread.
- Coca-Cola looked at a new world of online branding controlled by its customers and flinched, and has been paying a high price ever since. According to statistics at Compete, the number of people visiting Coca-Cola's Web site was down 16 percent since May 2007, whereas traffic to rival Pepsi's site, which features links to popular online content and its own social media, was up more than 40 percent in the same period.

Mentos caught on to a genuine social media trend and learned how to embrace it as an active participant that was willing to let the message be what the social media publishers and audience wanted it to be. Coca-Cola wasn't prepared to recognize the authority and influence of social media and tried to control the message unsuccessfully.

Interestingly, Coca-Cola and Pepsi find themselves in the emerging stages of yet another campaign for brand influence initiated by social media publishers. On the Facebook social networking Web site some Facebook members from Canada and Australia have started opposing Facebook groups for Coke fans and Pepsi fans who want to take a side in the "Cola Wars." Members get awarded status recognition points for the number of Facebook members that they invite into the group of their choice. Members post comments, photos, videos, discussions, and share their enthusiasm for one brand over another with friends on Facebook. Social media doesn't demand that products be unappealing, it only asks the products be polite about joining a conversation. Social media won't allow products to buy their way into conversations. Yet again, Content Nation decides to have fun with brands where and when it pleases, and shares its enthusiasm as it chooses to.

CONTENT NATION MARKETING RULE #9: *In social media viral marketing can create and mutate its own viruses at will and turn brands into what influential personal publishers want them to be.*

Be Careful What You Ask For: General Motors Gets Unexpected Feedback from Viral Videos

In 2006 automotive giant General Motors launched a contest for the best audience-created video featuring its large Chevy Tahoe truck model. Contestants could assemble videos using pre-filmed clips of their trucks in action and add music and text. It seemed like a good idea at the time, until the contestants arrived. What GM received was not glowing praise for its vehicles but people who used its toolkit to generate their own editorial statements about the Tahoe's size, lack of fuel economy, and impact on the environment. Some of the videos included references to pro-environment Web sites, turning GM's efforts into a promotion of the audience's favorite causes. Aware of the negative publicity that these videos attracted, GM took the contest Web site off the Internet. Not only had Content Nation made a statement at GM's expense on its own Web site; they also preserved their videos for viewing on Web sites such as YouTube. Tens of thousands of people have viewed these videos, continuing the branding of large trucks as these potential buyers would have them be branded.

It appears that trying to control people's endorsements doesn't work too well in Content Nation: people need to speak honestly so that their endorsement power will be authentic in the eyes of an audience that has ready access to all opinions on branded products, as well as opinions on the authenticity of someone who endorses a product directly or indirectly. If you're looking to use the influence of people in social media, you have to respect that influence at least as much as your own.

CONTENT NATION MARKETING RULE #10: *If you ask for a conversation about your brand in social media, you have to be ready to hear what you may not want to hear.*

Learning How to Have Conversations: Becoming a True Peer in Social Media through Facebook

Learning how to have conversations with markets does not seem to come naturally to many companies used to traditional marketing techniques. Like someone who has been good at charming a potential mate with smooth talk and good looks, being able to put some of the slick tools of mass marketing aside to engage in social media markets may seem a bit unnatural at first to those used to the appeal of traditional marketing methods. Social media doesn't require a brand marketer to make their products to become "wallflowers" to drive their appeal in social media; it only asks for a brand to be polite about how it joins a conversation and to try to buy their way into conversations where they're not wanted. This doesn't mean that advertising doesn't have its place in social media; many social media portals make a place for advertising that works reasonably well for people wanting to get messages across. Choosing your mix of methods can be tricky and can depend on the rules and expectations of a given social media community.

The Facebook social networking community offers interesting examples of how a brand can succeed when it takes on a role as a peer-endorsed source of interesting content and community contacts, an opportunity that's underused by most marketers. Very few major brands maintain a Facebook presence actively yet, but some that do are beginning to understand how to use a social networking community. We looked briefly earlier at how fans of Coca-Cola and Pepsi set up popular and rapidly growing groups on Facebook that attracted lots of enthusiasm for these brands, but with content created and selected by fans that may or may not fit either company's marketing themes. By contrast the official Coke and Pepsi pages on Facebook offer less raw content than the fan-generated "Cola War" pages, but still attract large numbers of Facebook members who declare themselves "fans" of these pages, and in doing so open themselves up for messages from these commercial page creators. In essence, fandom for a page creates an opt-in channel for marketing messages from the page creator. Think of how many marketers would have to labor to create such a willing audience for their marketing messages in other mediums; this is an extraordinarily powerful way to reach people who have a strong relationship with a brand or a product or service.

If that were all that Facebook did, it would be powerful enough, but in fact Facebook does quite a bit more. When a member becomes a fan of a Facebook page, Facebook will put a notification of their action on the Facebook home pages of their friends. So the personal endorsement of a page fan is automatically propagated to other members—automatic viral marketing, if you will. By some estimates the average Facebook member has links to 164 Facebook friends. This means that if I had 164 friends on Facebook and I had become a fan of a page, then 164 other people would become aware of my endorsement

of that page when they looked at their Facebook home page. If for the sake of argument none of the people who were fans of the Pepsi page on Facebook overlapped with the friends of all of the other people who were fans of that page, then that would mean that about 8 million people would be aware of people personally endorsing Pepsi's page.

Though due to overlapping networks of friends this is not a realistic estimate of the actual scope of fan endorsement, even if the total unique impressions of unique endorsements were just a third or a quarter of the typical Facebook members' friends network, there would still be millions receiving those impression endorsements. Moreover, for the friends that were overlapping with other endorsing members, those members would be viewing multiple endorsements for that page, and would be further persuaded to become fans of that page themselves. Facebook offers marketers the opportunity to put in a small text ad with a simple graphic and a link to a Facebook page in friend-notification messages, which helps to accelerate the power of that endorsement to attract new members to that page, but it's the personal endorsement itself from one or many friends that provides the basic marketing power.

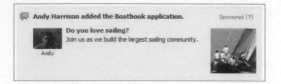

Facebook can also enable people to develop software that a member can add
to their page easily that can help to build brand value and marketing relationships. Some applications, for example, have the ability to send messages that
are graphic tokens of appreciation to friends, symbols such as a bottle of cham-
pagne, a birthday cake, and so on. A Facebook application exists that enables a
member to send Coca-Cola symbols to friends; the more friends to whom to you
send a Coke "gift," the more different kinds of Coke-product symbols will be at
your disposal. The data collected from this application can be used to analyze
how product preferences match up to different types of member profiles. This
is an interesting example of how altruism, the feeling that enables someone to
give to others with no direct personal reward in return, can be combined with
marketing goals such as brand endorsement and market research to enable a
freely given endorsement to be personalized to a recipient.

Facebook can also enable people to develop software that a member can easily add to their page, which can help a company to build brand value and marketing relationships. Some applications, for example, have been used by marketers to promote brands through fun features. A Facebook application sponsored by Coca-Cola for its Sprite soft drink brand enables a member to share with other Facebook members their choices for pro basketball player picks in the National Basketball Association draft. The data collected from this application can be used to analyze how product preferences match up to different member's profiles. This is an interesting example of how altruism, the feeling that enables someone to give to others with no direct personal reward in return, can be combined with marketing goals such as brand endorsement and market research to enable a freely given endorsement to be offered for two brands at once.

The ability of marketers to gain a position as a trustworthy peer in Facebook happens in large part because pages created by a marketer have no major differences in their capabilities from those created by an everyday member of Facebook. This limits the power of marketers to have unique control over their audiences through adding unique features. Yet, in a sense, having the same technologies at their disposal as everyone else enables marketers to gain more authenticity, to be seen as a true peer with an audience among peers much as any other person may have. The power of scalability comes not from being able to buy attention but by being able to leverage the scale of a community's endorsements. By using the same power that other peers use to gain those endorsements, marketers can become powerful and influential peers as they gain acceptance from other powerful and influential peers in a marketplace of relationships driven by social media.

CONTENT NATION MARKETING RULE #11: *The power of personal endorsements in social media places the ultimate power of marketing in the hands of the markets and not the marketers.*

Knowledge as a Marketing Tool: WikiAnswers Enables Experts to Build Relationships through Sharing Expertise

WikiAnswers is an online community that enables people to post questions on the Web and to have those questions answered by people who want to share their knowledge on a particular topic. The answers to questions accumulate over time and become a resource that people can search, and that comes up in search-engine results often when people type in a similar question. Like many social media communities, WikiAnswers builds up an enthusiastic core of people who answer questions on a wide variety of topics, but unlike some social media communities, WikiAnswers encourages companies that provide products and services in a particular marketplace to answer questions as well.

Other people on WikiAnswers are still free to answer a question answered by a company representative, but in the meantime the companies that respond to these questions have an opportunity to provide information that will be seen as an answer coming from a peer source. This enhances the position of that company to be seen as a trustworthy source of information in a way that would be hard to convey through a corporate Web site oriented toward traditional marketing or a company advertisement. In doing so companies gain access to the marketplace at a level of trust that costs little to support. The main commitment has to be to answering questions honestly in a way that will be respected by the peers on WikiAnswers. This is almost the inverse of the concept of traditional advertising, where words are chosen carefully to present a particular image of a company or a product. Simply giving direct and truthful answers to direct questions can be extremely beneficial to a company's brand value in the marketplace, if it's done in a community that explicitly and implicitly accepts them as trustworthy peers.

CONTENT NATION MARKETING RULE #12:   *When you become a trusted source of information in a social media community that competes openly with a community's peers for influence and authority, your brand gains marketable trustworthiness.*

The Super-Enthusiast: Building a Brand through Respected Social Media Peers

When people understand and respect a person's personal brand, good things can happen. A nice example of this can be seen in how some branded products work with enthusiasts who publish social media about their favorite pursuits. An interesting example can be seen in the Oh Gosh! blog of London, which highlights tips on mixing bar drinks, reviews of famous and trendy bars, and activities among the tipplers of Europe. In the process of doing so the Oh Gosh! blog drops many names and takes many photos, often including the names and brands of liquors and establishments. Although there's a commercial edge at times to Oh Gosh!, clearly it's a blog of, by, and for mixed-drink enthusiasts, with frank reviews of the fare in high-brow establishments (the famed Bar Hemingway in Paris drew a mixed review) along with photos of brand-sponsored events and personal accounts. Enthusiasts like to use the power of their endorsement with some care, but for those upon whom favor falls, cultivating relationships with bloggers covering niche markets can be a powerful level of endorsement from a blogger's personal brand that may motivate the trendsetters in that marketplace.

CONTENT NATION MARKETING RULE #13: *In social media all brands are personal brands.*

Me-dia: Social Media as a Place to Build Personal and Corporate Brand Messaging and Influence

Traditionally, companies spend lots of money and effort to get their senior managers in the media spotlight via press releases, interviews, and presentations at conferences. These remain important marketing tools, but one of the most important developments in promoting the brand value of senior managers is using social media to enable them to speak directly to markets. We saw an example earlier of GM's Bob Lutz, a self-professed car nut who is seen as an influential media figure, posting items on the FastLane blog. Certainly, examples of chief executive officers as bloggers now abound among prominent technology and content companies who are able to provide their companies with leverage in the conversations happening in those circles. Blogging as a tool to promote a business can work on any level of any industry seeking to build influence and to gain a personal marketing voice hard to deliver through traditional media channels.

An interesting example of how management blogs can help in a marketing effort for a company of any size comes from FirstRain CEO Penny Herscher, whose Market Mine blog covers events in the financial industry as well as highlighting her up-and-coming company's information-analysis products. Penny manages an interesting mix of timely topics, weaving in information that's useful to potential clients but first and foremost being herself—an insightful and well-spoken business leader—as she shares her thoughts. Penny Herscher once relayed to me the story of a blog post that she had written that resulted in a phone call from one of FirstRain's prospective customers. By reading her blog post the prospect finally "got" what FirstRain's sales team was trying to get across to him about their services, and finally arranged a valuable sales call that would probably have been much harder to attain without her blogging efforts. Penny is careful to provide links to her profiles in the LinkedIn and Facebook social networking services to maximize the business networking effect that she can attain from her efforts.

CONTENT NATION MARKETING RULE #14: *Sometimes your company's best personal brand is the person who drives the influential relationships that lead to sales.*

Sponsored Social Media:
The Good, The Bad, and The Ugly

Social media's marketing power comes from its ability to have genuine relationships between trusted peers act as market influencers. Unfortunately, many marketers who turn to social media view it as a medium that they want to exploit as just another media channel that can carry a commercial message first and foremost instead of a personal message. In other words, these marketers try to use social media as just another way to craft a sponsored commercial message. Like the payola scandals of years past in commercial radio, in which music publishers concealed their compensation of radio-station staffs to play specific songs, hidden sponsorship of someone's endorsement of a product can have very negative consequences. Most bloggers and producers of social media are careful to indicate when they have conflicts of interest that might interfere with their objectivity when speaking about a particular topic. Done the right way, as seen in some of the preceding examples, sponsoring social media can work when it's clear who owns and sponsors the content, and the people associating with that company or product actively endorse them. Sponsoring content in a way that represents a sponsor's intent honestly and openly can help them to gain the trust of their markets.

Unfortunately, this is not always what happens with social media. In the worst examples, companies sponsoring social media create content that's not only not legitimate peer communications but is downright deceptive. Whatever the technique, the desire of marketers to try to purchase deceiving influence via social media is an indication that there is something fundamentally different about its power. In Content Nation, people endorse one another openly and willingly. In traditional marketing, everything is done to purchase influence regardless of the market's openness to their influence or its value in comparison to others.

The Good: Be Honest About What You're Doing, Even if It's a Bit Commercial

Sometimes a brand wants to have a bit more "oomph" in a social media setting, and sometimes that can work out well, when it's designed to have its branding separate from other community publishers. A good example of this is the "Channels" feature of YouTube, which enables publishers to have their own branded section of the site in which to display their videos and to add marketing messages. Major brands such as the National Basketball Association can showcase their own videos as well as other YouTube videos that they find interesting, helping to underscore their membership in a publishing community. The same NBA videos can be found elsewhere on YouTube, but their own collection is highlighted in the "Channels" category of the site. This allows a brand to participate more powerfully in social media while enabling it to remain a peer source of content.

Another good approach to sponsored content is social media that provides useful information for a community but that promotes regularly products and services that people can purchase. Indie Sounds NY is a blog and newsletter produced by New York entrepreneur Pete Harris, who promotes local independent music acts and sales of their CDs from his Harris Radio Web site. Indie Sounds NY has content designed to appeal to people following the New York independent music scene in general, while including regularly links to new artists, songs, and content on Harris Radio. This enables Pete Harris to enjoy the benefits of being able to blog about general events as a part of this particular community while being able to keep his original Harris Radio brand in the spotlight.

CONTENT NATION MARKETING RULE #15: *There's nothing wrong with being commercial in social media, as long as it's clear how you fit into your community.*

The Bad: Blurring the Lines Between Community and Commercial Interests

Though Web presences like Indie Sounds NY and the NBA Channel on YouTube still have strong components of social media influence and leadership, marketers get into trouble when they try to combine commercial messages with community content too intimately. Though many of these efforts don't result in bad content, they do tend to bend the purpose of social media more toward trying to influence the ranking of another commercial Web site in search results from Google and other popular search engines. The Bath 747 weblog is an attractive blog with nice illustrations, popular topics with entries that are generally a short paragraph, each followed by a message to visit a Web site that sells bath products. When you look more carefully at the blog entries, each one really doesn't say much of anything important about the topic; it's just words that can be found by a search engine to make it appear to the search engine software that this Web site likes the bath product site it links to a lot. Though it may not appear to a search engine or a casual reader that this weblog is anything other than an independent view of a topic, this is content that's written specifically by people who are paid to promote the Web sites referenced at the end of each article.

SUNDAY, JUNE 22, 2008

Therapeutic Bubble Baths

Not only can bubble baths be relaxing, de-tensing, de-stressing, and even romantic, but they can also be therapeutic. Physiotherapy that is. Meaning, they can be treatments or symptom relievers when you are sick. This is not common knowledge and I'm sure that a whole lot of moms have done this with their children, but my mom used to put me in a cold, or tepid, bath whenever I had a fever. She did this when I was little and did the same thing when my brother and sister were little and it helped break our fever every time. That, and eating lots and lots of Popsicles. Next time your little one has a fever, try placing them in a cold or tepid bath, it is an at-home way to break their fever.

Visit BathandBody.com for the finest in quality bath and body products.

CONTRIBUTORS

BATH747
AMWOO.2007

Click Here!
Best Bath Store

| | | |CLICK HERE| | | |

FOR INTERNET INCOME SUCCESS

CLICK HERE TO
LINK TO MY BLOG

LINKS

BedBathStore.com--Largest Selection of Bedding and Bath Amenities From Leading Manufacturers

PREVIOUS POSTS

Therapeutic Bubble Baths

Not quite as deceptive, but still in a blurry zone for their value as social media, are services such as PayPerPost that pay people to blog about products and services and to offer their own opinions about them. PayPerPost has a code of ethics that asks the bloggers writing for a fee on a product or service to disclose that they are being paid to offer their opinions on a specific product or service, so it's clear that their opinions are not coming out of their own enthusiasm or interest in a particular product or service. Though the information in pay-per-post articles may be of a somewhat higher quality than in a service like Bath 747, designed to support a specific Web site or company, the articles are still sponsored messages with limited personal endorsement value. More importantly, they are likely to have the same net effect as a dedicated sponsored weblog, content that will be digested by search engines for getting better placement in search results and a potentially false sense of "grass roots" enthusiasm for a product or service.

CONTENT NATION MARKETING RULE #16: *Just because you're using social media technologies doesn't mean that you're creating social media—and some marketers don't really care.*

The Ugly: The Corruption of Social Media Marketing with Spam, Astroturf, and Misinformation

"Spam," the generation of mass quantities of low-quality marketing messages, is a problem throughout the Web in email inboxes, and unfortunately social media does not escape the efforts of spammers and other operatives who are intent on creating inaccurate or distorted information in social media. One of the most common attempts to hijack social media for spam are "splogs," weblogs that are like spam email messages offering no value in their content and no meaningful community, but instead only just content to trick search engines and to possibly gain some ancillary revenues from ads on the site. Splogs gained quite a bit of attention several years ago when there were few defenses against them, but search engines and social media services have become far more sophisticated in recent years, greatly reducing the effective use of splogs. Similar services that injected spam into the comment sections of weblogs also flourish, with similar anti-spam services from most major social media services.

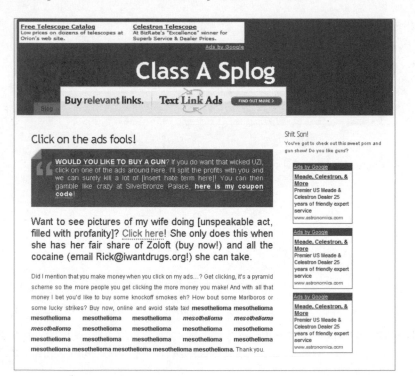

Of greater concern today are efforts to inject sponsored content into social media outlets that is supposed to appear as if it were created by people speaking independently. Sometimes referred to as "astroturf," this content is supposed to appear as if it's from "grass roots" opinion makers, but it is actually sponsored opinion. Though a practice that's specifically discouraged by the U.S.-based Public Relations Society of America, PR experts are sometimes called upon to create astroturf on behalf of their clients. Sometimes, though, organizations and individuals create their own astroturf, believing that they will not be detected. In 2006, for example, Sony was taken to task by bloggers and consumers who discovered that a supposed enthusiast's weblog touting the virtues of its PlayStation electronic game product was actually created by a contractor for its marketing department as a part of an effort to drive up holiday sales of the device over rivals' machines. Sony issued a statement apologizing for the effort, but the damage was done. In spite of improved controls and the consistent rejection of such efforts by social media audiences, the temptation to twist social media to provide the illusion of endorsements from everyday people remains very powerful.

CONTENT NATION MARKETING RULE #17: *It's not easy for many marketers to accept that their power in social media comes from the genuine support of everyday people.*

Putting it Together: Marketing as Building Relationships with Peers

In many ways marketers large and small are learning how to use the power of social media to identify markets, research them, and to communicate with them in market conversations that can lead to large rewards. Those who profit most from social media know how to use social media tools to build acceptance and enthusiasm among other influential social media publishers. They build their own "viruses," choosing their own paths through the marketplace. Smart marketers learn how to be a part of this crowd on their own terms. Flash and attractiveness are not penalized necessarily, but insincerity and exploitation of people's reputations will carry a heavy price.

From this perspective, marketing in Content Nation is a call to return to that basic premise of marketing: find people's real needs and fill them. With both buyers and sellers equipped with publishing tools that enable them to express their needs and their abilities to fill them more rapidly, there is less opportunity in Content Nation to overwhelm people with products and services that aren't really what people need or want based on a marketer's ability to buy people's attention through publishing. That attention can be attained, but it must be earned daily in the court of personal and public opinion if their messages are to gain leadership and influence in the marketplace.

In the meantime, those who are able to respond to niche markets more rapidly through a solid network of relationships cultivated using social media will help to drive both local and global economies to the Big Sombrero model, creating more value more rapidly for those who know how to converse with their markets most effectively and to benefit most directly from their endorsements. Content Nation will not kill mass marketing, but it will challenge it to think about how it can build relationships with markets based on leadership, influence, and respect among peers rather than seduction. In doing so new products, services, and companies will emerge that will challenge established brands to rethink how they serve the marketplace.

Though we've seen some good examples of how social media succeeds for marketers when used properly, Content Nation challenges marketers to take an approach to markets that may not necessarily align with their traditional strengths. Smart marketers are learning to adapt rapidly to social media, but it's as a part of a landscape that sees social media challenging marketers on a more fundamental level. For if social media changes how we market things, how do people organize themselves as a work force to serve markets most effectively?

The New Work:
Content Nation Transforms the Future of Today's Enterprises

In many ways, publishing as we have known it for centuries made the world's leading enterprises what they are today. If, as some say, knowledge is power, then managing the publishing of content has been the key to power for many enterprises. Major organizations have had the resources to equip their staffs with information from their own organization and from outside of their organization in ways that others cannot afford to do easily. From papyrus scrolls to the printed edicts of kings and queens to typed memoranda to photocopying to emails to electronic databases and Web sites, publishing has driven the ability of large organizations to assemble information that helps them to make effective decisions and that enables them to acquire and retain power, leadership, and influence.

Something is happening in enterprises and in public institutions where many people work today. Publishing content remains an important part of a work force's life, but a fundamental shift is underway in how publishing provides advantages to their organizations. Proprietary information such as trade secrets, high-level executive memos, and confidential reports remain closely held in today's organizations, but increasingly success is coming to those organizations that know how to use the rapid dissemination and sharing of information in their organizations to succeed. Often the lines between their own organizations and people from other organizations and the public are becoming blurred as organizations rush to succeed in global marketplaces that favor having people on all levels of an organization aware of the most recent insights inside and outside of their organizations and ready to put them to use.

In other words, the global economy, and the increasing importance of powerful local economies, needs the strengths of social media more than ever. The rise of social media in business and public institutions is in some ways a natural outgrowth of how things have been done in human society from its beginnings. "It's not what you know but who you know," is a familiar saying used to remind people at work that having the right personal connections can make or break your ability to experience professional success, but the phrase is taking on new meaning in the era of social media.

In the more paper-driven days of office work, people would receive important memos via inter-office mail, often passing a single document from one person to another. Who got that document when and how was often related to social connections within an organization. Business cards from contacts were coveted and held closely in private collections. Even when electronic information began to penetrate many large organizations, the electronic databases of one part of an organization were not always willingly shared with another part of the same organization. Emails, which were supposed to improve the immediacy and openness of communications, did so in some instances, but often emails simply underscored existing "who you know" struggles inside and outside of an organization.

Large organizations were created to take advantage of the combined knowledge and insights available in their staffs through well-managed hierarchies but found themselves in ongoing internal struggles for power, based often on the availability of information from one group or another. Publishing technologies, the means by which hierarchies managed their power through controlling the distribution of information, became tools of inner warfare as much as to support efforts to conquer markets and other external goals.

Enterprise Publishing: From a Tool of War to a Tool of Collaboration

In his classic 1943 book *Concept of the Corporation* author Peter Drucker credited the hierarchical command-and-control structures of the powerful 19th-century Prussian Army with having served with the model for managing modern industrial organizations. The management tools to turn a group of people into a successful war machine became the management tools for commercial success, and with those tools came the use of the hierarchical command-and-control structures of war for both internal and external business goals. Publishing tools were a key component of that effort.

In the Internet-driven era of the 21st century, though, Drucker's analogy of military organizations as a model for corporate organization faces an interesting evolution in how large military forces organize for success. Modern military organizations are more efficient than ever, to be sure, able to deliver highly sophisticated weapons to targets almost at will throughout the globe: the mass production of sophisticated weapons and the command-and-control systems to support them have been perfected.

Yet, in spite of these sophisticated military systems, much of today's emphasis in modern military organizations is on "asymmetrical warfare," fighting opponents with ample supplies of light, inexpensive, and plentiful weapons that can blend into landscapes and populations at will. To enable better military efforts against such opponents, modern military organizations are deploying new hand-held and helmet-mounted information systems that enable front-line personnel to communicate with one another and with their commanders far more effectively and to respond to battlefield conditions with more autonomy. Military logistics systems are focused on rapid deployment of resources to multiple battlefields for asymmetrical warfare, requiring more distributed control of rapid decision-making. Eliminating "the fog of war," the confusion that exists when communications break down between personnel during battles, places a premium on people sharing knowledge and collaborating on solutions as rapidly as possible. There must also be in modern warfare a stronger emphasis on learning how to build trust and effective communications with indigenous people; traditional warfare may last only a short time, whereas occupations of enemy territories can last indefinitely.

As it is in warfare, so it is in business and in other institutions in which people must work together toward a goal; collaboration via social media is enabling more rapid responses to asymmetrical threats and opportunities. To survive and to thrive, the people who are in these organizations are learning how to use social media tools to share the right information with the right people at the right time and to build the right relationships with the right people at the right time. In doing so, the outlines of successful enterprises are changing rapidly, and new kinds of work patterns are supporting the rise of new types of organizations that can respond successfully to quickly unfolding situations in the workplace. The concept of warfare still drives much thinking in today's workplace, but when today's opponents may be tomorrow's collaboration partners for innovative approaches to their goals, victory is relative to many different players, many of whom will benefit through social media communications.

Old Goals, New Tools: Tapping Social Media for Productivity and Innovation

The appeal of social media may not be apparent immediately to anyone who has had to deal with the ins and outs of enterprises both large and small. With so many tools already in use for creating and consuming content in the enterprise—email, Web sites, printed memos, databases, copying machines, internal libraries—why would yet another source of information help people to become more productive? A recent study by the professional-services firm Accenture noted that 59 percent of 1,000 surveyed middle managers in large companies miss information that might be valuable to their jobs almost every day because it exists somewhere else in the company, and they cannot find it. In addition, 53 percent said that less than half of the information they receive is valuable. The tools of enterprises that were supposed to improve productivity—email, central computer databases, and PCs—instead turned out in large part to be tools of mass information production churning out reams of information for people ill-equipped to absorb it all. Instead of content, people got noise and unabsorbable information.

The largest culprit in this mix has been email. As one of the earliest technologies used for personal electronic publishing, email remains the most popular resource for transferring valuable information from one person to another in today's enterprises, but being the one messaging system that unites internal and external resources, it gets overused and abused all too easily. A 2006 study by Harris Interactive of 2,400 U.S. adults found that 59 percent of those who use email at work admitted to wasting a lot of time searching for lost email. To add to the lack of focus produced by email, 61 percent of email users at work in the Harris Interactive survey admitted also to using work email for personal reasons. With the ability to publish to many people via "Carbon Copy" ("CC") lists and to "Reply to All" on long lists of people copied on an email, it's clear that email is a tool that helped to automate unproductive publishing patterns of the past while missing new opportunities for more effective ways to organize communications for more productivity.

Murry Christensen, director of learning technologies at JetBlue University, is assembling a wiki-based learning program to be delivered across JetBlue's complex organization. He notes that the desire to adopt these technologies stems from communication breakdowns caused by email, such as when people failed to forward critical information to the right staff members. "E-mail is unstructured and ephemeral," Christensen says. "With blogs and wikis, you can capture process improvements more visibly."

Information from social media sources outside of an organization are also becoming a key component of the flow of information into enterprise decision-making, complementing and enhancing traditional sources of business information. Newstex, for example, is a company that licenses content from selected influential weblogs and other social media sources, such as the Twitter social messaging service, and distributes it to other information services. Major business information providers such as LexisNexis and EBSCO license content from Newstex and make it available to their clients as an integral part of their information services. Ensuring that information is available from all of today's influential thought leaders is a key component of executive decision-making today, and social media is an increasingly important part of that mix.

Enterprises Invest More Efficiently in Productive Communications through Social Media

The need for improved publishing tools is very clear in today's enterprises, and they are beginning to respond with major investments in social media. A recent survey by Forrester Research showed that a majority of global companies with 20,000 or more employees were already purchasing new social media technologies for deployment inside their enterprises. Notably, only 20 percent of small businesses were purchasing social media services inside of their company. Why the small percentage of social media technology purchasers in small businesses? Because many of them have avoided the need for investing in social media technologies internally by investing in Web-based publishing services already on the Internet that can be used for business purposes.

Alacra, a growing company delivering content services to major enterprises, is an interesting example of a company that was able to use existing social media services on the Web very effectively. Barry Graubart, vice president, product strategy & business development for Alacra, explained to me recently how Alacra made the transition quickly to social media tools: "As a small company, we had no intranet. There was no way to easily share information among employees other than email. One day, as I was doing research on a new market, I wanted somewhere to store the research so that I could share it with colleagues in product management, sales, and marketing. Rather than going the traditional IT-driven intranet approach, I signed up for a JotSpot [wiki] account (before Google acquired them) and started to upload a bunch of documents. The best part was that we had no internal meetings or debates about whether to launch an intranet or what needed to be on it. It was basically a three-minute discussion between [my CEO] and myself; five minutes later, I'd entered my credit-card info and started to add info. About a week later, when I had reached critical mass, I sent around an email telling everyone in the company that we now had an intranet."

Though many larger enterprises still invest in installing their own social media software to tailor it to their own internal needs, Graubart's experiences point out an important factor for social media: with many social media services being offered as online services or as software with a free license for its use by most organizations, many growing organizations may never develop the elaborate information technology infrastructures that larger organizations have maintained for decades. Instead, they may evolve as organizations that have always used Web-based social media tools to improve their productivity, allowing them to invest far less in the "mass production" of information for the sake of information and far more in efficient information sharing and publishing through social media services.

Thinking of Drucker's comparison of businesses to military organizations, you might say that companies like Alacra are to today's large enterprises what grass-roots warriors are to today's large military forces: equipped with light, inexpensive, rapidly deployed technologies that enable them to scale up rapidly to meet their objectives before larger opponents can react to them effectively. The ability of new generations of potential competitors to scale their internal operations rapidly via social media may be one of the more compelling motivations for larger organizations to consider investment in their own social media tools.

CONTENT NATION ENTERPRISE RULE #1: *Social media isn't about technology. It's about adapting to more effective patterns of communication being adopted by competitors.*

Why Social Media for Work? Key Benefits of Social Media Publishing for Enterprises

Social media succeeds for any number of reasons in helping enterprises to communicate effectively. Here are a few of the key reasons why today's social media publishing tools offer vast improvements in communication productivity to an organization over time.

- **Effective social media tools enable people to choose who they want to be in their circle of communication.** One of the enormous weaknesses of earlier personal publishing technologies such as email is that they make it very difficult for an individual to define the people from whom they'd like to receive communications. Spam, CCs on emails, unsolicited communications from salespeople—it's very hard for an individual to control who provides them with content. With social media, the idea of an individual controlling their communications, rather than an institution, is paramount. Millions of people could possibly contact me via the Twitter messaging service or LinkedIn or Facebook or any other number of social media services, but unless I choose to allow them to contact me I will not hear from them. Enterprise-class private messaging services such as Reuters Messaging apply the same concepts with more-robust security and administrative controls to satisfy investment-bank clients. Senior executives have assistants who often can screen telephone calls and bring communications from important people to their attention; now anybody can have similar screening of communications via social media to keep them focused on the right messages from the right people.

  Effective social media tools enable people to publish to whole groups or organizations rapidly while reducing overload and disruptions. Whereas some social media tools enable people to filter out communications from others, tools such as weblogs and wikis can enable people to publish content to anyone who can reach their publications on the Web or their enterprise's own networks. In some instances, social media tools can be configured to enable restricted access to published content, but even then it's typical that there is universal access to that content among a known group of people. This can have a profound impact on people who adapt to this more public style of communications. Instead of pushing mass communications into personal-communications channels, social media allows mass communications to be picked up easily by anyone who has access to them and to leverage personal communications efficiently into broad communications when appropriate. Once people get used to the idea of certain publications being widely available, either inside an enterprise or on the Web, they learn that anything that they publish could be read by many people, a concept not always clear in email communications that get sent at first to one group and then to a much wider group by others. This is creating a new generation of publishers in enterprises sharing information more widely and more effectively inside and outside their organizations and spreading productivity and innovation in the process.

- **Effective social media tools make it easier to collect and organize communications from internal and external sources.** Social media tools provide the ability to filter content published by people on an opt-in basis using standardized technologies to collect content from a wide variety of sources. Social media tools enable the collection of information from specific sources by just about anyone without a lot of technical knowledge. Instead of visiting individual weblogs, for example, someone can "subscribe" to a feed of content posted to that weblog and have it delivered automatically to a Web page, a mobile device, or their email. Status reports, project updates, management messages—all these and more can be posted wherever an individual needs them most and organized in any number of display configurations.

  In many instances leading news services, corporate investor relations specialists, and even expensive electronic subscription services use the formatting and programming standards developed to deliver social media feeds to make links to their content available to their subscribers. With this ability to collect information from individuals, institutions, and the media in one common format, tailored collections of information can be assembled and adjusted in a moment. This can greatly enhance the productivity of people who cannot afford to trudge through dozens of emails or search results from sources that will not help them focus on their goals.

- **Effective social media tools make it easier to collaborate internally and externally to build and update valuable knowledge more effectively.** One of the continual problems in any large organization is building up a composite picture of valuable facts and insights that leverages as much internal and external knowledge as possible. Many different human and technology checkpoints or gatekeepers may exist in an organization to keep people from assembling that knowledge effectively. Social media tools make it as easy to build a common source of information collaboratively as easily as most people edit an email or a memo on their PC. This encourages both contributions and use that leads to more contributions and use. Once a social media resource is adopted as a definite source of information in an enterprise, it is rarely ignored and often is the most fresh and up-to-date view into processes and objectives.

Although these benefits of effective social media tools may be clear enough, support for social media in many large enterprises is only beginning to emerge. Change in information technologies in many large organizations can move very slowly, with information "gatekeepers" in many different roles. Corporate compliance regulations are also a concern that may slow down some social media projects, which add requirements to have all information generated by an organization available for examination in archived company records. The largest change may be the culture of large organizations: with generations of workers used to using more tightly held information as a means to personal success, it takes good examples of how to implement social media to begin to change institutional culture. With a large portion of the work force now used to social media tools from their personal lives, many powerful and influential institutions are beginning to deploy social media publishing tools successfully.

The Central Intelligence Agency: Building a Mission-Critical Knowledge Resource via Social Media

Few organizations on earth are offered the wealth of information tools for mission-critical job functions found at the U.S. Central Intelligence Agency. With its own venture-capital arm and countless technology projects underway, the CIA can deploy virtually any technology on the planet to attain its goals as it strives for absolute control and security over its knowledge assets. Yet, in the wake of attacks on the World Trade Center in New York and the Pentagon in Washington, D.C. in 2001, a brave group of technologists at the CIA began work on Intellipedia, a wiki collecting information from U.S. intelligence agents around the world.

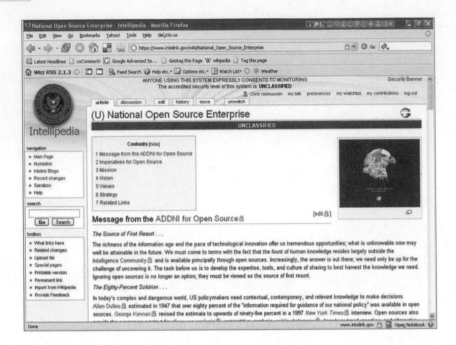

Intellipedia is based on the same type of freely available software that operates Wikipedia on the open Web, so its basic functions have been built at minimal expense. Intellipedia is a wiki that makes three different versions of its information available to U.S. intelligence agencies: one for those with top-secret access, one with secret access, and one for information that is sensitive but not classified. Intellipedia collects text, videos, and images that fill reports and profiles, with people collectively updating pages. As updates occur, the software used for Intellipedia enables people to see easily who edited what and when, providing a simple and effective audit trail for changes. Intellipedia is still growing after two years of deployment, helping the CIA and other U.S. intelligence agencies to combine their knowledge on key topics rapidly and to eliminate barriers to the flow of information.

The availability of Intellipedia is encouraging contributions not only from younger personnel but also from older agents whose knowledge can be retained and shared most easily—one of the most prolific contributors is 69 years old. Though more-sophisticated databases may help to structure information for more-detailed analysis, Intellipedia is succeeding both at encouraging people to be publishers to everyone in a community at a specified level of access, and in doing so overcoming barriers to widespread understanding of crucial issues. The CIA has also deployed secure instant messaging systems to enhance communications, one of the few ways to be able to cut through the information clutter in the organization and to reach key people rapidly.

CONTENT NATION ENTERPRISE RULE #2: *When knowledge needs to be shared widely and openly to enhance common understanding and open discussions, social media can break down barriers rapidly.*

Using Social Media to Drive Productivity and to Change Fundamental Business Processes

"This market has moved…two to three we'll have telepresences in all of our offices around the world, not just videoconferencing but true virtual presences," noted Cisco CEO John Chambers in an address at a recent conference. As a global supplier of computer network technologies for enterprises, Cisco needed to do more than control costs—it needed to improve productivity and increase innovation to respond to rapidly changing markets. Instead of just experimenting with social media, Chambers became a key driver for ensuring that for both its internal capabilities and its products and services, Cisco would be focused on social media tools. "Web services, online social networks, unified communications, telepresence, podcasts, mashups, blogs, and peer-to-peer all combined—we're already doing this across the company with tremendous speed," Chambers noted. "Consumers are driving business. There are a lot of ideas with social networks, and we are changing the business from a formal hierarchy to informal social network council implementations."

Chambers has deployed a wide variety of social media technologies, technologies to enable Cisco employees to communicate more effectively on their internal communications networks. A "Ciscopedia" wiki enables Cisco staff to keep a common reference of terms and methods used throughout their global organization. Cisco's I-Zone wiki is a platform to collect and build new ideas for products within the organization. I-Zone has generated 400 business ideas, with 10,000 people actively contributing to the ideas, ideas with billions of dollars' worth of potential new revenues. Text and video blogs help thought leaders and managers in the company keep people up-to-date on late-breaking developments and ideas, while social bookmarking tools are being explored to enable Cisco employees to highlight new sources of information and to generate "buzz" around ideas, events, and trends that are important to them. All of this is wrapped around Cicso's use of its own TelePresence videoconferencing platform.

Software that gathers information from these initiatives across the company and that generates performance metrics is a key for them to understand both the information being generated by Cisco and its business value. Cisco's expectation is that it will be able to measure a 10 percent improvement in productivity each year and to build new business units far more rapidly, thanks in large part to social media technologies that enable people to be liberated by technology to break down barriers to innovation and collaboration.

CONTENT NATION ENTERPRISE RULE #3: *When the future of your company depends on using the collaborative brain-power of your staff, social media can unlock new revenues and cost savings rapidly.*

Wells Fargo: Spreading Thought Leadership in a Major Bank via Blogs

Banking and finance is a highly competitive industry that requires constant innovation as well as stringent controls. Like many industries, it's one in which people have a hard time communicating new ideas and insights across an organization. Wells Fargo is a major financial institution that has embraced social media to build communications across the organization as well as to engage its clients. The first bank known to have established a client-facing corporate blog, weblogs thrive inside Wells Fargo now. At Wells Fargo hundreds of employees maintain blogs covering a wide variety of topics that propagate information and ideas across the organization as well as to clients in some instances. In a recent interview Steve Ellis, EVP of Wells Fargo's wholesale solutions group, noted that, "A blog is informal—a great way to get away from the corporate thing and let people inside our heads." Wells Fargo's employee blogs are one of the most popular information sources in Wells Fargo, but this does not mean that every employee is going to be a great or consistent blogger for their colleagues.

Although there are hundreds blogging at Wells Fargo, there are thousands of employees who had the opportunity to blog who have not. What a blog can do, though, is to enable an organization focused very intently on tightly controlled information resources to break out above the systems designed to ensure limited access to specific information and to begin to create a culture more focused on innovation and collaboration. Most importantly, these blogs do not clutter up email inboxes; they can be visited as one would visit any Web site to pick up the latest news and insights from people who see things from a fresh perspective.

CONTENT NATION ENTERPRISE RULE #4: *Give your staff the ability to provide thought leadership through social media and they will respond with it in ways that can drive your organization forward.*

BlueShirtNation: Best Buy Builds Employee Loyalty through Social Media

With thousands of consumer-electronics stores in North America and global retail alliances in China and elsewhere, Best Buy is a retail giant that lives and dies by what happens on its sales floors. Keeping its blue-shirted sales associates across this scattered network of stores motivated and in touch with the central management team was a major problem, a problem that social media was well positioned to help solve. Best Buy established an employee-only Web site called BlueShirtNation.com, equipped with a variety of social media tools.

The use of the public Web to give its staff access to the site was a crucial decision. Because most sales associates are engaged actively in sales and customer-support activities when in the store, a private Web site on the public Web enabled staff to access the site at home, and to give and receive insight and information that would otherwise be difficult to convey during store hours. On BlueShirtNation.com, employees can connect with employees in other Best Buy stores, offer ideas and suggestions on better sales and client-care practices, and get funding to try out some of their ideas.

With more than 20,000 employees using BlueShirtNation.com, it has become a part of the company's culture and has helped to deliver measurable improvements for Best Buy. Though employee turnover in most of its stores typically averages 60 percent, the employees using the BlueShirtNation.com Web site have a turnover rate in the neighborhood of 8 to 12 percent so far, according to the manager in charge of the social media project. In a business like retail electronics, which requires a knowledgeable sales staff to support buyers making decisions on complex technologies, such improvements in employee retention can help to power strong sales productivity.

CONTENT NATION ENTERPRISE RULE #5: *Giving fragmented groups of staff a sense of unity, intimacy, and influence through social media can influence your bottom line.*

Social Media Powers Data, Decisions, and Deals

The improved insights and collaboration enabled by social media publishing tools are good for many general business goals, but eventually people have to execute upon their enterprise mission with the best information possible. In many ways, social media is thought of as a tool for text and pictures and not for data, but, as seen in Chapter 3's example of Jigsaw's collection of business-card information from professionals that can be used to feed enterprise sales-automation systems, there is a wealth of opportunity to harvest useful data via social media and to use social media as a source of information for sophisticated analysis of individuals, companies, and markets. In enterprises, the importance of Content Nation is not just in what people publish in social media, but how it powers data, decisions, and deals.

Manta: Getting the Right Data on Businesses from People Who Care about Businesses

Whereas Jigsaw targets largely managers in major enterprises and early-stage technology companies, ECNext's Manta business-information portal focuses on the millions of small to medium-sized businesses across the U.S. In many instances, traditional business-information services collect information on this huge swath on companies through phone banks of people who call businesses to ask them to update information on their company in their databases. With rare updates solicited from major information services and many smaller businesses lacking Web sites or having only minimal information on them, it's not easy to harvest up-to-date information on many businesses from searching Web sources.

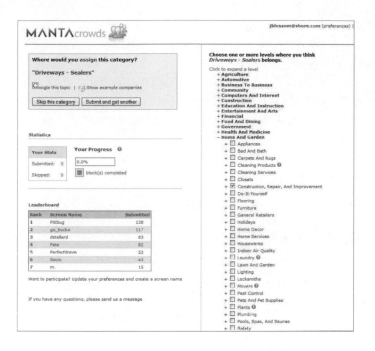

Manta's approach is to enable its members to edit information on millions of companies in its database. Members may edit basic information such as address, phone number, and Web site, but also important data such as the number of employees at a company and their revenues. Thousands of business records get updated every day in Manta. With small-business owners wanting to make sure that their business information is correct, minimal screening of updates is required by Manta's internal staff; most people want to, and do, provide accurate information. This enables Manta to deliver accurate updates to information on small and medium business faster than traditional business-information database providers.

Manta members are also helping to determine what categories should be associated with specific kinds of products and services. For example, if a company produces pavement sealant, should that be in industrial products or home repairs? By trying to apply these kinds of choices, Manta members "vote" for specific categories into which to place business with very specific products and services, information that is generally not available from other sources. Conceptually, this is not so different from a social bookmarking site like Digg, but it's a concept that's been applied to a very specific type of data-collection effort. Business information sourcing of this kind, both on the Web and by the staffs of major companies, is enabling businesses to get more up-to-date data through the collective insight of people who know the most about the topics that require data collection, instead of having to wait for traditional publishing methods to catch up.

CONTENT NATION ENTERPRISE RULE #6: *The personal perspectives offered by social media can be used to gather hard facts as well as insight and opinion.*

OneSource Information Services: An Information Company Turns to Social Media for Intelligence to Drive Strategic Decisions

Many companies provide information services to their staffs for intelligence on existing and potential competitors in the marketplace that helps to shape decisions on their product-design and market positioning. Though much of this information can be collected from company Web sites and news reports, social media plays an increasingly important role in providing competitive intelligence to enterprises, including companies that provide traditional sources of information on businesses. OneSource Information Services, a major provider of business data, research, and news, provides an internal Web site for its staff using software from RivalMap. With RivalMap, OneSource staff members are able to track news from both traditional sources and favorite weblogs on the Web that talk about very specific market niches. RivalMap also enables OneSource staff to create wiki overviews of companies and products along with structured tools for competitive analysis, competitive feature matrices, and segment needs analysis that can be compiled automatically into customized email summaries.

All these features are great, but it was the availability of ever-freshening content from weblogs that made it a resource that people at OneSource would put to work. Michael Levy, a product marketing manager at OneSource, notes, "I've long struggled with how to set up and maintain discussion portals around our competitors....a few weeks ago when RivalMap integrated [blogs] this enhancement led not only to improved competitive intelligence flowing through RivalMap, but a roughly 50 percent increase in usage as OneSource staff started linking from the expanded alerts....The lesson here is that you can build all of the communications tools that you want for an internal [Web] portal, but you need to have a steady set of compelling and current [content] links…to remind users about these internal assets."

CONTENT NATION ENTERPRISE RULE #7: *The many voices of social media attract people who are encouraged to contribute their own content to resources that drive decision-making.*

Rearden Commerce Uses Social Media from InsideView to Make More Deals

Making strategic sales for technology products in a highly competitive market sector is a challenge for any company, even when your product is great, but when you're trying to sell against other fast-moving technology companies to major enterprises, getting the right information at the right time is more than a matter of convenience; it can be a matter of a young company making enough sales to survive. Rearden Commerce produces software for mobile devices that make life easier and more productive for executives on the go. Selling to major companies through its own sales force and through backers such as American Express and Chase, Rearden needed to have information on when and where people were ready to hear sales pitches to keep its sales force focused on the best opportunities.

Rearden Commerce turned to sales-productivity specialists InsideView to get content that would get it pointed in the right direction at the right time. The InsideView service is able to combine information from a wide variety of subscription information services and to combine it with information from weblogs and social networking services such as LinkedIn and Facebook. InsideView filters this information through software that analyzes it for patterns that will indicate that a sales prospect is ready to hear a sales pitch.

Using information harvested from social networks and internal sources InsideView then helps salespeople to understand who the right contacts would be for a sales call and what relationships they have that might lead to obtaining an effective introduction to those people. Using these capabilities, Rearden Commerce was able to reduce its re-call research time from 30 minutes to 10 minutes and to increase the average number of sales calls from 30 a day to more than 60 for each sales representative. This year, Rearden Commerce is expected to double its sales, thanks in part to social media that makes it easier to understand how to get to the right people at the right time.

CONTENT NATION ENTERPRISE RULE #8: *Social media makes it easier to know who is ready to say "yes" to a deal and how to get to them.*

Reaching across Boundaries: Social Media Builds Benefits outside of Companies

Although enterprises are reaping rewards from using and developing social media inside their own organizations, one of the greatest benefits of social media is that it can act as a powerful bridge between an organization and the people and the organizations and individuals that it serves. Increasingly, enterprises are finding through social media that there is a great deal of value to be found in "the commons," the arena of publishing that enables people in various roles from many different kinds of enterprises to come together and to share knowledge, ideas, and solutions. In some instances, these cross-role and cross-organization meeting places made available through social media enable not just problem-solving and collaboration, but these social media meeting places also offer a new sense of common purpose. Social media can bring organizations and individuals together in ways that create relationships and end-products that may have a greater value to all participating in their common efforts than the sum of the parts.

Oracle Forums Take Market Conversations Beyond Marketing

As one of the world's leading technology companies, Oracle competes fiercely to build a loyal base of clients who will rely upon them for enterprise software. One of the keys to Oracle's success is its system of online forums, in which anyone can find or provide answers to technology questions and interact with Oracle's global staff of software developers, product managers, and support specialists. Millions of people visit Oracle's forum pages each month, which are equipped with social media tools that enable people to track the most popular topics, forum members, and topic description tags applied by members.

They come not for the razzle-dazzle of the Web site—it's well designed, but downright plain-looking—but to communicate openly and clearly with one another.

ORACLE

Welcome, Guest
Sign In / Register
Guest Settings
Search
FAQ

Forum Home

Welcome to our online community. Please choose from one of the forums below or log-in to your user account to start using this service.

Forum / Category	Views	Topics / Messages	Last Post
Technology Network Community			
Community Feedback and Suggestions (Do Not Post Product-Related Questions Here)	192,767	7,504 / 15,973	Jun 28, 08 01:05 PM by: Hans-Forbrich »
Downloads	196,892	3,488 / 6,783	Jun 27, 08 11:04 AM by: Hans-Forbrich »
Documentation	78,125	667 / 1,796	Jun 25, 08 06:10 AM by: Hans-Forbrich »
Certification	24,332	277 / 982	Jun 28, 08 09:30 AM by: Sabdar Syed »
More...			
Database			
Database - General	4,009,573	78,865 / 385,270	Jun 28, 08 02:02 PM by: jocave »
Installation	308,846	10,441 / 28,473	Jun 28, 08 10:13 AM by: Hans-Forbrich »
SQL and PL/SQL	4,175,827	69,375 / 375,626	Jun 28, 08 02:11 PM by: mihe »
Advanced Compression	1,741	2 / 3	Jun 11, 08 02:16 AM by: damorgan »
More...			
Fusion Middleware			
Application Server - General	393,831	14,639 / 50,211	Jun 28, 08 10:18 AM by: user635847 »
OC4J and Java EE	540,807	12,738 / 35,994	Jun 28, 08 11:25 AM by: user642052 »
Identity Management	232,931	1,700 / 11,626	Jun 28, 08 01:21 PM by: user633262 »
Business Process Analysis Suite	22,096	204 / 999	Jun 27, 08 08:31 AM by: user9anmu »
More...			
Developer Tools			
JDeveloper	2,328,313	55,238 / 182,382	Jun 28, 08 08:07 AM

Popular Threads
- PLS-00123: program too l... Replies: 15 Last Post By: qube at Jun 28, 2008 Forum: SQL and PL/SQL
- I have problem with data... Replies: 6 Last Post By: Paul M. at Jun 28, 2008 Forum: Database - General
- Can any help me out Replies: 4 Last Post By: John Spencer at Jun 26, 2008 Forum: SQL and PL/SQL
- Oracle profile and passw... Replies: 3 Last Post By: jocave at Jun 27, 2008 Forum: Database - General

Top Users in Category
forumuser20605 (15)
user449647 (10)
usercontent_ww (3)

Popular Tags
11g 1nf/00 acknowledged adf apex application bi-4j calendar captcha certificate dbms_metadata editor express flag flying_spaghetti http jdeveloper lock mail mod_plsql

Company-sponsored online forums like Oracle's have been around for years, but what's interesting is how being able to have discussions with both peers who are using Oracle products as well as Oracle staff members is becoming a key draw for Oracle's marketing purposes. Judith Sim, senior VP-CMO of Oracle, noted at a recent Business Marketing Association conference that Oracle's marketing budget has been going down every year for 10 years. "Oracle believes in doing more with less," Judith Sims said. She became concerned, though, when in recent months people visiting the home page of Oracle's Web site had declined 4 percent—a trend that is becoming far more common for corporate Web sites. What she discovered, though, was that in recent months the number of users visiting Oracle's forums had increased 22 percent, with 94 percent more postings from members inside and outside of Oracle. In other words, instead of coming to the branded, marketing-oriented home page to solve problems, people were moving directly to the forums as the starting point for engaging Oracle. Overall traffic to Oracle's Web sites has nearly doubled in the past year, according to Compete, driven in large part by these online forum conversations between people coming together to learn and to solve problems.

In the process of engaging with people via its forums, Oracle is learning truly how to have conversations that engage its markets, and learning that simple, person-to-person communications that lay aside the smoke and mirrors of typical marketing presentations can provide not only client loyalty but real engagement with its markets that puts everyone on the same side trying to solve problems together. The power of Oracle grows through this conversation, but serving the conversation itself through social media in ways that people find to be honest and constructive becomes the real source of influence and leadership for whoever uses this form of personal expression to drive revenues.

CONTENT NATION ENTERPRISE RULE #9: *Solving problems and building influence and leadership through social media is becoming the center of an enterprise's brand value.*

Connotea: Building Scientific Understanding through Social Bookmarking

The Nature Publishing Group has experimented with a number of social media tools that will enable scientific and medical researchers and people applying the lessons of research in product development and medicine to exchange knowledge with people outside of their own institutions. With conferences at which research papers are presented—an expensive and time-consuming option to share knowledge with peers—social media seemed to be a logical choice to enable people to share information and insight more frequently.

One of the most successful of Nature's experiments in social media is Connotea, a social bookmarking service based loosely on services such as Digg and del.icio.us. Connotea enables its members to collect links to articles on topics on the Web that interest its members, to organize them by topic tags, and to share comments on them with other members. Many of the articles bookmarked by Connotea members are "hard science" produced in peer-reviewed scientific journals, for which Connotea makes it easy for scientists to extract bibliography information that they may use in developing their own scientific papers. Bookmarks and comments can be shared with everyone or organized by specific topic interest groups.

The response to Connotea has been very strong in the scientific community, which values open access to research but also guards closely its ability to publish research that will give individuals a boost in their career goals. Connotea offers these professionals the ability to share, organize, and discuss topics that keep them in touch with their professional peers and to use their insights to propel their own thinking without having to spend a lot of time at a conference or to search the thousands of publications in which scientific information is published. Search engines can help scientists to find what information is of general interest and relevance, but Connotea allows them to rise above the general and to get to the specific articles that are drawing the interest of people with similar interests in very specific fields.

SOCIAL MEDIA ENTERPRISE RULE #10: *When most of the people who know something about your specialty aren't in your own organization, social media can help professionals to build knowledge and relationships.*

ALM: Enabling Lawyers to Build Blogs and Data That Lead to Business

Lawyers get business from people who know their work, but getting people to know your work when you've had success with very specific types of litigation is not always easy, and advertising techniques are often not an option for helping people to get to know your work objectively. ALM is a publishing company that has come up with two innovative approaches that enable lawyers to leverage their own publishing in a setting that builds their reputation. ALM's Law.com Blog Network is a collection of more than two dozen of the leading weblogs by lawyers with a variety of legal specialties. ALM provides ads that run on each of these independent blogs and highlights the best of these in its Legal Blog Watch "blog of blogs." One of ALM's most popular content features, legal bloggers get to expose their expertise in a community of experts, something that a corporate Web site or marketing program would be hard-pressed to provide.

The other ALM resource built on social media principles is VerdictSearch, a database in which lawyers may deposit for free information about recent legal cases that they've been involved in. Laywers provide details on cases that would otherwise be inaccessible, including details such as expert witnesses that were used to support their case, awards provided in verdicts, opposing lawyers, and many other details about their day-to-day professional work. The ALM editorial staff reviews these submissions before posting them in the database, and in the process of reviewing the submissions, the staff identifies newsworthy cases that can be highlighted as news in ALM publications. ALM sells subscriptions to the VerdictSearch database created by these submissions from lawyers, which they can search in great detail to find just the type of information and expertise that they need. ALM gets great content to sell and lawyers collaborate to build a valuable resource that helps them when they need to do research and that their potential clients use to find the right lawyer for a particular kind of litigation.

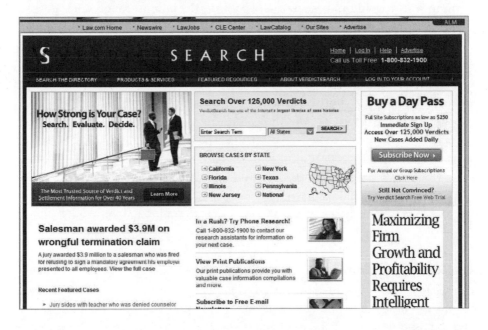

SOCIAL MEDIA ENTERPRISE RULE #11: *Even in highly competitive marketplaces, professionals can collaborate outside of their organization to build highly valuable content that can help them to reach their goals.*

Managing a Career: Building Lasting Relationships through Social Media

Although major organizations work hard to break through their hierarchical restraints to compete in global markets, the effort to respond more rapidly to changing conditions means that many people are no longer as tied to specific organizations as they used to be. The U.S Department of Labor estimated recently that by the age of 38 the average American worker will have had between 10 and 14 jobs. Their statistics also show that 1 in 4 workers is work-ing for a different company from a year ago, and that half are working for a different company from five years ago. Cradle-to-grave job security, always a myth, but long a promise of many economies, is clearly not a reality for most people in today's shifting enterprise workplace.

With many organizations offering mostly transitory benefits to the typical worker, it's no surprise that one of the most popular social media applications among working adults is social networking. Keeping in touch with people who we've met along the path of our lives turns out to be a major focus of many social media applications for adults in the workplace. Social networking among professionals is not limited to services that help people look for jobs or find work assignments; many are turning to services, such as Facebook, that connect people with both colleagues and personal friends. The merging of personal lifestyles with work lifestyles into an "always on" society is bringing people to social media to find relationships that will help them to survive and thrive. Social media is becoming the constant in today's electronic lifestyles that work often promises to be but often fails to be.

The impact of social media on how people manage their careers can be seen in part from a comparison of social media sites to traditional job-seeking sites. Traditional resume-posting services such as Monster and CareerBuilder.com are showing stagnant or falling traffic to their Web sites, while social media sites such as Facebook, Craigslist, and LinkedIn are growing strongly. Social media enables people to develop and call upon trusted relationships within a community instead of just inserting information into a database. Instead of being just a commodity, a person gains more value in the context of their relationships. Enterprises in turn are beginning to understand the power of social media as a tool for recruiting new talent, leveraging the existing relationships that people have in their organizations through social media to identify people already known to their staff.

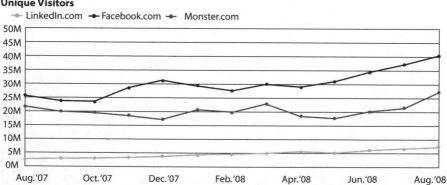

Unique Visitors
LinkedIn.com — Facebook.com — Monster.com

LinkedIn: Leveraging Trusted Professional Relationships for Business, Jobs, and Knowledge

LinkedIn is the leading social networking service for business, enabling more than 20 million professionals to establish a network of relationships that they can use to locate business, work, and information. LinkedIn enables members to link their personal profiles to others on LinkedIn, which in turn helps them to understand who their colleagues know well enough to arrange a possible introduction. LinkedIn members can send private email messages to one another without exposing their email addresses, enabling people to communicate easily while maintaining a level of privacy.

The personal profiles that people fill out on LinkedIn are quite detailed, which enables them to filter through contacts with possible skills, personal connections, or affinities that might be useful for a specific purpose. Endorsements of a member's work from colleagues help to provide potential hirers a sense of the strength of their skills. The LinkedIn Answers feature enables people to pose questions to colleagues and to get back answers from people who are right in the thick of many key topics. Instead of having to commission expensive research projects to locate, qualify, and interview professionals, questions can be posed quickly to hundreds of members and answers can be provided quickly, often within minutes or hours of having asked them. A person's profile on LinkedIn can also link members to people on other Web sites. Hiring departments in some major organizations include LinkedIn data in their Web portals to make it easier for LinkedIn members to identify staff in a hiring organization who they know already and who might be able to help accelerate the hiring process through their personal knowledge of a candidate.

In other words, LinkedIn provides many of the benefits of professional relationships that one has to struggle to build both inside and outside an organization, usually at great personal or financial investment. Old colleagues appear and link a member to new opportunities. People update their profile data on LinkedIn to ensure that it is fresh for people's viewing, making LinkedIn's database of contacts one of the more authoritative sources of professional work histories.

As LinkedIn grows its membership it is becoming a default place to identify oneself to peers in a trusted environment, so much so that some major organizations use LinkedIn messages as a preferred way to contact people outside of their organization, instead of having a message lost in a person's email inbox. Instead of worrying about losing contacts when moving from one job to another, people are able to keep their professional networks intact and to stay alert to new opportunities. With a service like LinkedIn, Content Nation can face the future with at least the assurance that their personal network of colleagues will be well-organized and ready to help them meet new challenges at a moment's notice.

CONTENT NATION ENTERPRISE RULE #12: *In a world of increasingly temporary relationships with enterprises, social media builds bonds that keep people connected to the influential relationships that can help people to survive and thrive.*

Facebook: From School to Work to Play

Whereas LinkedIn is a place to hang one's professional hat, Facebook is a social networking venue that lets people stay in touch with colleagues in a more personal way. Originally a Web site that enabled high-school and college students to connect, Facebook has expanded its appeal as early adopters brought their enthusiasm for its social networking tools into the workplace. Today, both young professionals and professionals in more senior positions, including CEOs of major corporations, maintain personal and enterprise presences on Facebook to stay in touch with friends, clients, and colleagues and to find out who's doing what with whom. The "what with whom" can revolve around people becoming Facebook "friends;" joining affinity groups; inviting people to events; sharing photos of recent get-togethers; becoming a "fan" of a company, cause, or product; or sharing links to videos and text that interests them on the Web.

Though the profiles on Facebook are more limited than those on LinkedIn and its mix of interests as much about fun as about business, Facebook is an increasingly important example of how "always on" lifestyles require a different kind of personal communication at times to make the most of professional relationships. With the tenuousness of so many relationships with enterprises on the increase and the bonds built through social media growing ever stronger, social media services like Facebook are ways to get to know people who are in one's professional life in ways that used to take conferences or personal get-togethers, such as golf outings, to develop. Now we can peer at our colleagues' most recent family photos, hear about their favorite activities, and share moments of fun or serendipity in an instant, and, perhaps, build a deeper personal relationship that will lead to important influence on a personal or professional basis later on. In Facebook, our personal worlds become our media.

SOCIAL MEDIA ENTERPRISE RULE #13: *In a world where many enterprises use people as disposable "human capital," social media helps people to build their own multi-dimensional human capital that can last a lifetime.*

Breaking the Isolation: myLayover Helps Truckers to Connect in a Mobile Lifestyle

Whereas people in office jobs are now discovering the benefits of social media as a tool to help their personal and professional lives, in some ways the truckers of the world have been there and done that for decades. Equipped with citizens' band radios and their own particular language for broadcasting to one another on the road, a trucking sub-culture has developed to support people who live out of their rigs a good part of their lives. It's not surprising, then, that the increasing availability of high-bandwidth mobile communications networks is enabling social media to connect truckers on the road with a new generation of tools to keep in touch with their tightly knit community.

myLayover.com is one of several online social media services now available to truckers who want to create and share content with one another. Launched by Layover.com, one of the leading Web sites for information on the trucking industry, myLayover.com offers social networking tools, blogs, forums, videos, music, photo galleries, job postings, and polls to enable people in the trucking community to build relationships with one another on the go, and a "small town" feeling that helps people working in a very specialized profession that blends work and family in its own intimate way. Though getting smaller social media communities to scale effectively can be a challenge, the rapid initial growth of myLayover's audience is an indication that blending work and personal lives in a profession that encourages their overlap can help them to come together even more closely, even when they're rolling down the road.

SOCIAL MEDIA ENTERPRISE RULE #14: *When your work life becomes your personal life, social media can help people to build influential bonds that bring both worlds together.*

Content Nation and the Cloud: The Changing Shape of Enterprises

Social media is having a major impact on enterprises large, small, governmental, corporate, independent; virtually every profession on earth has been touched by social media or in all likelihood will be touched by it sometime shortly. While many social media tools are succeeding using software installed within major enterprises, many of the enterprise success stories for social media that we've touched upon are tools that work both inside and outside of the enterprise or outside of them altogether. In many instances social media is succeeding without a company having to involve its own technology staffs to get the services up and running. Today social media tools and other publishing tools can be made available to an enterprise's staff over the Web quickly and used at desktops and on mobile devices as if they were a part of the company's own internal infrastructure.

This trend toward using social media tools as services rather than as purchased software reflects a broader trend in enterprise technology. Though many enterprises have large technology staffs to provide for the development and support of information systems, many of these staffs have neither the time nor the budget to deal with anything other than technologies that impact the core operations of an enterprise. As a result, more and more content services needed by enterprises are being provided by external service providers on a subscription or ad-supported basis via a connection to the Internet or a similar communications network. Because communications networks are depicted often in technical diagrams as clouds that pass information from one place to another, this delivery of information services from external communications to internal communications networks is referred to sometimes as "cloud computing."

A recent study by Gartner information industry analysts indicated that by 2011 the leaders in adopting enterprise information technologies would be delivering up to 40 percent of their information services via cloud computing without spending on internal infrastructure to deliver them. Instead, these services will come in to their enterprises from external service providers, including social media service providers on the Web. Although companies will continue to use information technologies to give them a market advantage, fewer and fewer of those services will come from their own technology staffs.

If so much of the crucial infrastructure needed by enterprises will not even be in an enterprise because of cloud computing, and if so many of the services provided by social media succeed best when they are enmeshed with people and information outside of an enterprise, then some troubling and pressing question come to mind: Are the kinds of organizations that we have today really producing the kinds of unique intellectual assets that will allow them to succeed in the future? Is the prevalence of social media and other content that flows in and out of major enterprises with increasing ease because of cloud computing indicative of a more fundamental shift in leadership and influence in the workplace being accelerated by social media?

A Nothing but Net Enterprise: What Happens When Social Media Defines Everything?

Hints as to what social media's role will be when these changes occur can be seen in a more radical example of how social media is transforming people's work lives. Serena Software, for example, is an up-and-coming software-development firm that decided to keep its young work force motivated by using private groups on the Facebook social networking service as their main internal infrastructure for sharing information with co-workers. Because all of their customers are also willing to use Facebook, it's easy for Serena Software's staff to stay in touch with customers and to be able to communicate with people inside and outside their organization at all times, regardless of where they are and what they're doing—with no training of staff on software that's special to their organization and no investment in the hardware that is required to support it. Significantly, this will help them also to reduce and in some instances eliminate the need for emails, because messaging is build into the Facebook platform already, and in essence put all of their intellectual assets on a public service.

It's another way of saying that the property in which enterprises need to invest is increasingly out of their complete control. The software upon which they rely for such externalized operations is not their own and they don't even own a license to it; they simply own the right to use someone else's software on the Web as a service. The information upon which they rely will be fully accessible, but although the information and ideas that are stored in such services may be the property of an enterprise by law, they will not own the relationships that people have via the social media platforms that helped to create and store this information. In a sense, today's large, hierarchical enterprises are running out of things that they can own that will actually make money, provide leadership, or influence people.

Economies of scale are no longer necessarily benefiting directly from the scale of hierarchical organizations. Instead the ability to scale productive, collaborative relationships through communication tools such as social media may be enabling another kind of asset to dominate the success of organizations, the asset of a trusted network of personal relationships that will exist for individuals with or without the presence of specific institutions to sponsor those relationships. The asset of relationships pushes us further into an economy focused on delivering services, with intellectual or physical assets providing a less prominent option for delivering value through trusted service relationships.

Creating New Channels for Demand: Farmavita.net Shows How to Market Pharmaceuticals Expertise

A further hint that social media is an important alternative for building economic success can be seen in the pharmaceutical industry. The pharmaceutical industry is beginning to resemble the Hollywood movie industry in that it relies more and more on the intense marketing of a small number of expensive "blockbuster" drugs and treatments for its revenues. Many pharmaceutical companies are actually spending more on advertising and marketing for new products than they are on the research and development required to produce them, trying to ensure maximum market demand for a product during its protection under patent-law protections before it becomes a generic drug that can be produced by anyone. With fewer and fewer potential market winners in the product-development pipeline, pharmaceutical companies are challenged to deliver the profits that their shareholders demand, especially from sales in developing nations in which expensive drugs are rarely an option for impoverished people.

A possible model for improving the markets for pharmaceuticals is being tested by the Croatian social network Farmavita.net, which offers an opportunity to turn the pharmaceutical business model inside out. Instead of focusing on major marketing campaigns to mass markets, Farmavita provides an online community in which initially anonymous companies can make potential clients aware of their expertise in preparing both patented and generic drugs ready for the marketplace. Buyers from developing nations can make sellers aware of the skills and materials that they require to manufacture drugs in their local markets at prices that people will be able to afford in those markets.

Instead of trying to focus on selling specific drugs with a very short duration of high profitability Farmavita.net invites the producers of such drugs to consider that the most valuable thing that they may have to license is not a specific product but rather their insight into how to create and market drugs successfully. In the Big Sombrero market model (see Chapter 4), pharmaceutical companies could take fewer risks and reach potentially greater rewards by facilitating conversations globally with many smaller global markets via social media and learning about how to meet the needs of a greater number of existing markets for existing products more effectively, though with more competition from other enterprises with similar skill sets. The "new work" that social media facilitates may be pointing us toward the importance of leadership and influence through social media rather than ownership as the key drivers to our local and global economies.

If social media can have such a potentially world-changing impact on leadership and influence in today's enterprises, you can be sure that social media will have an equally great impact upon an arena of human endeavor in which leadership and influence are its very lifeblood: politics.

6

The New Politics:
Content Nation Redefines How Citizens Influence Governments

"All politics is local," observed Tip O'Neill, a former Speaker of the U.S. House of Representatives. O'Neill was a congressman from Cambridge, Massachusetts, who learned this maxim of politics when he lost his first political campaign—a race for a seat on his local city council—by only 150 votes. When O'Neill asked some of the people in his neighborhood why they hadn't voted for him, they told him "You didn't ask for my vote." O'Neill never forgot this lesson and went on to a very successful career in politics in which he was known for his ability to lead and influence the most unlikely combinations of political allies to get their votes—and to get business done. The art of politics is indeed all local, based on building bonds of trust and delivering on personal promises to people who have entrusted someone with their personal political endorsement.

Social Media in Politics:
New Tools for Conversations

If ever there were an activity that was perfectly tailored for social media, politics would certainly be it. Political systems may vary from one location to another, but the art of politics is a universal human discipline that calls upon the most powerful tools of human communications available to build leadership, endorsement, and influence. Rarely has there been a substitute that would trump a politician meeting personally with people to build influential relationships, but social media enables masses of people to participate in political processes in personal ways that make all politics a local affair on a scale never before achieved in human history.

To underscore the universality of the lessons to be learned from the use of social media in politics, I have tried to write this chapter from as neutral a political position as possible using examples from across the world's political spectrum. Given that many of the most compelling examples of the use of social media in politics stem from situations with major political impact, that's not such an easy thing for an author to do. Some of the political figures and organizations in this chapter may appeal to you; some may not. Whatever the person or political view being portrayed or my portrayal of them, I hope that you can focus on the lessons to be learned about social media from a particular point of view, and not on the political views of the people and organizations being used as examples.

From Monarchs to Conversations to Dictation: The Evolution of Publishing as a Political Tool

Earlier in the book we looked at the availability of affordable publishing tools and venues popular during the time of the American War of Independence that allowed everyday people to discuss political ideas with fellow citizens, and to take decisive political action. Publishing, once the political tool of monarchs, became a tool for building citizen awareness of political issues. In the 19th century the rise of mass-produced newspapers, journals, and books built a wide awareness of political issues and theories that resulted in massive political changes in Europe and elsewhere. This broadcasting of ideas that formed the core of modern politics provoked new thinking and produced powerful new political movements. The 20th century witnessed the rise of electronic media used for politics, adding radio, recorded sound, and moving images to the arsenal of political communications. Literacy was no longer a requirement for mass political communications. With these tools, powerful political messages could quickly galvanize entire nations to do the will of its political leaders, sometimes with beneficial results, sometimes with disastrous results.

With the rise of television broadcasting in the late 20th century, the techniques of mass marketing blended with politics to create political television advertisements and influential news-opinion television shows that began to shape politics as a consumer marketing discipline, packaging candidates as if they were household products and shaping their positions on issues as part of a brand strategy to appeal precisely to the tastes of specific well-researched groups of citizens. Political discussions on a personal level were still important, but somehow the ability of citizens to use publishing to fire the discussion of political ideas with peers as the primary channel for political decisions and actions had been lost to the political process in many nations by the end of the 20th century. Thomas Paine's *Common Sense*, the simple pamphlet by a lone citizen in the political wilderness of colonial America, was all but forgotten as a model for motivating fellow citizens to take political action by the dawn of the 21st century. Conversation among citizens had given way to dictation to consumers.

Early Web: Promising Tools, Small Audience

The first hints of the power of social media to influence politics via Web-enabled publishing were already evident by the 1997 death of Diana, Princess of Wales. Although the event became a global media phenomenon via broadcast television, it was likely the first event with global impact that had been carried via live online video services. Fuzzy, tiny pictures rolled across computer screens around the world, enabling people to witness another nation's state funeral as if it were a funeral of one of their own. People could retrieve video clips of the event on the Web later on at will, enabling people to participate not only globally but at any convenient time. People could listen in to some comments at Princess Diana's memorial service that were sharply critical of Britain's head of state. All of a sudden, any time could be the right time to engage in a moving political video experience for people around the world. Nonetheless, these video clips were for the most part simply repackaging existing television-broadcast reports.

Early weblogs and other Web-based social media experiments in politics were significant, but more as a way to feed established media outlets than social media tools in their own right. The Drudge Report's famed 1998 breaking of the story of President Bill Clinton's relationship with White House intern Monica Lewinsky was a key breakthrough that highlighted the potential power of bloggers as a channel for leaking stories from political sources, but the Web site's notoriety and power came primarily through established media outlets picking up the story and amplifying it to the public. There was, at that time, a fairly limited cadre of Web enthusiasts who were in a position to follow political events on the Web, much less comment on them in weblogs.

By the time of the 2000 U.S. elections, social media was beginning to be seen as a tool for helping political campaigns, but it did not influence the outcome of national elections in any significant way. Comments in Web forums and news sites generated some enthusiasm for candidates, but the Web was still being used mostly as a one-way medium for the dissemination of information from central providers.

Former U.S. vice president Al Gore, an early promoter and enthusiast for the Web and a presidential candidate in 2000, provided on his campaign's Web site links to sign people up for email and instant message communications, live video-camera shots of their campaign headquarters, and the ability for people to design simple personalized pages where they could express their positions on political issues. Though demonstrating many of the early best practices of Web site design used in that era, the Gore campaign Web site and similar campaign sites built by other candidates were mostly experiments in building interaction among the growing but still relatively limited number of citizens who were using the Web in 2000 to learn about political campaigns.

The Howard Dean Campaign

By 2004, social media technologies on the Web had matured to the point that a rapidly expanding online audience equipped with rapidly improving Web publishing technologies could be engaged for political messages and activities with a far greater scope than ever before. In the United States candidates for political office began to engage citizens through social media and political activists began to leverage social media for their own efforts to organize and motivate citizens. Though social media may not have played a crucial role in the year's elections, its power was evident and growing quickly.

The presidential campaign of Howard Dean used many social media tools that proved to be key elements his U.S. presidential campaign. As the governor of Vermont, Howard Dean was well known to an inner circle of politicians but relatively unknown to most voters beyond his own small New England state. His national profile changed rapidly when his campaign used social media tools to recruit and train people supporting his campaign, gather campaign contributions, communicate with supporters, and use them to rally additional support. Early opinion polling showed Dean's efforts paying off, but with campaign-management issues, strengthening opponents, and the repeated playing of a now-famous Dean "scream" from a televised campaign rally, Dean did not go on to become his party's candidate for president. In the process of operating his relatively short-lived campaign, though, the team behind the Dean phenomenon had stumbled on to several key methods that began to put together the outlines of how to use social media tools effectively in politics, as follows:

- **Using social media as a virtual and physical organizing tool.** The Howard Dean campaign made extensive use of the then-new Meetup social networking tool, which enabled people to organize campaign enthusiasts for online meetings and in-person meetings at locations across the country. Web forums were used to help gain feedback on issues and to foster discussions about possible campaign tactics and messages that could be provided to voters, and enabled campaign enthusiasts to draft letters to potential supporters. None of these concepts in and of themselves was particularly new, but the efficiency and ease with which new social media technologies could be deployed enabled citizen involvement and interaction with political candidates and their enthusiasts to scale very rapidly across an entire country in thousands of local communities with little central intervention.

- **Using social media concepts to encourage small campaign contributions on a massive scale.** Although campaign Web sites had been used for several years to solicit campaign contributions via credit card donations, candidates would generally focus on raising the maximum contribution possible from relatively few donors. The Howard Dean campaign was the first to engineer very large numbers of very small contributions, using emails and viral marketing techniques to spread enthusiasm for donations with person-to-person solicitations for small donations similar to those used for non-profit causes. Though Howard Dean was not able to outraise other candidates in total funds, he did raise a then-unprecedented $50 million from Web-based donations and surpassed records set by earlier presidential campaigns in his party for funds raised in a three-month period. Instead of raising funds from a small number of large donors to be used to persuade citizens, the citizens themselves were persuaded to support a candidate and provided contributions and active involvement in a campaign as a form of personal endorsement.

- **Using social media to design a campaign.** A core of a few thousand enthusiastic Howard Dean supporters, known as "Deaniacs" by some, became expert at spreading enthusiasm and points of view across the Web. They wrote weblogs and commented on other people's weblogs, sent out emails, and contributed passionate thoughts on forums. Most importantly, though, was their ability to define via Meetup, other Web sites, and in person how best to use social media tools to spread the word to other people. This self-organizing group of about 3,000 enthusiasts was able to leverage social media via their own efforts to become more than 140,000 enthusiasts in a few short months. "We fell into this by accident," Dean noted in an interview. "I wish I could tell you we were smart enough to figure this out, but the community taught us. They seized the initiative through Meetup. They built our organization for us before we had an organization."

The Dean campaign set precedents in how individual citizens could use social media not only to comment upon a political campaign but actually to shape that campaign. Citizens deciding to organize themselves for political action based on their own compelling political ideas had shaken off the dust of the ages and had seized powerful new publishing tools in an era of global electronic communications.

Ron Paul: When Citizens Define a Candidate's Power and Influence

Congressman Ron Paul was a relatively unknown Texan in the U.S. House of Representatives who in March of 2007 began a campaign for his party's presidential nomination that most in his party considered to be quixotic at best—that is, until he was able to leverage his appearances in televised debates into campaign cash and strong grass-roots support through social media. Having run for the presidency as an independent candidate in 1988, Paul had a sense of how to campaign, but his greater sense of how to pull off a long-shot bid for a major-party nomination came from his 2006 congressional campaign, in which he raised virtually all of his campaign funds online from small citizen donations by emulating many of the techniques used by the 2004 Howard Dean campaign.

With knowledge of how to use social media and leveraging bloggers and the rapidly emerging strength of online video services and emerging social networking services, such as Facebook and MySpace, Ron Paul had a strong grassroots organization already in place when he caught the attention of national audiences in televised presidential-campaign debates. Largely discounted by both political analysts and reporters, he was able to transform his television performance into enormous waves of small online campaign contributions and a rapidly expanding network of citizens expressing their support for him online in video clips, discussion groups, and viral marketing campaigns.

On November 5, 2007, an online fundraising campaign built around the British holiday commemorating the defeat of the anti-government figure Guy Fawkes, a figure celebrated in the popular 2005 movie *V for Vendetta*, triggered $4.2 million in campaign contributions in 24 hours for Ron Paul's presidential campaign from small online donors—a then-unprecedented record for online fundraising. Though Ron Paul was unable to translate his Web-based support into wide support for his party's presidential nomination, he established that any candidate with any message has the potential to tap into strong sentiments among citizens, and that when citizens are passionate about political views it can translate into powerful political support that transcends the leadership and influence of traditional political power brokers.

CONTENT NATION POLITICAL RULE #1: *Powerful social media tools enable political power to grow from everyday citizens who organize and inspire one another autonomously and locally on a massive scale.*

Political Blogs—Influence from Anywhere

Along with political campaigns seizing social media, the 2004 elections also witnessed the widespread rise of people using weblogs to promote political opinions and to incite people to provide their personal support to politicians and political initiatives. While prominent political weblogs provided great influence, it was also noteworthy how anyone's willingness to create a post on a weblog on a candidate or an issue could gain attention and influence rapidly. Links from other weblogs and from search engines that were programmed to surface content to which other Web sites were linking made it possible for influential voices to appear out of nowhere. This has enabled a much wider discussion of a much wider array of political opinions than ever before. The proliferation of influential voices via today's social media publishing outlets makes it seem as if Thomas Paine had been cloned a million times over in a matter of a few months: everyone was inciting everybody into discussing and taking action on political issues, with or without any official political allegiances.

One of the more surprising instances of the spontaneity of political weblogs that arose in the 2004 election was a topical weblog that existed actively for only a few weeks, yet nevertheless gained enormous attention. In one of the televised presidential debates some viewers noticed rumples in the rear of then-candidate George W. Bush's suit coat that appeared in their minds to be a piece of electronic equipment to relay audio to an earpiece in Bush's ear. This incident was noticed briefly by some prominent weblogs but the creators of Is Bush Wired, an anonymously authored weblog, decided to stick with the story and to collect information that accumulated about this incident.

The weblog attained such widespread and immediate interest from prominent bloggers that it was frequently overloaded with viewers to the point of being unavailable, but when it was available it provided a story-specific conduit for all of the latest and greatest information and links relating to this emerging news item. The weblog had been set up on Blogger's free facility that enables a weblog to be set up in seconds. There was absolutely nothing unusual about the weblog, except that it had intense interest almost instantly. The ability of anyone to create a politically influential publication on a moment's notice clearly was changing the way that politics would unfold forever after.

Weblogs also enabled people who would normally gain political influence through print, radio, and television to build audiences on the Web that in many instances helped them to create their own independent brands as political commentators. Michelle Malkin was a journalist whose syndicated political-opinion column was popular with several major newspapers, but when she began her own weblog during the 2004 U.S. elections she found that her popularity among her Web audience began to take on a life of its own. Although her opinion columns are still syndicated to major newspapers, her willingness to begin to use social media has enabled her to develop her independent brand as a personal publisher among other bloggers while there was still a clear opportunity to stand out from other established journalists. Michelle Malkin uses all of the tools of blogging to make her independent presence possible, including a style of writing that mixes observations about her personal life with political observations that enables her to appeal to her audience as a person with everyday interests as well as political interests.

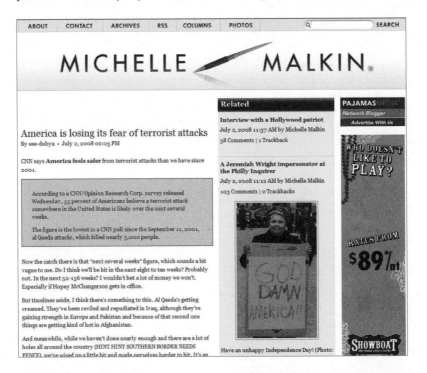

Political activist Markos Moulitsas, known widely as "Kos," started his Daily Kos political weblog in 2002 and gained an audience rapidly with his frankly worded blog entries, but he is most significant in that he turned his personal brand into a very powerful group brand for political blogging. Most systems that support blogging enable more than one person to post entries to a weblog, a feature that is rarely used by most people but that was put to good use by Kos starting in 2004. Kos attracted bloggers who were able to contribute "diaries"— a collection of weblogs—to the site, and which were edited by Kos and others to provide content for the site's main weblog. This enabled Kos to focus on building the influence of his publication on a personal basis with media appearances and with conferences in which people who were readers of Daily Kos could interact with its weblog authors and discuss politics. By cultivating the weblog's influence among political enthusiasts, Daily Kos's endorsements of candidates and its views on key issues are taken seriously by many political insiders and organizers, as well as the more than 700,000 political enthusiasts who visit Daily Kos monthly.

The 2004 election also saw the questioning of weblogs as reliable sources of information. On the night of the November 2 elections in the U.S., a number of weblogs, including the political-gossip site Wonkette, carried exit-poll results from various sources that did not reflect the ultimate result of the presidential election in several of the polled states. Traditional media outlets took bloggers to task as lacking journalistic integrity in releasing these exit polls prior to the close of national voting. Regardless of the rightness or wrongness of these leaks, it was clear that traditional news outlets, well known for their own publishing of leaked documents, were now encountering competition from weblogs on breaking news about major political events on the most crucial day of political coverage. Presumably these exit-poll numbers came from people on the inside of the political process, so one assumes that the bloggers given these leaked exit-poll numbers served their political purposes. In other words, those with political power had recognized the power of weblogs to influence citizens. The use of social media for both information and disinformation to influence politics had begun in earnest.

Wonkette!

SEARCH

NOV 02 2004

Birdies All Atwitter
6:50 p.m.
6 p.m. exit polls – not internals.

K/B:
FL 51 49
NC 48 52
OH 51 49
Missouri 46 54
Ark 47 53
Mich 51 47
NM 50 49
LA 43 56
CO 48 51
AZ 45 55
Minn 54 44
Wisc 52 47
IA 49 49

CONTENT NATION POLITICAL RULE #2: *Social media allows anyone from anywhere to influence politics on a massive scale—including the powerful and the influential.*

The Voice of the People: Blogs, Videos, and Communities Speak Out

As much as social media has benefited candidates for a high-profile office like President of the United States, it has also enabled people to speak out about any political issue on any scale. Many times social media's greatest impact is being felt by politicians in more local environments, enabling people to become aware of and get involved in local issues and to take a new look at local politicians who may have otherwise received relatively little scrutiny. If all politics is local, then local communities are certainly a part of social media's story.

The Partrick Open Space Alliance: Confronting Political Power with Citizen Involvement

An interesting example of social media in action in local communities is almost within sight of my home. A tract of undeveloped land is an unusual commodity in my home town of Westport, Connecticut, which is within easy commuting distance of New York City and is a prime target for real-estate development. When an undeveloped 55-acre tract of land became available in 2002, not far from my home, it was no surprise that a developer purchased the forested land and planned to use it for a major housing development. The catch: about half of the site was a swamp sitting atop a site that a century ago had been an industrial site still littered with toxic substances. In an area in which large open spaces are rare and where many residents rely on well water for their homes, the community near the parcel of land would be impacted significantly by this development.

Starting in 2002, a group of concerned citizens started an email mailing list to notify people of efforts to oppose the development. Soon after that the Partrick Open Space Alliance, named for a scenic road near the parcel of land, launched a Web site that provided news, background documents, letter-writing tools, links to public opinion, and online fund-raising to build opposition to powerful real-estate and political interests who were intent on the development of this land. The Web site was publicized on photocopied flyers and roadside signs, enabling more people to learn about the issues regarding the development of this land and to receive the group's email alerts. Dozens of activists turned into hundreds rapidly and enabled a strong coalition of interests to bring their side of the issue to public hearings and town meetings and to heighten coverage in local newspapers. Highly motivated citizens who informed one another and influenced other residents and local government officials via social media brought a development once thought to be unopposable to a standstill for more than four years. The net result was a meaningful compromise: fewer than half of the original number of homes would be built on the site and the wetlands portion of the parcel was donated to a land-conservancy trust in 2007. In a town in which most people are commuting to their jobs and not able to commit much time to local causes, social media enabled a community to act like a community, using just the most basic online publishing tools and a good deal of commitment.

CONTENT NATION POLITICAL RULE #3: *If local media doesn't take interest in a community cause, social media can enable people to create their own independent influence rapidly and effectively.*

Local Political Blogs: Nobody Special Influences Political Leaders and Elections

My home state of Connecticut is generally a quiet place, but our local politics now come into the spotlight in exciting ways thanks to social media's ability to change the balance of power in influencing local politics. Connecticut has developed a thriving community of local bloggers who work together often to cover local and state political events and to build community interest in issues and campaigns. Equipped with mobile video cameras and using freely available video-editing tools, their blogs are capturing the flavor of local politics as much as they are capturing local information and opinions. Bloggers post videos to YouTube and embed them in their blog posts, enabling them to build exposure rapidly for local politicians. Politicians who might otherwise never be known or heard by the local electorate may find their statements being broadcast via the Web, although not always with flattering consequences. In one particular video interview on the Connecticut Bob weblog, a politician says to his interviewer on camera, "You have any idiot [that wants] to run against me in this town and I will crush them." This is the raw face of true everyday politicians in true everyday local politics that would be seen rarely if ever via local commercial media outlets that are tied very closely to the interests of their advertisers. Instead we find these views of local politics in a blog published by a computer-network engineer with no particular qualifications as a publisher or a political expert other than his own abilities and enthusiasm.

Local and nationally focused political weblogs played a key role in the 2006 elections, which saw Ned Lamont, a relatively unknown citizen with only limited town-level political experience, run for the U.S. Senate. To get his party's nomination he had to face Senator Joseph Lieberman in a primary election. Lieberman, who had served in the Senate for 12 years and had been a candidate for U.S. Vice President in the 2000 election, was a very powerful politician on the national stage. It seemed to be a daunting task to take him on in a party primary, but the Lamont campaign provided an extraordinary challenge to his opponent by embracing bloggers as a key to communicating to local citizens and to gaining attention among political enthusiasts and media outlets in other parts of the nation.

Lamont often wrote personally on his campaign's own weblog, which included links to key local and national weblogs and attracted an enthusiastic community of commenters. Like in the 2004 elections, Lamont leveraged this network of online political enthusiasts to gain thousands of small contributions rapidly and to build a network of campaign volunteers. Lamont made himself available to local bloggers on a frequent basis for video interviews that were uploaded to sites such as YouTube to provide a readily available outlet for his opinions. Nationally focused weblogs drew attention to local bloggers, who in turn drew attention to the national weblogs, creating a reinforcing cycle of attention to citizen-generated media. By contrast the Lieberman primary campaign made little use of independent weblogs, did not allow comments on their campaign weblog, and in general relied upon Lieberman's decades of political and media connections to build support.

The result was staggering: Lamont defeated a three-term icon of Connecticut and national politics in the primary election by a narrow margin. Nevertheless, Lieberman then went on to win the general election for the Senate as an independent candidate by a healthy margin, leveraging his much larger base of established donors and support from national political supporters and local politicians to overwhelm the base of support that Lamont had been able to build through social media. Social media's power to change politics took a step forward in this particular campaign, but awaited a broader audience and more refinement to turn influence by citizens into broad leadership.

CONTENT NATION POLITICAL RULE #4: *Social media can build influential political support rapidly, but it requires a broad base of people in a community who use it and understand it to be completely effective.*

A Police Incident Becomes a National Political Phenomenon: The Unyielding Eye of Social Media

One of the most potent aspects of social media from a political perspective is that any moment could become a political moment though the all-present eye of social media. George Orwell in his 1949 novel *1984* foresaw an era in which "Big Brother," a dictator in a police state, was using surveillance cameras to monitor the activities of all citizens. With social media, in many ways, the tables of that fictional account have been turned. Now, the citizens of the world keep an eye on their governments and share what they see with fellow citizens, sometimes creating strong political reactions among citizens in the process.

In September 2007, John Kerry, a U.S. senator and former presidential candidate, was speaking at a forum held at the University of Florida in Gainesville. A student came to a microphone in the audience to ask Senator Kerry questions relating to the 2004 presidential election. After about 90 seconds of questions and quotes from a book that included some colorful language, police in the auditorium grasped the student and carried the student to the rear of the auditorium, where they used an electronic taser weapon to subdue the student. "Don't tase me, bro'!" yelled the student as the police applied their weapon to him.

We know these facts because of videos recorded by students present at the forum who uploaded them to the YouTube video-publishing service. It is reported that with 24 hours of it having been posted on YouTube the video had become the top virally distributed video on the Web. Versions of the incident were viewed, copied, shared, and modified until various versions of it had reached more than 2.4 million people within a few days and millions more afterwards. The video became the inspiration of many "mashup" remixes of the footage into political songs and statements. Traditional media outlets reacted to the phenomenon and provided their own commentary from prominent political opinion-makers, but the footage of the incident itself and the remixes, comments, and sharing by everyday citizens enabled them to make their own opinions of the incident known to one another with relatively little intervention from political pundits. If a week in politics is a lifetime, as is said often, then in a week of intense viewing and participation the Web created a lifetime of political opinions nationwide about a local incident with little facilitation by traditional media and politicians. Citizens were making themselves aware of what was important politically.

CONTENT NATION POLITICAL RULE #5: *Through social media anyone's politics could become everyone's politics.*

Showing Local Issues in a National Spotlight: BlackBox.org's Eye on Electronic Voting

Investigative reports are well known to most people who follow the news, but social media has given citizens the ability to focus on issues that most news outlets would ignore entirely or look at from just a local point of view. In many instances, though, political issues at a local level found in many localities add up to nation-wide issues that require political action. BlackBoxVoting.org is a Web site set up by Bev Harris, founder of the nonprofit group Black Box Voting, Inc., to watchdog voting rights in U.S. elections. Though the use of electronic voting is encouraged by the Help America Vote Act, as they are currently implemented these machines count votes in secret and transfer power from the citizenry to government and vendor insiders.

The founders of BlackBoxVoting.org started noticing at first issues in specific locations with electronic voting machines and then began to compile and investigate issues with voting machines and their administration that were being found across the nation. BlackBoxVoting.org makes extensive use of its own video recording of incidents and online forums to collect and disseminate information on problems with voting machines experienced by citizens. Today, BlackBoxVoting.org is an influential citizen-driven national clearinghouse for information on voting rights in the U.S. that continues to compile investigative reports on election accuracy and fairness, which add up to a national political issue.

CONTENT NATION POLITICAL RULE #6: *If you think that your politics are only local, social media can make you think again.*

Follow the Money: Social Media Becomes an Engine for Citizen-Driven Fund-Raising

As much as modern American politics are known for their use of advertising and marketing techniques for spreading a political candidate's message, the key factor that has underwritten these efforts has been fund-raising. Without the massive amounts of funds, a campaign's advertising and communications don't get seen by citizens. In the 1960s U.S., political action committees, or PACs, started using mass-marketing techniques to identify potential campaign donors and contacting these donors through targeted direct mail campaigns very similar to those used for promoting commercial products and services. These techniques were highly successful and helped to raise millions in campaign funds in major elections. Direct marketing was complemented by traditional fund-raising efforts such as dinners where contributors to campaign committees would provide thousands of dollars to hear a candidate speak, appeals to leading businesses and trade associations, and phone banks used to appeal to potential donors directly.

The Howard Dean campaign of 2004 demonstrated that online fund-raising could bring in millions of dollars for a candidate running for national office from very small donations on a massive scale using social media techniques. This inspired political activists to try to extend the principles of social media fund-raising further to support a broader array of candidates and political issues. One of the most successful of these efforts to date has been ActBlue, which started in June of 2004 to build a system that would enable candidates and causes to set up their own Web-based funding networks and to receive small-donation funding from people nationwide. Within seconds any candidate or cause supported by ActBlue members can establish their online fund-raising capabilities, which they can connect to their own Web sites but also use through the ActBlue Web site and affiliated Web sites to encourage contributions. Weblogs supporting candidates and causes can embed ActBlue fund-raising tools, making any Web site, weblog, or other online publishing presence a potential fund-raising presence for any local or national candidate. ActBlue provides reporting and management functionality that simplifies reporting required by government election-oversight organizations.

Since 2004, ActBlue has raised more than $56 million for a large number of candidates, with full accountability for the funds raised and easy viewing by anyone visiting the site of which people, weblogs, and causes are supporting which candidates via ActBlue. The site enables a person to split a donation easily between candidates supported by a particular fundraiser, making it easy for local candidates to receive small donations from all across the country. Bloggers and others with influential political opinions can lend their endorsement to a group of political candidates to get others interested in their campaign efforts.

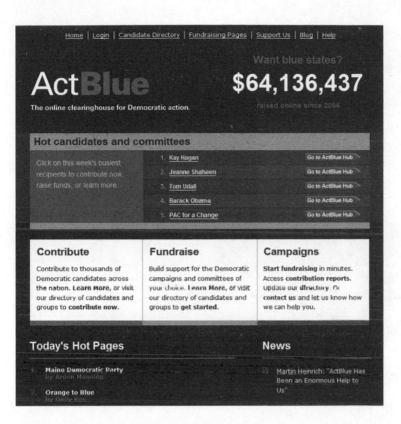

Comparable Web sites have been established recently by people who support candidates and causes from a different part of the political spectrum, but not without some early failures. Rightroots was a Web site that tried to emulate the ActBlue formula in a general sense, but it lacked many of the citizen-directed features of ActBlue and had little interaction with political webloggers helping to raise funds. It was also supported by a political action committee backed by the Associated Builders and Contractors, Inc., which gave the Web site less of a sense that it was empowering citizens. In January 2008, a new site called Slatecard was launched that incorporated many of the social media features of ActBlue, most especially being careful to position itself as a technology to promote political fund-raising from citizen activists rather than promoting specific political issues itself. Though early yet in its development, Slatecard seems to be repeating the early successes of ActBlue for another group of citizens.

CONTENT NATION POLITICAL RULE #7: *If those who have the gold make the rules in politics, social media is putting citizens in the rule-making spot for campaigns large and small.*

The Obama Campaign: Perfecting Social Media in Politics Means Listening to Citizens

In many ways the 2008 presidential campaign of Barack Obama was the culminating proof that social media has the power to transform politics as we have known it in an era of mass electronic communications. From viral videos to small-donor online fund-raising to organizing and training campaign volunteers to a vibrant online community all its own, the Obama campaign demonstrated that it could use social media to support the success of a major political candidate in its efforts to win political battles against the most well-backed opponents focused on more traditional communications methods. Designed by one of the founders of the Facebook social media portal, the Obama campaign's use of social media was designed from its inception to be a highly influential and transformative tool for politics.

The philosophy of the Obama campaign's approach to social media has been one of "open source politics," an allusion to the use of freely available programming code for many kinds of software that encourage open development of its capabilities from anyone. This meant that the Obama campaign would allow any member of its campaign Web site who followed simple ground rules for conduct to set up their own weblog on the campaign site to form issue-oriented groups and to communicate and comment freely on the campaign's tactics. Because the site attracts mostly enthusiasts and active contributors, this turned out to be a huge plus for the most part, enabling citizens to inspire one another and to build enthusiasm for the campaign rapidly.

This openness created both challenges and opportunities for the Obama campaign. In June of 2008, some supporters of Senator Obama's campaign grew concerned about the strength of his support for changes to pending legislation addressing U.S. wiretapping laws. These members established a discussion group on the Obama campaign Web site that was asking Senator Obama to vote on the wiretapping legislation according to their views. Within a few days the group's membership had grown to more than 10,000 Obama supporters, becoming the most popular group on the Obama campaign Web site. This kind of influence usually comes from external sources of political insiders; here the citizens supporting Obama's campaign were exerting their own political influence through the campaign's own Web site.

The resolution of this issue in the short term was a simple and elegant solution: Senator Obama replied to this group in an entry on the campaign's own weblog which was posted by campaign staff. Many members of the campaign's Web site commented on Obama's blog and several campaign staff members replied to concerns, because Obama himself was not available at the time. In other words, social media was used both to raise issues to influence a candidate and to enable the candidate to respond as a peer of that social media community. This was a political moment in every way, but one which demonstrated that the power of social media to enable citizens to have influential conversations with political leaders had reached unprecedented heights.

CONTENT NATION POLITICAL RULE #8: *Social media challenges politicians to use the empowerment of citizens to drive their own political power, a task that requires a willingness both to support and to engage in real conversations on real issues.*

Bending Truth into Truthiness: Sponsored Social Media Corrupts Citizens' Conversations

One of the uncomfortable truths about politics is that often tools get turned into weapons very quickly. Social media has tremendous power to enable people to communicate honestly and openly in politics, but it also has the ability to enable political operatives to disguise themselves as everyday unaffiliated citizens while promoting their political points of view. As we saw in Chapter 4's discussion on marketing, this "astroturfing" inevitably creates as many problems as it tries to address, yet those who are used to publishing being a way to dictate a message to citizens will try to use social media for something other than genuine political discussions.

One of the most common practices is for a political operative to pose as an unaffiliated individual and post comments or links to news stories in a social media service. The practice is widespread and difficult to stop, but often people practicing this are discovered or assumed by the members of a social media service to be representing more than their own interests.

An interesting instance of two political opponents getting caught in "astroturfing" occurred recently in a hotly contested battle for the U.S. Senate. The email address of a "Buck Smith" used to post comments on the Burnt Orange Report political weblog was traced back to an aide of Senator John Cornyn. In turn, the Cornyn campaign discovered that an aide from the campaign of his Senate campaign opponent Rick Noriega had posed as a blogger under an assumed name to obtain information from the Cornyn campaign. Political affiliation is no guarantee as to who will try these techniques.

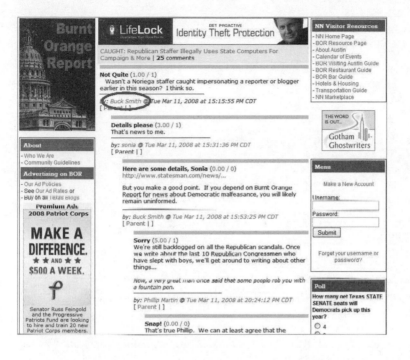

A larger problem in politics is the use of social media Web sites designed to appear as if they are representing an independent point of view without indicating the site's sponsorship by a political organization. An interesting example of this appeared in the 2008 U.S. presidential election when the Clinton Democrats Web site appeared. The Web site openly disavows any affiliation with the former Hillary Clinton presidential campaign and the Hillary Clinton campaign disavows any affiliation with the Web site as well. Yet the Web site has weblogs and other social media aimed at the supporters of Hillary Clinton to dissuade them from supporting Barack Obama, the eventual nominee for her party's presidential bid. The weblog posts on this Web site are by anonymous figures and the Web site as a whole has no indication of its sponsorship. This type of Web site uses the tools of social media, but clearly it is being used by political advocates to have their points of view appear to be coming from large groups of everyday citizens rather than from their associated activists.

CONTENT NATION POLITICAL RULE #9: *Social media publishing tools can become publishing weapons when politicians fear honest conversations with citizens.*

Global Localism: Politics Shaped to Any Scale ▪

The power of social media as a tool for politics is quite evident in the United States, not just from the ability of campaigns and bloggers to influence citizens but as well from the ability of individual citizens to influence one another without the intervention of politicians and the traditional media. I have given so far examples that apply mostly to the United States, but social media is a publishing phenomenon with global impact as well, most especially in developed nations with long-established traditions of open communications, but in other nations as well.

Though there are many nations whose governments control and monitor Web-based communications more closely than others, voices around the world are beginning to start making political statements in weblogs, videos, and social networking communities. Although government control of political communications is an important barrier to the growth of social media in many nations, a larger barrier may be culture. The concept of criticizing or challenging public figures is not something that comes naturally to many societies, both because of long-standing cultural traditions and fears of reprisals by the powerful. Yet, even where there are such barriers, the inborn nature of humans to be publishers drives people inevitably toward social media as a political tool.

Another factor pushing social media into the global political spotlight is the rapid expansion of a global economy that depends upon the efficient communications of the Internet and mobile communications networks to enable commerce. As the Web pushes ever further into the economies of the world's nations, the benefits of social media outlined already for marketing and efficient communications in enterprises are helping to expand its use rapidly. The enormous benefits of having a nation's economy being driven by social media are pushing many nations toward more experimentation in social media that will lead inevitably to more political expression through social media. This enables everyday citizens from any community to build influence within their community and to extend that influence rapidly to people in their own countries and to other people around the world who share their interest in political goals.

Myanmar: Feet on the Ground and Awareness around the World through Social Media

The Union of Myanmar, known also as Burma, has experienced significant political unrest in recent years. In September 2007, demonstrations rose up in the streets of Myanmar, led by Buddhist monks and with participation by many citizens. The media of Myanmar, controlled closely by its government, did not provide accurate coverage of many of these events, but citizens equipped with text- and video-enabled mobile phones and concealed video cameras were able to capture many key moments of the protests and to find ways to transfer them from their phones to people outside of the country. News and pictures made their way to the world's media organizations via the Web, which heightened the initial awareness of these events in the world and, for a time, in Myanmar. The interest of traditional media outlets was intense for a period of time, but then died down, as other headline-grabbing stories overtook stories from Myanmar. Social media had cracked open the doorway to world awareness via citizen publishing, but the door threatened to close as quickly as it opened.

That might have been the end of this story except for one key factor: although the eyes of traditional media may have looked elsewhere for novel stories, social media enabled people to continue to communicate their concern and their support for the people of Myanmar. One of the keys to accelerating the awareness of issues on an ongoing basis was the initiation of a group on the Facebook social networking service in September 2007 by a 19-year-old Canadian college student and a recent college graduate in the United Kingdom who focused on the monks' protests. From a start of just a few thousand members, the group now counts more than 370,000 people who became aware of Myanmar issues through members of the group, which includes prominent CEOs as well as everyday people. The May, 2008 storms that killed thousands of people in Myanmar accelerated awareness of the plight of this nation and helped to drive even more membership into the Facebook group, which assists with both issue awareness and fundraising. What was a curiosity in world headlines for a few days became a global cause through social media, helping to broaden political support from leaders in nations aware of the leadership and influence enabled by on an ongoing basis by social media.

SOCIAL MEDIA POLITICAL RULE #10: *Traditional media finds political causes that pay for a few commercial breaks and then moves on. Social media finds causes that can grow into movements that carry personal endorsements into lasting influence.*

Where Politics Can Be Difficult: Global Social Media Paves the Way for Local Political Expression

In a world in which at least one nation's parliament is considering legislation that would provide the death penalty for anyone in that nation who is found to be blogging, political expression via social media is not always easy to experience in every nation. Cultural barriers, lack of advanced technologies, or fear of reprisals by political figures can also limit the willingness and ability of people to express themselves, even when social media services are available locally. Where the world does seem to express itself politically with more openness is on social media Web sites that are more oriented toward global markets.

YouTube, the social media video service, has videos focusing on politics uploaded by its members from nations all around the world. News footage of legislators around the world fighting with one another in their meeting chambers is popular fare on YouTube, but the depth of political coverage goes much deeper than such novelties. There are already more than 2,600 videos on YouTube focused on politics in India, for example, many of them viewed by thousands of people with dozens of comments from YouTube members.

Some of the political videos on YouTube oriented toward India are clips of news shows or documentaries, and others feature personal interviews and footage of local political scenes. One political video, for example, is a local-language compilation of movie footage, news footage, and local interviews relating to a proposed government project to dredge a shipping channel through what appears to be the remains of a legendary bridge celebrated in Hinduism. Viewed by more than 4,000 people and with dozens of comments, this video is typical of any number of politically oriented videos from around the world, available to a global audience on YouTube but focused on very local issues. There are already several Web sites within India that encourage sharing of politically oriented videos via social media features, but YouTube's global presence puts it above local politics and social outlooks and gives its content a bridge to a global audience of Indian nationals as well, helping to drive viewership to levels above many social media video portals in India that are still in the early phases of development.

Another social media publishing service with a global focus is Orkut, which provides social networking, photo sharing, and group discussions similar to other social media services. Orkut is popular in many nations across the world, including Pakistan, for which Orkut offers more than two dozen groups that focus on politics in Pakistan. The largest of these groups has more than a thousand members and features discussions both in English and in local languages, focused primarily on Pakistan's internal politics but also taking a look at how Pakistan's politics relate to global politics, giving people in Pakistan a bridge to a broader political outlook.

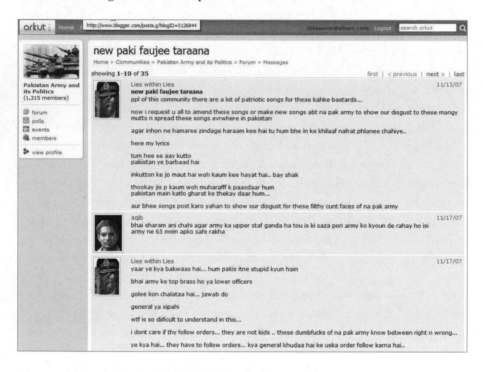

In the use of social media services such as YouTube and Orkut for local political concerns, it is clear that people in Content Nation recognize that talking about politics openly as a citizen requires at times a sense of global empowerment, even when the audience for a particular political statement may be quite local. People are glad to participate in their local and culture-specific politics via social media. In many ways social media helps people to preserve and accentuate a sense of localness and cultural tradition in approaching political issues. In a world in which open political expression via publishing is not something taken for granted in many cultures, though, globally oriented social media publishing services beyond the reach of local politicians can enable people to speak both to their own nation's citizens on local issues as well as to the citizens of the world. Whether through local or global services, in most every nation on earth there are social media enthusiasts who are learning how to express themselves politically through their own social media publishing.

CONTENT NATION POLITICAL RULE #11: *In a world filled with different cultures, global social media services can offer people steps toward political openness that may lead to more local openness.*

Politics beyond Borders: International Activism via Social Media

Al-Qaeda is well known as an organization dedicated to the overthrow of many governments around the world. With a form and organization known well to very few, its adherents are a shadowy group that speak to the world through news outlets at times but otherwise seem to keep a very low profile in their communications. In some nations, laws that protect the privacy of people using the Internet can be leveraged by Al-Qaeda to use social media Web sites that facilitate their communications with the world. *The New York Times* conducted an interview in 2008 with a secretive woman who had created her own "cause within a cause" to enlist women to join Al-Qaeda, an organization that does not openly admit to accepting women as members of its cause. Her Web site is a forum with more than a thousand articles posted in which she exhorts people to join her political movement. A resident of Belgium, the Web site's founder is apparently under constant surveillance but continues to publish information to the world in her members-only forum.

Her words from her interview are a sobering reminder that social media has power that can have influence beyond the control of governments: "I have a weapon. It's to write. It's to speak out. That's my jihad. You can do many things with words. Writing is also a bomb." She is one lone voice in a very small minority of people using social media. Certainly, we cannot afford to eliminate the power of social media because of a handful of carefully monitored political extremists using it any more than we could afford to take mobile phones away from the people of the world. The power of social media to do good for the world far outweighs such negative views. Yet it should remind us that speaking out politically to a global audience can empower people with radical views as well as those with moderate views.

CONTENT NATION POLITICAL RULE #12: *The ability of anyone to communicate via social media to a global audience can have powerful political consequences that are difficult to control.*

The Voice of Government: Learning How to Have Conversations with Citizens

Once someone has won a battle for political power....what then? Governments have long been the source of publications communicating the official policies of their nations, but as much as politics are a person-to-person art, many governments don't go a great job of having conversations with their citizens. Government officials will receive and respond to correspondence, telephone calls, and other communications from citizens, but generally it's on the basis of one party having a great deal of power as individuals and the other not having much power at all as individuals. Even with "e-Government" initiatives taking hold in many nations, the emphasis is on outgoing communications for the most part, with not great advances in making more peer-to-peer contact between government officials and citizens. Yet, social media is helping government officials to learn how to tap into the insights of their citizens and to rub shoulders with them more effectively as they ready themselves for their next campaign for office.

New Zealand Police Act Review Wiki: Crowdsourced Legislation?

Call it a pioneering effort or call it a publicity stunt, the New Zealand Police got a lot of attention from around the world with their efforts at obtaining public feedback on changes to the regulations governing their operations via a wiki in September 2007. With anonymous contributions and heavy "policing" by police staff after a day's contributions to ensure clarity of language and organization, the end result reflected some collective wisdom that helped to inform the revision of the 2008 New Zealand Policing Act. The built-in auditing features of the wiki made it possible for people viewing the wiki to understand the "before" and "after" versions of page revisions. After two weeks of use the police closed the wiki and left the resulting documents online for people to view.

Although the resulting legislation drew upon this experiment only for ideas, as well as from more traditional forms of feedback, some of the ideas collected via the wiki were provocative and reflected positive contributions such as the suggestion that "all citizens and residents of Aotearoa/New Zealand are obliged to help uphold the law, keep the peace, prevent crime, and bring offenders to justice." A suggestion that the minimum age for recruiting candidates for the police be raised to 25 gained wide note, but suggestions that "individuals will be given the legislative tools to help uphold the law by ensuring they can defend their property with whatever force is required without fear of being charged and can catch and hold criminals, even at the point of a gun until police arrive" did not gain as much attention.

If nothing else, this exercise was a reminder that one of the key reasons for having representative governments—so that people can assemble legislation for self-governance—stems largely from an era in which the simple functionality of a wiki that allows collaborative editing of a document from any citizen did not exist. Does this mean that we're ready for the "wisdom of crowds" to assemble complex legislation that complex nations will have to live with for years to come? Perhaps not, but perhaps we are nearing the time when technologies such as wikis can be used to enable wider input into a wider range of legislation, and more accountability for who had their fingers in it.

CONTENT NATION POLITICAL RULE #13: *Just because social media brings the voice of the people to government doesn't mean that it's ready to replace government. Yet.*

Webcameron: Trying to Reinvent a Political Party's Leadership with a Social Media Brand

Leading a major political party in any nation can be a challenge; leading it in the face of having being out of power for more than a decade can be more challenging yet. For the United Kingdom's David Cameron, part of the answer to this challenge is to attract people to the political party that he leads by using social media to engage existing and prospective constituents in a real dialogue about political issues. His Webcameron Web site is a step toward placing his party in the forefront of political social media.

At first glance you wouldn't think that it was a Web site about politics at all. Slick graphics, extensive use of video, blogs with comments, and links to major social media services where his materials can be found are all used. It is the productization of politics cast in a social media light. The differences between this productization and the productization from political candidates in the 1960s couldn't be more striking: where the older political "brands" were about pre-packaging a candidate through market research, the David Cameron "brand" evolves through conversations with his political "market," his constituencies. Instead of trying to sell a politician like a bar of soap, Webcameron helps citizens to tell a politician what kind of soap it is that they need and to get to know the soap craftsman through personal conversations. The result is, hopefully, a politician more aware of the real needs of citizens and better legislation to meet their needs.

CONTENT NATION POLITICAL RULE #14: *In the marketplace for political ideas, social media doesn't eliminate marketing: it just makes it more conversational.*

Instant Messaging as a Political Medium: A Congressman Twitters His Way to Public Awareness

Like any member of the U.S. House of Representatives, John Culberson is never more than two years away from facing an election in his congressional district in Texas. Even as he nears the completion of his fourth term in office Congressman Culberson still looks for better ways with which to keep in touch with his constituents and to carry his brand of politics to a wider audience. John Culberson was the first member of the U.S. Congress to use the Twitter instant messaging service as a channel for his personal and political outlook. Members of Twitter can follow any other member on Twitter on an opt-in basis and receive their instant messages as they post them. This enables an individual to post one short text message from a mobile phone or a PC or other device connected to the Web and to have that message broadcast immediately to all his or her followers.

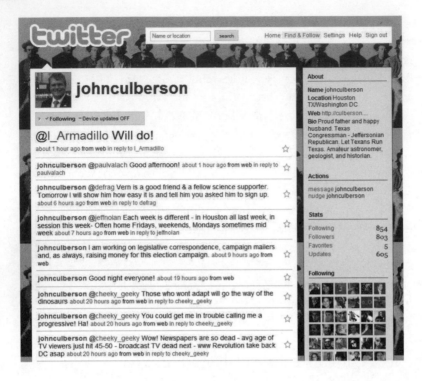

Congressman Culberson's Twitter messages reach a younger and technology-savvy group of voters, the kind of people who are influential in political opinion-making and who will represent the future of his political aspirations. He peppers his Twitter messages with personal observations—"Raising money campaigning and having fun!"—to more issue-oriented communications— "Awesome—thank you—with the worlds third largest oil reserves Iraq can certainly afford to pay much more of its own way." At the same time, Congressman Culberson uses Twitter to alert people to other social media content that he publishes, which allows him to interact with the public on a more personal level. It's a method of keeping up conversations with citizens that he believes will have a major impact on politicians seeking to build a conversational relationship with citizens usually found only in trips home from Congress. With Twitter he gets to bring those local conversations with him right into the halls of Congress. As Congressman Culberson observes in one Twitter message, "I am trying to change the rules for representative gov't and put We the People in every room and every dark corner." "All politics is local," indeed.

CONTENT NATION POLITICAL RULE #15: *If you're in a position where you claim to be speaking for the people, you had best be in a position to be speaking with the people on their own terms.*

Politics in the Hands of Content Nation

Although social media has enormous potential to shape politics throughout the world in ways both large and small, it will not change the fundamental nature of politics from being the art of influencing people to attain a goal. The primary benefit of social media in politics is that the "selling" of political views by politicians is becoming less empowered than the "buying" of political views by citizens.

In the world of marketing, social media helps to shape products and services into conversations that influence marketplaces already empowered by a wealth of publishing relationships at their disposal. In politics social media does likewise, providing a way for people to make their own informed political decisions using influence and information from peers as a key driver in their decision-making processes.

Political peers could be local and using a local language, or anywhere in the world using a common language to express political thoughts. Whatever the scope of their interest and actions, social media enables more groups around the world than ever before to think and act together as they shape the outcome of political matters. With social media, any and all politics can become local politics, the politics of one person having personal influence over another.

We have seen now how social media is permeating our markets, our work lives, and our politics. Truly, it is a phenomenon that is shaping the very nature of our world's societies. We are only at the very beginning of the growth of Content Nation, yet even so the outlines of a new kind of society are taking shape among its citizens.

7

The New Society:
Content Nation Redefines How People Live Their Lives

The rise of social media is more than just a "new, new thing," more than just a fashionable way to buy or sell things or to get a job done or to elect someone to office. Social media is in fact the beginning of a new way of living for the people who make regular use of its capabilities. I say "beginning" because it is truly only the very early days of a movement toward citizens as the world's leading publishers. Content Nation may be as large as many of the world's leading nations, but it is an assemblage of people who in many ways are like people on a busy street. We see the people passing by, we know that we're part of a crowd, yet to call that crowd a group with a purpose or even still a movement would be a mistake. Just for the moment there are a lot of people going in the same direction, each for their own reasons, or in different directions, but perhaps with a similar purpose, but then, suddenly, something happens—and there is indeed common purpose. Things align, take form, and then there is an enormous amount of power to compel people all in one place.

The Sharing Society: Content Nation Shares New Spaces for Common Experiences

It is no real surprise that the power of social media to shape human society catches people off guard so often, because the potential for that power has always been around us in the form of personal communications. Like a substance that crystallizes in just the right conditions but remains liquid in most other conditions, people using social media go unnoticed most of the time until they join forces to assume a common form for a common purpose.

Frozen Grand Central: The Predictably Unpredictable Power of Social Media

An interesting example of this concept of crystallizing human power through social media can be seen in the work of Improv Everywhere, a group that organizes live performances in public places, often using people who follow their exploits on their weblog and who are informed of upcoming events via a mailing list. Social media is used to organize their events and in turn is used to communicate the power of their events. One of their recent projects was called Frozen Grand Central, in which 200 volunteers entered the main concourse area of Grand Central Terminal in New York City and at a precise chosen time they froze in place in whatever position they were at the time at whatever place they were in at the time. This assembly of random people frozen in random positions in a common area all of a sudden startled passersby: What did this mean? Why were all of these people stopped in these positions? Was it funny? Was it serious? Was it dangerous? The police began to investigate. Then, exactly five minutes after they had begun, the figures "unfroze" and went their individual ways as if nothing unusual had happened. Video recorders captured the scene from many angles and the group posted the edited results on the Web, turning what would have been otherwise just a moment in time into a moment that could compel people for a long time.

So it is with social media. We are seeing the potential for its power to influence how people behave as a society in glimpses, small projects that scale rapidly to take on huge significance and huge numbers of small projects that may stay small individually but add up to major changes. There is not a major motion picture in the world that is filmed, edited, and distributed with the notion that a few of the producer's friends might see it and eventually make it popular with millions of people. With social media, that is exactly what happens time and again, day in and day out. A few people align themselves on a whim, an idea takes hold, and before you know it people around the world are experiencing something new. Individually, we can dismiss these events of influential publishing, much as we can dismiss soon enough random figures frozen in place for a few minutes at a train terminal, but over time, the regular occurrence of these events changes society as we know it. The rhythm of life changes. Our flesh, our clothes, our food, and most other things in our lives may be all quite the same for an indefinite period of time, but our toes and our fingers are tapping out a new beat. Eventually it becomes everyone's beat in their own unique way, until it is part of everyday society by default. Eventually the notion of everyone *not* freezing randomly for five minutes every now and then becomes intriguing and, perhaps, even quaint.

A Horseless Carriage?: Trying to Imagine a Society Built around Social Media

If social media's emerging impact on society is so significant, then why is it that so many people have a hard time accepting its importance? The answer to this question can be found in part by acknowledging that, as popular as social media has become, it's still a phenomenon that is in many ways packaged into the technology and mindset of previous generations of human communications, including early Web communications. Although the Web was conceived from its inception as a vehicle for peer-to-peer communications, it took a long time for the Web technology to get to the point where it began to support social media functions on a massive scale, efficiently. Even today the relentless drive to adapt social media to the existing marketing strategies of many of today's established companies obscures much of the real value available through social media that has little to do with today's marketing concepts.

It may help to understand how the full potential for social media's impact is misperceived by some people if we look at the early history of another innovation that transformed society: the automobile. When, in 1885, Karl Benz invented and then manufactured the first practical self-propelled vehicle for personal transportation, it looked more like a light horse carriage of the era than anything like today's automobiles.

Widely known as "horseless carriages," these new inventions looked much like their horse-driven predecessors for many years, even though they functioned quite differently. They still ran on the same roads as horse-drawn carriages, which dominated traffic and required automobiles sometimes to follow traffic laws ridiculously stringent by today's standards (a still-enforceable law in Redlands, California: "Motor vehicles may not drive on city streets unless a man with a lantern is walking ahead of it.").

Eventually, the personal and commercial advantages of the automobile became popular enough that roads, laws, and manufacturing technology adapted to their importance to the point that the thought of an automobile being a carriage without a horse seemed antiquated and inappropriate. Improvements in technology and new features that made sense only on automobiles eventually made automobiles look altogether different from the original self-propelled vehicles, even if they served much the same function. Their functionality also significantly changed how we behaved; in some places, driving a block or so to a store to pick up a bag of snack food is considered a normal way to go shopping. Not all changes created by new technologies are equally beneficial, of course.

Today we are just beginning to emerge from the "horseless carriage" phase of social media. The very fact that we use the phrase "social media" is indicative of the fact that in many ways people expect social media to act the way that traditional media does, only in a more personal way. At the same time we expect social behavior to be pretty much the same as any other situation when we use social media, only in a more media-oriented way. We try to apply regulations and social standards to social media that make sense to our current culture, but that may make little sense to people far less than a generation from now. Currently the U.S. Congress is investigating the implications of putting official materials on Web video services, such as YouTube. Even today, many media companies are deeply concerned about the implications of doing likewise with their television programming. Are these the "lamps in front of the horseless carriages" of today that will seem silly and senseless all too soon?

A Nation of Publishers Is Also a Nation of Inventors

As seen in the parallel themes in the rise of the automobile, social media is not just one particular kind of technology for one particular kind of purpose. Social networking, instant messaging, weblogs, wikis, social bookmarking, remixes and mashups of other people's content—all these and many more represent an explosion of communications technologies in the hands of individuals who are using them creatively. The Museum of Modern Betas, a Web site that catalogs promising new Web publishing products in pre-production beta testing, has listed more than 5,600 beta publishing products introduced on the Web since April 2004, most of them related to social media collection and publishing. Often, several new social media product betas will appear in a single day, and those are just the publishing products and services developed by programmers to facilitate social media. The people who use those products often have the ability to create their own unique programs or services using those publishing tools. Factor in the development of social media tools for other cultures around the world not covered by the Museum of Modern Betas, and the global innovation coming from social media tools is a breathtaking phenomenon.

Out of thousands of social media publishing tools that have come into existence in just a few years, many of them have spawned thousands of their own tools in turn and millions of customized publications using those tools. This is more than mass customization; this is mass invention on a scale that human communications has never experienced before. Content Nation is not only a society that is a nation of publishers, but as well a nation of pioneering inventors who no longer rely on a handful of sources for creativity and innovation. If Tim Berners-Lee was the Karl Benz of social media and publishers like Facebook and Digg are the next-generation Toyota and General Motors of social media, then there are still countless creative independent toolmakers and tool users out there creating social media independently in ways that will challenge our ideas about how its power can shape society for years to come.

A Society of Third Places: When the Coffee House Becomes Your Life

Interestingly, the roots of social media's impact seem to go back to those coffee houses and taverns in which Thomas Paine's pamphlet *Common Sense* was discussed. You may recall that, although the pamphlet was powerful in its own right, it was the awareness and the discussion of the pamphlet in meeting places that rapidly accelerated opinion about Paine's ideas through the American colonies. There was something about ideas in a gathering place away from work and home that opened people up to influential ideas and the willingness to endorse them in front of other people.

In his 1999 book *The Great Good Place* author Ray Oldenburg noted that gathering places like coffee houses and cafes that encouraged people to take in the scene and to chat with old and new friends were key to the health of a society and its public institutions. The concept of a "third place" was packaged and marketed by the Starbucks chain of coffee shops quite successfully. Starbucks recognized that in a mobile society people are in search of a "third place" with which they're comfortable in a wide variety of places around the world. A perfectly good local cafe may be right next door to a Starbucks in many places, and yet Starbucks has become the brand to which many people gravitate in a place that's new to them, in part because they feel comfortable there, socially. Yet Starbucks is not a brand that people can call their own; it is a corporate brand in which they participate only by purchasing items at its shops. The employees, the furniture, and the food are all chosen and managed elsewhere by the Starbucks corporate staff. This can affect the quality of the experience at these locations significantly. Recently, Starbucks had to re-train workers in more than 7,100 of their stores in the art of making a good cup of coffee.

By contrast, in a truly local cafe, such as the historical Cafe du Monde in New Orleans, Louisiana, known for its great coffee and pastries, the owner is likely to be present almost always, the employees may be friends or relatives of the owner and may know many local patrons very well, yet people from far and wide may be attracted to its unique flavor and appeal. This does not make a local cafe altogether better than a Starbucks. If people are in Beijing and need a bit of the flavor of home in a distant country, or need the experience of a foreign country near home, a Starbucks may serve an important purpose. By the same token, if the owners of a local cafe don't keep up the quality of their establishment, loyalty to their business will last only so long before people choose another one. Being local and being global each have their own advantages, and in any particular situation, a person may choose one over the other for any number of reasons.

This example illustrates that engineering a social experience is a matter of both what makes people feel comfortable enough to walk through the doorway of an establishment and what makes them feel comfortable enough to stay there a while and, perhaps, to keep coming regularly. In social media, we see the same phenomenon being played out on a massive scale via the Web and in ways that mix the feel of a local experience with the feel of a worldwide experience. The "cafes" of social media form themselves into whatever shape makes people comfortable, which helps them to attract the community of people who will sustain its value on an ongoing basis. Like a coffee house, it takes work to make a social media service a success; rarely does it succeed just by having the right technology in the right place at the right time.

Unlike a Starbucks or a Cafe du Monde, however, social media offers many different kinds of "third places" in which people can congregate. Thinking of the example of the thousands of different social media services that have been tracked by the Museum of Modern Betas, and of the millions of people who have used those tools to make pages on a social media site more powerful experiences, you might say that social media has enabled thousands of different *types* of Starbucks and local cafes to span the world and millions of different ways to build and decorate them. The number of possible combinations of social media publishing tools, communities of people attracted to them, and variations on their use is unthinkably enormous.

Moreover, people using social media can be "present" at these "third places" in any physical place at any time. Often, people can be found using *several* social media services at the same time. On any typical day I may find myself bookmarking content on Digg, checking out friends on Facebook, sending or watching messages appear on Twitter, participating in a video phone call on Skype with someone halfway around the world, writing or commenting on a weblog and, oh yes, checking my email. I may be somewhat extreme in this regard because of my interests in social media, but looking at younger generations of people using social media, it's safe to say that social media's "third places" are becoming primary places through which more and more people around the world experience life.

As a result, local personal influence becomes global personal influence through any number of channels simultaneously, and global influence impacts local influence as well in the same time frame. People we encounter in our social media "coffee houses" are becoming our families, our work mates, and our villages, even as our villages, our work mates, and our families are becoming a part of a global coffee house through social media.

CONTENT NATION SOCIAL RULE #1: *In social media, any place could be the right place to find a third place in which to create meaningful social exchanges.*

The Global Cafe: Qik Invites Anyone and Everyone to the Scene

Qik is a relatively new service that enables people who use the video-recording features of their mobile phones to post videos on the Web as they're being recorded. Qik provides features that enable people made aware of these live events via text messages to look at and hear what's happening elsewhere via these live videos and to send live text messages to people watching the live video session. When a text-messaging service such as Twitter is used to broadcast links to these sessions, hundreds of people could be "stopping by" to join a scene anywhere in a world—a conference, a coffee house, a pub, a jazz club, someone's home, a disaster scene, or, in one recent broadcast from Congressman John Culberson, the halls of Congress. Once these recordings and messages are complete, they remain on the Qik Web site for others to experience and share later on.

Qik video and discussion services are an illustration of how easy it is not only to be socially engaged with others around the world on a moment's notice through social media, but also how easy it is to experience it together with people who are a part of a live scene and with people who are experiencing it virtually via the Web. With social media, the lines between "being there" and "hearing about it" begin to blur to the point that one wonders, What was the real nature of the experience? Was the experience the things that were seen in the video shared with others or was it the interaction of the people there and on the Web with one another? For the people who experienced it later, did they have to "be there" when it happened to "be there"? Social media is begging us to consider these questions, but even more, asking us to consider that, regardless of our personal answer, the changing behavior of people will form their own answers regardless.

CONTENT NATION SOCIAL RULE #2: *Anyone, anywhere, at any time can make any social experience a social media experience.*

Facebook: A Public Space That's Strictly Personal

You've heard about the club from your friends. It's the hottest place in town, so much more interesting than that place where you hung out when you were younger. It's where everything that people talk about is happening. You check it out with other people, perhaps someone a bit more conservative; they're going there, too. You get an address. You go down an alley and there, lit dimly by a menacing light, is a plain doorway. You're told that it's public, that you can go in, that anyone who goes in there is a member of the club, but first you have to go through that door and trust that everything on the other side of it will be as you hope it will be, that your friends will be there and that you'll have a good time. Finally, you approach the door…and it opens. Just like any other door.

So it is for many people who approach the simple entryway to Facebook, one of the most popular social networking Web sites in the world. Facebook offers a bare-bones home page, with only a place for current members to log in and prospective members to register. How can this almost anti-social entryway into Facebook be such a popular destination? By contrast the MySpace social networking portal is filled with promotions for famous musical groups, ads, lists of most popular songs, blogs and videos, search boxes—all of the things that someone would expect to find on any media Web site. There you have the major difference between MySpace and Facebook. Both offer social networking, both offer the ability to become fans of people or members of a group, but where one is like hanging out with your friends at the music store at the mall, the other is a place where real social things happen with real people.

This is not to say that MySpace is a commercial failure. Even though Facebook traffic is up roughly 50 percent since a year ago in 2007 while MySpace's growth has stalled, there is still roughly double the people who visit MySpace. Where MySpace seems to be driven largely by very young members—many not even in their teens—and as well by people with real or assumed identities promoting products and services through aggressive ads and promotions, Facebook has always concentrated on trying to build trustworthy relationships between real people displaying their real identities. Facebook members are invited to call upon their real-world network of friends and enables people to keep their networks and profile on Facebook as limited or as exposed as they would like.

Facebook is a powerful media property in its own right, but it has avoided assuming that the world of traditional media is a good place from which to build the assumptions that power social media. Instead, it focuses on the power of communicating with peers, learning about what they're doing, what they're endorsing, what they're joining, who they've met, and who on Facebook might be worth having as a friend. All of this builds into a rich network of content that people share through Facebook. Commercial entities are an important part of Facebook's membership, but Facebook members build relationships with those entities the same way that they would anyone else. Trust has to be earned. Endorsements of others are weighed. If it looks too tacky or self-promoting, a company is not likely to succeed with promotions on Facebook. Fun is a big part of being on Facebook, but it has to be a genuine kind of fun to get most people's attention. There has to be something that draws people together in truly common bonds.

In Facebook, people share their vacation photos, fun games, videos, personal triumphs and insights, and what they're trying to do professionally, often. All of your life is on Facebook, not just a fantasy image of what you want people to think is your life or just your business life. Facebook is a place where people learn how to express themselves in public with friends in a way that is at once both very personal and very public. Except for some occasional ads that are clearly marked as separate from personal communications, Facebook is social media without the assumptions of traditional media, without someone trying to push their message more loudly than other people's messages or with tricky slogans repeated again and again or ads that splash over what you're trying to read.

There are some who pay lip service to the concept that markets are conversations and who then turn around and enable splashy ads and promotions over their social media service that enable traditional marketers to shout at audiences instead of having a conversation with peers. They are like prostitutes who will go to social spots and try to seduce people into using their services, pretending that they really like someone, but everyone knows that they're in it for the money. They make money well enough, but they miss out on the real relationships that are the real gold in life, the relationships on which all good personal transactions are built.

Facebook challenges marketers to learn what real conversations among friends and peers sound like. It also challenges everyday people to realize how valuable they are to one another, and to build upon the value of their conversations in a largely public venue to enhance their lives and to influence other people's lives in a genuine way. Being yourself in a public place with others who are just trying to be real human beings sharing real lives is a lot better social experience than hanging out at the music store with some bored friends down at the mall. Furthermore, you can do it at anytime, anywhere, with any number of people in the world.

This isn't just a game-changing experience; it's an indication of just how fundamental a change social media is from traditional media and how much more complex and richer it can be compared to traditional social venues. Facebook challenges us to be ourselves in public places with people who know us and to enjoy it. It's a simple enough human concept, but one that many modern societies have left behind as they've ceded power over public venues to governments and traditional media and entertainment companies, and forced both our personal and our public lives into ever-smaller social spaces. In social networking communities like Facebook we learn to remember that the public is made up of real people, people from anywhere and everywhere, people who can be, by and large, our trusted friends. Companies and products can be a part of this conversation, but first they must gain our trust.

CONTENT NATION SOCIAL RULE #3: *Social media challenges us to treat our trusted relationships with people and institutions from around the world as the basis for a rewarding way of life that's both public and personal.*

Muxlim: Using Social Media to Create Social Identity Out of Cultural Identity

Europe has more than 12 million followers of Islam in its midst, but many of these people live in isolated communities, with little cohesiveness as a presence across Europe or within the nations in which they live. It should come as no surprise, then, that one of the fastest-growing Web sites in Europe is Muxlim, a social media Web site started by Scandinavian Muslims that is said to have attracted more than a million registrants since its 2006 launch from 190 countries around the world. Muxlim has weblogs, member-uploaded videos, forums, polls, interest groups, photo sharing, and member-profile pages that facilitate online social networking. Most of the members of Muxlim post content that focuses on personal and religious topics, with just a thin vein of political insights and opinions on the site. Notably many of Muxlim's members are Muslim women, who seem to find in its pages an opportunity to express themselves in ways that they cannot do easily through more secularly oriented Web services or in their native cultures.

In all of this, Muxlim creates a breadth of content not too different from any other social media Web site, but shaped uniquely by a community that has an intense focus on both its faith and on expressing itself passionately on topics of interest around the world. Sometimes cultural borders are hard to work out with political borders. For the group "Political Muslims" the location of the group is listed as "birmingham prefer-not-to-say," an indication of concern over government scrutiny. This self-censorship may limit political expression, but it needs to be taken in the context of what is happening in the wider world of Muslim social media. At the time of this writing, the predominantly Muslim nation of Iran's parliament is considering legislation that would provide the death penalty for anyone in that nation who is found to be blogging, making the relatively modest efforts at self-expression on Muxlim all the more important. Cultures of many nations as well as the culture of Islam must find common ground in this publishing service.

A new generation of Muslims in Europe and elsewhere are breaking through their isolation to define a cross-border community with people of similar faith and faith-driven culture, shaping through their public expression and discussions a common understanding of one another apart from the institutions of family and national culture. For people who have lived in a world where Western culture was never their own culture, social media offers an opportunity to forge a new sense of constructive collaboration guided by their fellow believers. Perhaps from the pages of Muxlim will come a new sense of Muslim culture, a Content Nation devised from that global understanding of themselves and their worlds.

CONTENT NATION SOCIAL RULE #4: *Social Media can enable existing cultures to define a new sense of their own society through new channels for local and global public expression.*

Bringing Your Community to Your Content, Bringing Your Content to Your Community

Many social media publishing services use technology that can allow anyone to assemble content from many sources into one unified display on a computer screen. This ability to embed content from many sources into a Web page enables anyone's Web publication to become a social media experience or to expand the depth of the content in their existing social media pages. Shelfari is an example of a service that can enable people to embed content about their favorite books in social media sites. In doing so, the Shelfari service can connect its users with people who have similar interests in books. Shelfari members can build a virtual "bookshelf" of books that interest them, rate them, review them, and learn about what other people think about them. If I embed a Shelfari content tool in my Facebook page, for example, I learn instantly who else on Facebook is interested in the books that I read—and what they say about them. In a matter of moments I can go from having no one else to talk with about a book to having a whole world of people connected to me by our common interest in a book.

Embedding content from a social media service into a weblog can enable communities to develop in these social media services also. MyBlogLog is a service that enables people to embed on pages in their Web site a listing of people who are members of the MyBlogLog social network that have visited their Web site. MyBlogLog is used by bloggers frequently to enable people to see who else is interested in their content who may not have left other signs of interest such as comments on their weblog or bookmarks to their weblog on other Web sites. Clicking the links to a MyBlogLog member's photo and name in an embedded MyBlogLog listing will bring you to their profile page in MyBlogLog, where a MyBlogLog member can display their own content via feeds from their various social media services. As people visit the MyBlogLog pages of people appearing in the weblog-embedded member listings, they can then follow links to those members' own social media sites, where they will encounter more listings of MyBlogLog members who have visited those sites recently. It's a gathering that moves on and on, like moving from one discussion at a social gathering to another, recombining with new and familiar people again and again. With MyBlogLog, any page on the Web could be a place where one encounters people whom they know and encounter people whom they may not know with similar interests in a given topic.

The interchange of social media worlds can go in seeming circles at times. Lively, a virtual reality service under development by Google, enables people to move a virtual-person avatar through three-dimensional virtual rooms where they can encounter and have text chats and "physical" interactions with other people's virtual figures. You will also be able to embed content in a Lively room, such as videos from YouTube or photos from a photo-sharing service, and comment on them with other people in the virtual room. In turn, a Lively virtual room can be embedded in a Web page, enabling people to experience both a virtual world with content embedded in it and a Web page's content with a virtual world embedded in it, all at the same time.

If this seems to be a little confusing, well, it can get that way sometimes when virtual worlds are embedded in other virtual experiences.

In all of these instances there is a key common element: people like content that includes contact with influential people who they they'd like to get to know better as a part of the experience of "being there" at a Web page. Whether we bring our content into our social media community or whether we bring our social media community into our content, we are seeing the presence of social networks in everyday content as key elements of its value. The content becomes a launching point for expanding our relationships with people as much as the relationships in our social media communities become a launching point for expanding our insight into content. Social media challenges us to recognize that the power of personal relationships is needed more than ever to make a public media experience valuable to people.

CONTENT NATION SOCIAL RULE #5: *Social media enables the power of personal relationships to transform any public experience into a personal experience.*

FriendFeed: Creating an Inner Circle of Friends

Sometimes there's the party within the party within the party—a certain group of people on whom you focus most intently, no matter where they may be. When those people are posting content to dozens of potential social media outlets, trying to keep up with them can be truly exhausting. We can't all be social butterflies, after all.

FriendFeed is one of a number of social media services that enable people to consolidate updates that they post in their social media services all in one place. Instead of having to go to several services to keep up with a special group of people, you can concentrate on them on FriendFeed and have a quieter, more private environment in which to offer short comments. In a sense, FriendFeed turns everyone's social media publishing into a consolidated weblog of all of your favorite people and publications, including social networking, social bookmarking, weblogs, photos, videos, music, and other key sources. You can refine this process even further by creating a private "room" on FriendFeed to which you can invite an even more select group of people to discuss a particular topic or piece of content. Social media is learning through tools such as FriendFeed to enable people to have multiple levels of social engagement that parallel what people expect from their real-life relationships.

CONTENT NATION SOCIAL RULE #6: *Social media enables relationships to unfold on multiple levels in multiple venues, each appropriate to a specific group and purpose.*

The Organizing Society: Content Nation Aligns People to Achieve Goals

Though getting to know people through publishing is a good goal unto itself in social media, eventually there comes a time when we actually want to accomplish something with these publishing tools. We need to solve a problem. We need to get timely information. We need to figure out what's really important. Traditional publishing tools can help to address these needs, but the challenge is not always met easily by their capabilities. In traditional publishing, we rely upon the insight and skills of a specific group of authors and editors producing a publication to come up with quality information that will help us to achieve our goals. Social media challenges this method of relying on a specific organization to come up with answers by calling upon people to contribute and organize their own answers through publishing. Who knows who has the right answers? The answer to that question can be surprising when social media tools are applied.

What's the Right Hotel? Twitter Offers the Answer Out of Thin Air

When Scott Monty, a Web marketing specialist, visited New York City recently, he was in a bit of a bind. He realized that his travel plans would require an unexpected overnight stay in a hotel, but rooms at less-than-astronomical rates in a convenient spot were not to be found. Scott turned to his Twitter network of friends by typing a text message into his phone that was forwarded to the hundreds of people who followed his messages on their computers and mobile phones. Almost instantly he got replies flowing in with suggestions from his contacts, including a Twitter message from a business friend who had his travel coordinator get in touch with him through Twitter. The travel coordinator contacted a specialist in hotel reservations and, a few minutes later, Scott Monty received a Twitter message with a reservation at a hotel that fit his needs quite well.

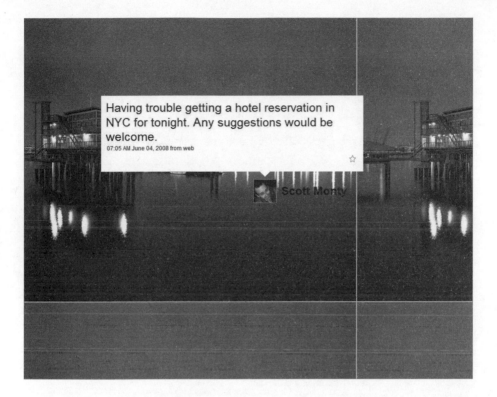

Could Scott Monty have reached his goal some other way? Sure—if he had been willing to wait for people to pay attention to emails or for phone calls to be returned. By thinking of himself as a person with a publishing audience through Twitter, Scott Monty was able to tap into hundreds of people who follow Twitter on a moment-by-moment basis to keep up with short messages from their contacts. Twitter was just the right medium to focus his personal network on his problem, which they were only too eager to do. Why? Because they were eager to share their knowledge as part of their social publishing relationship with Scott Monty. The rewards of helping were both personal and public: Scott Monty reached his goal by publishing his needs instantly to a community of people willing to focus on him through their publishing; his friends in turn shared their ideas both with him and with others on Twitter, creating an instant brainstorm of ideas that could be used both immediately and later on by people searching through Twitter messages. One person's need became an instant publishing event with a solution that is now part of the knowledge available through Twitter.

CONTENT NATION SOCIAL MEDIA RULE #7: *Social media can turn immediate problems into worldwide searches for answers by people aligned through influential publishing.*

NowPublic Aligns Citizens to Report on the World

Many social media Web sites collect links to pages on the Web contributed by members but NowPublic has been a pioneer in building a community of people dedicated to making and sharing real news in communities around the world. With members in 5,500 cities in more than 140 countries, NowPublic enables people to write their own news articles on events and have other members contribute additional content such as photos, videos, and links to their own stories and comments. Members can vote up stories in popularity for more visibility on their Web sites, but collaboration on collecting news matters on NowPublic as much as competition for attention.

The importance of collaboration in news-gathering was especially important for NowPublic members in 2005 when they organized to facilitate news and information flowing into and out of New Orleans, Louisiana in the wake of massive damage to the city by Hurricane Katrina. With local news-gathering organizations crippled, social media from NowPublic and other organizations was a key link in helping people to understand local conditions and to locate missing relatives. More recently a major electrical failure in Vancouver, British Columbia demonstrated how the growing and maturing NowPublic community can deploy itself rapidly to cover a major local event. One central news article became the point of collaboration for dozens of photos, quotes, and links to supplementary stories filed by NowPublic members, as well as comments from people offering information on the impact of the outage in their area. Traditional news organizations have performed these functions for centuries, of course, but with NowPublic, the public itself can establish its own unfiltered coverage of events, prioritize events according to the interests of a community instead of an editorial board, and reach a new kind of goal for journalism enabling a community to tell its own story and to strengthen the community by becoming its own publishers.

CONTENT NATION SOCIAL RULE #8: *When a community publishes together it aligns itself toward the goals that are most important to the community.*

Organizing Sensitive Technology Manufacturing through Social Media Collaboration

Many organizations are experimenting with social media as a means to improve workplace productivity, spurred on by the gains from companies that learn to implement social media practices effectively. One company that is serving as a role model for many others is Lockheed Martin, a major aircraft-manufacturing company with many contracts to develop advanced airplanes for the U.S. military. With layers of control to manage sensitive and complex government projects, Lockheed Martin might not appear to be the most logical candidate for social media, but in part because of the habits of working in an organization that had a lot of segmentation in its work roles, it was necessary for Lockheed Martin to come up with a better way for people to work together. Existing tools for collaboration—email, a file-sharing site, scattered social media projects—were not resulting in teams fostering strong collaboration on key design and production issues.

The solution that Lockheed Martin implemented was Unity, a customized publishing platform that integrated information from across the enterprise using social media publishing tools. Using the popular Microsoft SharePoint Server enterprise collaboration platform integrated with social media software from NewsGator and other social media tools, Unity brought together all of the shared information resources across a given team and made it easy for people to monitor people's contributions to Unity across the organization, keeping issues such as government security clearances in mind. The result looks somewhat similar to a system developed by NewsGator for another client.

Unity takes many of the key concepts found in social media services on the Web and applies them to the people who work with one another in aeronautics design and manufacturing. People using Unity can follow colleagues' contributions to Unity as they would their friends on Facebook: bookmark Web page links for others to view, add keyword tags to content that can be tracked by other team members to be alerted to new kinds of content, encourage internal weblogs, wikis, Web conferencing, and other social media tools integrated into Unity to minimize the use of person-to-person emails and to maximize the amount of publishing available to their teams. Instead of information staying tucked away in email folders and people being unaware of what others were doing, Unity fostered an internal culture that saw collaborating through social media as the default behavior for getting work done in an enormously complex development and operations environment. The results from Unity are good enough that Lockheed Martin's efforts with Unity are the source of great interest from their clients, improving and deepening their relationships and helping Lockheed Martin to be seen as a thought leader in developing efficient workplace environments through social media.

Though many enterprises are beginning to explore social media very seriously to improve their own operations, it makes some institutions uncomfortable. Work for many organizations is still about strict hierarchical distribution of information, hidden networks of knowledge to protect a person's job security and secrecy used to accrue power over other people in an organization. Though these types of behaviors that inhibit collaboration at work are likely to be a part of society for many years, it is interesting that fostering an environment in which employees think of themselves as publishers collaborating with colleagues as a default behavior is becoming so critical to the success of so many organizations with extremely complex and critical tasks to complete.

CONTENT NATION SOCIAL RULE #9: *When everyone sees themselves as publishers, everyone is empowered through common knowledge to work flexibly and rapidly toward common goals.*

The Giving Society: Content Nation Builds New Value from Altruism

One of the aspects that is both most powerful and, for some people, most troubling about social media is that so much of it appears to be "given away." To someone first encountering social media, it seems as if it's all about giving away something and expecting nothing in return. People think often that this "something for nothing" type of transaction is known as altruism.

We'll examine the full influence and impact of altruism expressed through social media later in this book, but for now it's important to recognize that altruism is not really a "something for nothing" transaction. Altruism is really about people who give something to a community that has something more to offer them than just money, goods, or services as a reward for their immediate actions. Altruism is a human trait that helps people to recognize that people benefit from a society that can offer them rewards on many levels.

The rewards that come to people from altruism are not always about philanthropy or the general betterment of mankind. In thinking of some of our earlier examples from the world of business, the altruism of social media can have many very concrete benefits for the people giving and receiving content. Altruism is about more-complex transactions between individuals, organizations, and society as a whole. The elements of altruism that are at the core of much of social media, then, are really at the heart of a much more complex economy based on more complex social relationships than those usually experienced in the world of commerce. We may not always see money changing hands in social media, but through the concept of altruism there is definitely value passing from one party in a social media transaction to another, value that is changing how people define their lives and their society.

The "Give to Get" Equation: The Value of Providing Content to Get Something Back

Why should an individual provide content to someone else for free, especially information that reveals to the public who they are? It's a question that's still a mystery to many used to traditional publishing models, but one that millions of people answer every day. The answer is simple: people learn to understand the value of doing so.

When the social media search service Delver was launched recently, the home page of the Web site asked the question that was on the minds of people visiting the site: "Why should I sign up to Delver?" The answer to that question was in plain language: "Your [social] network will be kept permanently, you will be able to access your network from any computer and your friends will also benefit, you'll see." This is a "give to get" transaction as much as when someone buys a magazine or a movie ticket, but the transaction is based on contributing something other than money to gain access to the "get." The "get" is the promise of both personal and social benefits for contributing some information to the service. Yet the promised benefits are vague: the person signing up for Delver is asked to trust that the service will deliver on its promises, based on the assurances of…someone.

Millions of people wanting to use social media services confront similar types of messages and promises when they sign up for a social media service. People really don't know what the benefits will be. In the instance of Delver, a person gets the ability to search for and find social media content on the Web and to learn about how they are related to the people who produce it. Instead of just searching information, you're searching through current and potential social contacts who not only may have the answers that you're looking for, but also may be able to help you personally through establishing personal and social media links. By making yourself a little bit vulnerable you get the potential of enormous insight and enjoyment from others who can enrich your world both through the social bonds that are created and through other opportunities for career advancement or commerce through personal relationships.

CONTENT NATION SOCIAL RULE #10: *Social media requires us to become a little vulnerable personally to make the connections necessary to get broader personal benefits from publishing.*

The 2004 Tsunami: Altruism Invents a Social Structure to Respond to a Disaster

When the second-largest recorded earthquake in history, off the coast of Indonesia, triggered widespread tsunamis in December 2004, more than 240,000 people in south Asia died from the enormous waves and their aftermath, with millions more having lost their homes and their livelihoods. It was an event of global proportions that overwhelmed the governments of the nations impacted by the tragedy as well as world relief organizations. Because of the suddenness of this widespread disaster, just getting basic information on the scope and scale of its impact was difficult.

Social media played a critical role on many levels in the aftermath of the tsunami. People equipped with video cameras uploaded the scenes of destruction and made a worldwide audience aware of the impact of the news almost immediately. Many social media outlets, such as the pioneering ICQ instant messaging service, set up special bulletin boards for people to share needs and information. Members of Wikipedia set up a new page on its site to cover the event, with people collaborating from around the world to piece together events as they were unfolding. Dozens of weblogs relayed what was happening at the scenes of devastation, helping governments and relief organizations to see where help was needed before they could even deploy their own assessment teams.

The relief efforts from this massive tragedy also benefited from media outlets that incorporated purely social goals into their otherwise commercial goals. Links to relief-organization Web sites were promoted online on many commercial and non-commercial Web sites donating space for ads promoting relief efforts, enabling them to obtain massive amounts of aid money rapidly and then to funnel relief efficiently to where it was needed the most. Many of these Web sites also opened up their own message boards to help coordinate relief efforts and provided consolidated listings of relief resources.

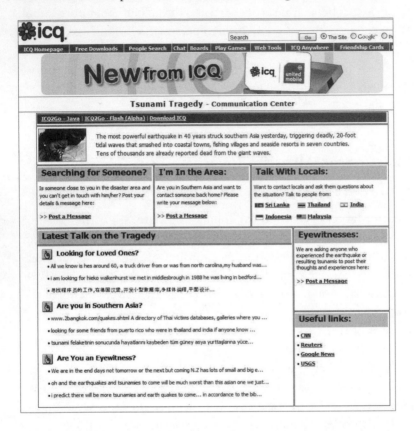

The greatest tragedy in this event is that although individuals in the area were receiving alerts via email and other message services on the earthquake that triggered the tsunamis hours before the tsunami waves struck the affected areas, apparently many government officials failed to translate these early warnings of impending disaster into actions that could save lives. Many governments did not have the organizational structure or the infrastructure in place to communicate the danger to settlements in harm's way, even though information was available. Yet in spite of social media being a very new phenomenon in 2004, it was able to provide massive amounts of information, coordination, and publicity and to contribute enormously to the relief efforts in its aftermath. Very few if any of these efforts were done for personal profit, yet the world as a whole profited enormously from the sum of these individual efforts.

With an event that was unprecedented in modern human history, humans collaborating with one another independently created their own solution to a humanitarian crisis. The hierarchies of government and traditional media work well when there are relatively fixed patterns of problems to solve, but faced with a unique crisis, social media enabled people to organize themselves on both a local and a global scale to respond to a novel problem rapidly and relatively effectively. There appears to be a problem-solving aspect to altruism that challenges many of the ways in which humans have organized themselves in modern societies.

CONTENT NATION SOCIAL RULE #11: *The natural communication abilities of people can combine with the natural problem-solving abilities of people through social media to provide society with benefits of almost any scale imaginable.*

I'm Talkathon: Why Some Marketers Have Such a Hard Time Doing Altruism

The folks at Microsoft, having done some research on the impact of altruism on the marketing value of a company's brand, decided recently to do a nice thing; they decided that for a limited time they would donate to charity a portion of the ad revenue every time someone used their Windows Live Messenger instant messaging product or their Windows Live Hotmail webmail service. The basic concept: the more messages you send, the more Microsoft would give to charities. Microsoft called this product promotion the I'm Talkathon, an effort that seemed to be hitting all of the right buttons. Microsoft was honest about what it was trying to accomplish ultimately (promote its products and services); all you really had to do was to register at the event Web site to have your messages count toward the charitable goal. So far, so good—people like to do the right thing, and a fund-raiser was a concept more likely to generate use of the products than any sort of small rebate or other direct financial incentive would.

Then came Parker.

Parker appeared as the author of a weblog associated with the I'm Talkathon campaign, saying in a note on the home page of the weblog, "I'm just a guy with a computer and good intentions. A couple of months ago, I found out about the i'm Initiative…I hope you join me. Thanks for checking out the Talkathon!" Parker's blog entries had links to his pages on major social media outlets, the ability to post comments, embedded videos—all the things that one would expect from an enthusiast's weblog.

There was just one problem. Parker was fake, an actor hired to play the role of a blogger along with "friends" who would appear in videos. A disclaimer at the very bottom of the weblog notes:

> "If you're reading this, your BS detector is chirping like a smoke detector with a dicey 9-volt. As you've probably guessed, this blog is fictional, but the causes, and the i'm Initiative most certainly are not. The purpose of this blog is to raise awareness of the i'm Initiative and the worthy causes it helps. If we rubbed you the wrong way in the process, that wasn't our intention, so "sorry, our bad." The alternate was something called an 'e-mail blast.' But, believe us that's not nearly as exciting as it sounds."

Funny in their own way, perhaps, but words that came no doubt from McCann Worldgroup, an advertising agency hired to develop and to promote the fund-raiser. The weblog was received for what it was, a promotion that was entertaining, but not real, but the weblog received few comments and its YouTube videos were viewed by a handful of people. The link to Facebook was to a page where graphics were posted; no person, real or otherwise, was there to respond.

Promoting charities is a good idea for marketers, but if your aim is to position your company's brands in the marketplace as being more sincere and in touch with your customers, why would you use a pretend spokesperson instead of a real person? If altruism in social media is about allowing yourself to become vulnerable enough to offer something to a community who will give back to you social rewards, why would you be afraid to put someone out in front of the public as a spokesperson who was real? Why use a medium that's all about genuine conversations to promote a cause based on genuine conversations by using social media to provide fake conversations? Most importantly, why go out of your way to pretend to be linked in to other social media networks and then allow people to see that these were fake presences?

People accept that companies are trying to use social media for their own marketing, and people accept that actors can be entertaining, even in social media outlets, but it's probably a mistake to try to create something that's supposed to be promoting altruism with an actor pretending to be a person doing something for purely altruistic reasons. It may be an indication of how much some companies struggle to engage a public that has grown cynical from mass marketing in general, but it's also an indication of how hard it is for some people to accept that altruism is truly about getting benefits back from society as a whole where and when society as a whole is able to give them.

CONTENT NATION SOCIAL RULE #12: *It's possible to mix your own commercial goals with social goals through social media, but pretending to be sincere about social goals is not a good way to go about it.*

Pregnancy Blogs: Sharing the Common across the World

Few life-changing experiences are more common than having a baby, yet each pregnancy, or attempt at getting pregnant, has its own story. With the growth of blogging on the Web, many women decide to write their own blog about their experiences. Why blog about something that is going to happen anyway? Why blog about something that happens to so many people? It turns out that pregnancy blogs are quite popular, a resource for those who are pregnant themselves or just wanting to share in another person's experience in a way that fills their lives a little more. Sometimes these bloggers are very witty even while capturing the frustrations of their problems.

The "a little pregnant" weblog is a currently popular example of pregnancy weblogging, written anonymously by "Julie," who says of herself, "I'm 35 years old. I'm married to Paul, who's 48, and we live in a small town in New England. We conceived our son after four rounds of IVF. Along the way we experienced an ectopic pregnancy, a miscarriage, a complicated third pregnancy, and, finally, the birth of our son, Charlie, 10 weeks premature." Julie is pregnant again, so her weblog continues with the adventures of a second pregnancy. Julie's weblog captures the frustrations, terrors, and joys of her situation with graphic honesty for nobody in particular and for no real reason in particular except to share her experience with the world. All of a sudden the world becomes her cheerleaders, sharing hundreds of comments on each of her posts and building a community around a real but anonymous person. Julie gives of herself freely and through her anonymity she can talk about things in a way that might be difficult otherwise. People around the world give back to Julie freely as well, inspired by her honesty, her creativeness, and her wit to share a little bit of themselves with her and with the world.

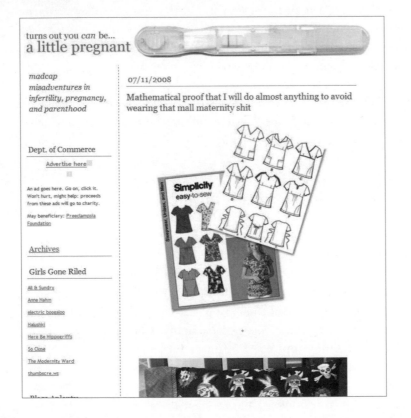

This kind of sharing happens across the world in countless numbers of topical online forums, user groups, and online chat rooms in which people are giving of themselves to share experiences, ideas, and camaraderie that breaks across barriers of time, location, and culture to bring people together in common experiences for the sake of just being human. Weblogs in particular help the most talented and poignant storytellers to rise above the crowd to become heroes or heroines of their followers, still very much life-sized but standing on their own as unique talents and able to bring the world together in their common experiences. Such personal stories used to have to wait for a publisher to discover them, but now people can discover them in social media on their own through recommendations from friends, other social media outlets, or search engines. In a world seeking caring and seeking to offer it, social media enables people more than ever to break the isolation of their lives and to become a part of a community of like-minded people, just for the sake of being human.

CONTENT NATION SOCIAL RULE #13: *Sometimes the gift of just being yourself as you are in the moment is the most valuable thing that you can offer in social media.*

The Educating Society: Content Nation Discovers New Ways to Learn

One of society's key functions is to help people to learn from one another, to teach us about things that will help us to survive and to thrive. Education is a basic human institution, but with the advent of widespread publishing, advanced education began to move beyond a handful of elites to society as a whole. Today's schools and universities are awash in valuable content, but it is social media that increasingly plays a role in educating the world both in formal settings and informal ones. Though social media is not replacing the tradition of instruction from formal textbooks in education, it is changing people from being passive vessels into which knowledge is poured into active creators and distributors of knowledge.

Wikipedia: Let's Educate the World Just for the Fun of It

Few online publications get tongues wagging more quickly in academic circles than Wikipedia, the ongoing project of the Wikimedia Foundation to assemble an authoritative source of reference materials on topics that span far more than a traditional encyclopedia is able to cover. Teachers and university professors discourage students often from using Wikipedia as a reference source because its articles can be edited by anyone who registers for a Wikipedia account. At times companies, governments, and other entities have edited entries on Wikipedia to bias its materials toward their points of view, attempts that are regularly identified by Wikipedians and corrected. These are the typical negatives that can occur in any social media project dedicated to assembling objective and accurate materials that educate people.

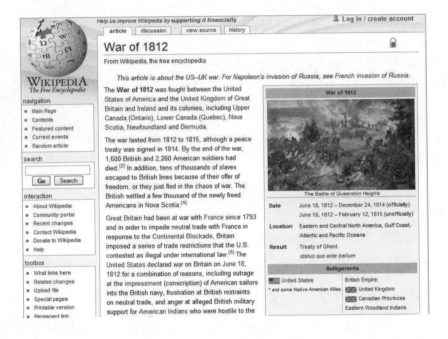

Yet more than 50 million people visit Wikipedia each month for quick facts and links background documents in Wikipedia's millions of articles on everything from the War of 1812 to computational genomics to breaking news that gets folded into its reference materials even as it's occurring. Why do people come to Wikipedia again and again for learning? In large part because people find its information to be very useful, accurate, and up-to-date. A 2005 study by the prestigious scientific journal *Nature* found that scientific articles in Wikipedia were at least as accurate in sum as those found in the long-established *Encyclopedia Britannica*. A later study from the University of Nottingham focused on how experts in a given topic viewed Wikipedia articles versus non-experts. To the surprise of some people, the subject-matter experts rated the Wikipedia articles to be more accurate than those non-experts reading them.

In other words, people know very well how to assemble their own educational materials if given the proper collaborative environment. It doesn't happen without a certain amount of forethought; there are ground rules for Wikipedia authoring and editing, enforced by volunteers who monitor Wikipedia for needed corrections and improvements. Articles aren't written perfectly every time, but Wikipedia has established once and for all time that human learning is a collaborative process that can be empowered by social media to reflect a summary of knowledge available from humankind on a given topic more efficiently and more effectively than any other method. If humans are by nature publishers, we are also by nature teachers who can use social media publishing to donate our knowledge to humankind, knowing that an educated world is our best tool for survival.

CONTENT NATION SOCIAL RULE #14: *People trust the world to teach them about the world.*

Wikis for Kids: Collaborative Education Creates a New Generation of Publishers Who Learn

Even as students reach out to the Web to learn from social media, students are using social media to create their own learning experiences. Social media is powering many education efforts around the world, enabling students to collaborate on studying a subject and reporting their findings. Wiki software similar to that used by Wikipedia is powering many innovative projects in education.

Though many of the initial efforts at using social media in education are focused on teaching writing and technology skills collaboratively, some are beginning to work their way into mainstream education. In New York City, a class studying civil-rights issues has used a Web-based wiki to capture their views of the subject, adding and revising their materials as the class moves on to new views of the subject. The students learn not only about the subject, but get to reshape their thinking again and again as they learn more and more about the topic from the teacher and from one another. In the process of doing so, collaborative publishing is becoming ingrained in them as a new learning and teaching method as surely as earlier students moved from writing on bark to slates to paper and to computers for their personal publishing. With social media, students will learn from their earliest experiences that their publishing is highly scalable, able to reach the world and very focused communities within the world with their insights. As they do so, learning will never be the same.

CONTENT NATION SOCIAL RULE #15: *Social media changes how we learn from the world and how the world learns from us.*

Demystifying Education: Teaching and Learning as Default Behavior

As social media permeates our lives from childhood onward a new picture of human learning is taking shape. Education remains an extremely vital and important element of society, but as society, its technologies, and its economies become ever more complex, it becomes increasingly difficult for people to make informed choices. The education of our youth prepares them to begin life as an adult in society, but by the time young adults enter adulthood to put their education to use, the world has already changed significantly. Books used to capture the distilled sum of human wisdom, which was collected by experts and then distributed to the world. Now, as our problem-solving needs shift from moment to moment, our need for education cannot wait for a book to put everything that we need to know together. Life moves too quickly; we need the world to tell us about the changing world. By the time you have read this book, my blog and countless other blogs like it will have updated the world thousands of times over on the progression of these ideas.

This means that to a large degree we are becoming a society that has a constant need to teach and to learn from everyone through publishing. Social media makes us teachers and learners on a constant basis, sharing both our insights and our need for insight nearly every day of our lives. When I look at a social media service like Yelp, which collects reviews and ratings on restaurants, I see educators and learners as much as I see enthusiasts. People organize their content using taxonomies, much as an educator or scientist would; they respond to questions, they grade one another, working together independently and collaboratively to create both knowledge and learning, and, of course, it's fun, just what your teachers and professors always promised their courses would be. It's fun because people are invested in their teaching and their learning; they want to influence people, they want to expose their value to society, and society, both collectively and individually, rewards them through their own use of publishing. Traditional education will live on indefinitely, but as we become more used to being teachers and learners on a constant basis our perception of society will change into one where we see ourselves being in front of and in a classroom constantly.

CONTENT NATION SOCIAL RULE #16: *In a world where everyone is a teacher and a student through social media the learning never ends.*

The Publishing Society: Content Nation Becomes a New Way of Life

What does it mean when we're always teaching and learning from one another through publishing? What does it mean when the world shares itself with the world on a constant basis? What does it mean when publishing is one of the most important and rewarding things that an everyday person can do in society?

It means that society has changed fundamentally. It means that instead of being a society that uses publications created by a few elite organizations for the world, we are a society in which publishing has become one of the most common and basic human functions with which people can communicate with anyone throughout the world, with or without elite publishing organizations. We challenge the world's nations in our responses to disasters of historical proportions. We learn how to give and to get from one another in ways that industrial titans never dreamed of. We teach one another around the world, even as the world teaches us. We share our humble humanity with the world, and the world embraces us. Content Nation is no longer just a concept, a statistic, or a catchy slogan. Content Nation reflects the current reality of our global publishing society, unified in their way of looking at publishing even as they use it to communicate and to organize themselves both globally and in very focused groups.

A Nation of Publishers: Prometheus at the Arena Rock Show

The nature of this nation of publishers is still hard for us to imagine sometimes, but it can be seen perhaps more clearly in a relatively new phenomenon being seen at concert performances: the mobile-phone encore. With smoking cigarettes banned in may public locations the tradition of lighting a match or flicking on a butane lighter to encourage an artist to perform an encore has given way to people holding up their mobile phones instead, their lit screens flickering in the dark of arenas, auditoriums, and cafes, many of them in the hands of people taking photos and videos of the scene to share with others elsewhere.

In the age of flickering matches and lighters asking for an encore performance it was fire, the most basic tool of humanity, that people used to summon the creative spirits to return to them. The legends of the Titans from ancient Greek mythology tell us that Prometheus had stolen fire for mortal humans from Zeus, who was angry with mortals and wanted to keep them ignorant. Today Content Nation offers performers the new basic tool of humanity in tribute, millions of people lighting up the world with their own creative spirits, sharing in the moment as performers themselves in the creation and global distribution of content, uniting the world through their influential publishing. The performers on stage give them an experience to remember. The audience replies, yes, we do this, too. Prometheus's torch was a gift to us.

The world has become a nation of publishers. Society is changing fundamentally through social media, moving past our old archetypes of how humans survive and thrive far more rapidly than the early motorcars passed by the horse-drawn carriages. Society must embrace these changes brought about by Content Nation, not as a convenience or a courtesy, but as a necessity. For the very survival and success of humanity is now in the hands of Content Nation.

The New Survival: Content Nation Redefines the Future of Humanity

As we have seen so far in this book, social media has had a wide-ranging impact already on many of our most essential institutions and ways of living. Clearly, the scale and the scope of this impact is shaping the way that people survive and thrive in the world in ever more profound ways. Just how profound is social media's impact on human civilization? Is it just another way to communicate with people that will have little change on society as a whole, or is there some more basic change occurring due to social media that will have far-ranging implications? The significance of any new technology on the long term prospects of humankind is difficult to predict with any real accuracy, but let's consider the impact of social media in the light of how other significant innovations in technology have impacted human civilizations in the past and in the present. In looking at these examples of humanity's struggle to adapt to changing conditions we may find some very important lessons about the role of publishing in these struggles for human survival that will shed light on what role social media may have in helping us to ensure the future survival of humanity.

Two Fables: When the Present Repeats the Past

Twenty-seven hundred years ago, the plains surrounding the Tigris River, in what is today southern Iraq, were awash in grains and prosperity, thanks to an innovation that enabled the rulers of Babylon to support a booming population: irrigation. The wealthy and powerful Babylonian empire, nearing its height at that time, was controlled by the rulers of a city-state in the midst of this lush scene of fertility. With a civilization that had lasted already for a thousand years Babylonia had every reason to be optimistic about its future.

Through the years, though, the very innovation that helped to fuel the rise of Babylon led to its ultimate downfall. For though irrigation was a wonderful way to grow more crops on the land in the Tigris River flood plains, it was also a technology that had a problem associated with it: salinization. Inevitably, the forced flooding of farmlands that made the soil of the irrigated land moist and more fertile also made it salty, making it harder and harder for crops to grow. A thousand years after its final peak of glory Babylon was in ruins, the once-fertile plains surrounding it glistening with salt. The most fertile lands in early civilization had become a desert.

Although this may seem to be a fable that points out the weakness of earlier civilizations, it is a fable about the survival of today's civilizations as well.

Not far from San Francisco and the so-called Silicon Valley, the birthplace of the Internet and many other advanced technologies, lies the San Joaquin Valley, one of California's most productive farming regions and the source of a quarter of all U.S. agricultural products. Though the San Joaquin Valley enjoys the benefits of today's modern agriculture technologies, like the kingdoms of Babylon this fertile region also relies on irrigation and fertilizers for its productivity. With a geology very similar to that of the Tigris River valley upon which Babylon relied for its food, the San Joaquin valley suffers mightily from the salinization of its farmlands. Most scientific estimates calculate that at least 25 percent of the San Joaquin Valley's farmland is already affected severely by salinization.

Though the parallels to Babylon's difficulties with farming and those found in California today are troubling, what's more troubling is that the problems with salinity in the San Joaquin Valley have built up in little more than 60 years; the infertility of Babylon's irrigated farmlands took thousands of years to unfold. As seen in Figure 8-1, which indicates problems with salinity that degrade farming, the salinity numbers in the San Joaquin Valley have grown steadily since World War II. At this rate some scientists believe that the San Joaquin Valley will be un-farmable as early as 2080. If left unchecked, we are racing toward Babylon's destiny at an alarming rate.

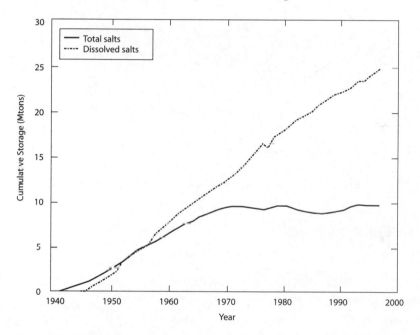

Figure 8-1: Dissolved salts in the San Joaquin Valley soil

When I say "we" I am referring to the world, of course, because the world's use of agriculture methods largely similar to those used in the U.S. puts us all on the same accelerated path toward a reckoning with our ability to survive using the farming techniques of the past 60 years. Global statistics on the impact of farmland salinization parallel those compiled for the U.S. very closely. Though I am pointing out a global problem with agriculture, I am using the San Joaquin Valley as a key example of this problem to underscore a broader point: why is it that in the shadow of the world's most technologically advanced region of the 21st century we have problems that are a clear near-term threat to the survival of humankind, problems that are very similar in their essential nature to those encountered in Babylonia thousands of years ago? Why has the vast store of knowledge available about the impact of salinization on farming failed to change the course of this phenomenon?

The answer to this question lies in many places, of course, but there is one key technology that contributes both to our inability to face the major crises of modern humankind and to the opportunities that we may have to meet those challenges: publishing.

The Race for Human Survival: Is Publishing's Past Threatening the Future of Humankind?

To some it may seem to be a little dramatic to consider social media as having the potential to change how humankind responds to situations that challenge the survival of humankind. If you look at the history of how publishing helped civilizations to rise in the first place and how publishing is positioned in modern civilizations, it may become clearer just how new and important social media may be to our survival as a species.

Innovation and the Quest for Survival: The Persistence of Short-Term Ideas That Keep on Working

As much as I love social media, one of the things that I don't like about it sometimes is that many new social media products and services seem to favor short-term solutions over long-term goals. Thinking back to The Museum of Modern Betas' rapidly building list of new social media publishing tools, it reminds me a bit of what happened in the 19th century just beyond the San Joaquin Valley in the Sierra Nevada mountains. When, in 1848, John Sutter discovered an abundance of gold in the Sierra Nevadas' American River, his discovery didn't remain a secret for very long. By 1849 hundreds of thousands of people were heading to the mountains of California to become gold miners. In some ways the "get rich quick" schemes of that era never left, with the culture of Silicon Valley sometimes feeding the ambitions of entrepreneurs as intent on striking it rich through publishing technologies as were the '49ers of California's "Gold Rush" to turn some quick and hard sweat and a bit of luck into their own fortunes.

Though the entrepreneurial spirit of California's gold miners no doubt inspired an aggressive "can-do" attitude among Silicon Valley technologists, there is one key difference between them and the Gold Rush miners. Where the gold miners of the 19th century in California sought riches from natural resources, the 21st-century entrepreneurs of Silicon Valley were seeking riches from the publishing tools that they build through their intellect and insight. The gold of the California mountains never lived up to the huge expectations of entrepreneurial miners, but there is no real limit to the potential economic benefits from the human mind applied to tool-making. Though the tools that are generated for social media may seem to be short-sighted at times, their astounding variety and their sheer numbers ensure that there will be an enormous number of options for developing models for publishing social media that will be tried, tuned, rejected, or adapted to new circumstances rapidly.

By contrast, most print-based publishing for the past 500 years has been based on one single invention that revolutionized publishing: the movable-type printing press. When the German goldsmith Johannes Gutenberg introduced the first practical version of his invention in 1450, it had metal-based movable type that could be created in large quantities easily. The crisply printed letters, durable inks, and relatively affordable design of Gutenberg's invention enabled printing to become a trade that could flourish in the growing economy of 15th-century Europe. This invention enabled many significant changes to human society, but the invention itself was largely unchanged for centuries. Even today the only truly significant difference between most major printing operations and Gutenberg's invention is the efficiency with which they produce a printed page.

The stability of the technology used for print publishing is not terribly different from the stability of irrigation technologies used by the Babylonians to flood their farmlands. There were no doubt improvements through the years in the efficiency of the equipment and techniques used for irrigation, to be sure, but in essence, the fundamental concept and the underlying farming methods remained unchanged. A tool found a stable place in society, little needed to be invested in the improvements of farming methods, and Babylonian civilization flourished, until the limitations of their farming technologies became evident. What seemed like a long-term solution turned out in fact to be relatively short-sighted in terms of the long-term need for human survival.

The ability to grow populations and farming away in unexploited regions kept people reinvesting in the same basic Babylonian irrigation concepts again and again. If it worked for thousands of years for them, after all; why shouldn't that be good enough? When modern fertilizers and water-pumping technologies enabled the Babylonian concepts of irrigation to be accelerated to a new scale of productivity, irrigation-based farming was able to sustain soaring world populations as never before. Human technology has been able to outrun the growth of human populations with ever-increasing commitments to modern farming techniques, but inevitably this continual amplification begged a greater question: what would happen should all of the world's farmable land turn into salty deserts? We carried a single, highly scalable technology through thousands of years to the point where its limitations for all of humankind are apparent both for the short term and the long term.

In a similar way, publishing was a short-term human invention that kept on getting used again and again as human society grew, becoming part of the fabric of human life and developing into new forms through more efficient technologies. Even the electronic publishing technologies of the 20th century, which enabled mass communications with illiterate people through audio and moving images, accelerated the impact and reach of publishing but still carried over key traits from the publishing of Gutenberg. Most importantly, like print publishing, 20th-century electronic publishing was based largely on centralized mass production: a single item was created and reproduced by a central source for a mass audience. Like the modern technologies used to accelerate farming, the implications of accelerating earlier strategies for deploying technology on the survival of human culture were poorly understood by many people. Like human tools from the dawn of time, they were tried, and what seemed to work in the short run kept on being repeated as long as it seemed to drive the success of human civilization.

Now we appear to be reaching an impasse as to how the combination of human society and human technologies transforming both nature and society will enable the survival of humanity as we know it today. In many ways, though, we are not changing our underlying assumptions about how a civilization should go about responding to this impasse. Like the farmers who irrigate the San Joaquin Valley, most responses to the global challenges to human survival are pulled off of a relatively short menu of options that have worked for thousands of years. Although technology has changed in some dramatic ways since the days of the Babylonian empires, civilization as a whole is still running the same game plan for survival as the Babylonians: *transform nature uniformly through technology and use centrally controlled publishing to compel people to act uniformly in a society transformed by technology.*

This is a formula for developing civilizations that has worked pretty well for more than 7,000 years, but as humans begin to stretch the limits of how the world can sustain human life at an astounding speed, we need to consider what may need to change in the basic formula for successful human civilizations. Inevitably, considering the role of publishing in this formula is an essential component to unraveling its role in the survival of humankind, and to considering the value of social media as tool that can help civilizations to respond more effectively to today's challenges affecting the future of civilization.

The Code of Hammurabi: Publishing as a Tool for Natural Selection

Thirty-seven hundred years ago, Hammurabi, the ruler of Babylon, decided to create a standard set of laws that would be known well by everyone in his growing empire. Because stone and clay were popular publishing media in that era, he chose to erect in public places large stone tablets, or *steles*, to publish his code of law. Many of the laws prescribed punishments for not following the Code of Hammurabi. Often, the punishment for breaking a law was dismemberment or death. This was the price that people would have to pay if they could not help society to be organized and managed in a predictable way.

Why was predictability so important? Because it seemed to ensure survival. If the Babylonians followed Hammurabi's laws, people would be able to live in safety, they would be able to organize effectively to defend their land against potential invaders, and they would have an efficient economy based on well-understood rules for supporting the state government through taxes and obedience to regulations. The assumption in providing a death penalty for not following Hammurabi's laws was that, based on past experience, rule-breakers would threaten the survival of society as a whole. It would be better to destroy people who threatened the ability of Babylonia's gene pool to flourish than to enable them to challenge what had been "written in stone" as the keys to survival. The publishing of Hammurabi's code was in effect an extension of human DNA, the genetic coding inside every human cell that determines the form of a human life that is likely to survive into another generation. People who could conform to these laws were promised a high chance of survival in a society that was influenced as much by human technology and relationships as by natural circumstances impacting humans.

Most people adhered to Hammurabi's laws, out of fear in part, perhaps, but also because of a basic human trait related to human genes that had allowed the growth of human civilization beyond small groupings of people: altruism.

Altruism and Scalability: How Publishing Fueled the Growth of Civilization

Altruism is often depicted as selflessness, the willingness to put one's personal interests aside to enable others or society as a whole to gain. Author Nicholas Wade observes in his book *Before the Dawn* that altruism is a trait that existed in the ancestors of human beings as well, but on a more limited scale.

Chimpanzees and gorillas, our closest genetic relatives in today's world, also exhibit the ability to demonstrate altruism. Both of these species of animals will collaborate to ensure the survival of those of their kind who are not certain genetic relatives. In other words, they see benefits to the survival of their own bloodline through ensuring the survival of others in their social groups who may benefit their own genetic survival indirectly. Some scientists believe that this may be due in part to the indiscriminate mating patterns of these animals, which make it hard for an individual chimp or gorilla to determine whether another particular individual is a blood relative. In a sense, animal altruism is a deep-seated survival response to threats to others in their social groups that tells these animals, "Well, who's to say whether these others who are threatened are my relatives? I had better help them just to be on the safe side."

It turns out, then, that though there may be a noble aspect of sorts that drives altruism, its roots are grounded in an individual's desire for their bloodline to survive another generation. Animal altruism is, in a sense, healthy self-interest that gives others the genetic benefit of the doubt. The altruism of animals can only go so far, apparently, and similarly so in primitive human societies. In his study of the isolated tribes of the Amazon rain forest, anthropologist Napoleon Chagnon noted that it was rare that these tribes ever exceeded 50 to 100 people. It appears based on numerous studies that until the rise of civilizations large groups of people were rarely if ever organized toward a common cause. Something more than the possibility of a genetic relationship was required to create a broader kind of altruism.

A possible explanation for what drove human civilization forward from clan-based altruism to society-based altruism may be found in the clan depicted in the preamble to this book. As the ice ages waned thousands of years ago and new tools and methods enabled more efficient hunting and gathering in a more stable climate, surpluses of food and crafted materials accrued more regularly. This made the prospect of trade with neighboring clans and, eventually, far-away clans, more attractive. To make this system of trade work, Nicholas Wade argues, trust was a necessary ingredient. Trusting someone outside of one's clan for the purpose of trade was like a temporary granting of clan-like reliance on someone else to ensure one's survival. Even today in some cultures oaths or contracts are confirmed sometimes with a cutting of fingers and the mixing of blood between people to signify a family-like connection between people trusted for business dealings. Trust is like a virtual extension of one's DNA-based circle of altruism.

There was no guarantee that reciprocity with a trading partner from another clan could be relied upon in early human commerce, but gradually trading partners built up that trust, extending the reach of altruism's power. Organized human behaviors began to expand significantly beyond small clans and hunting groups. As trade relationships became more complex and memories of what had been entrusted to whom became more difficult to maintain, it became clear that something more than trusting in one's memory of a commitment would be required to ensure that trade transactions could be carried out correctly. Having records of transactions and contracts became essential to enable altruism to scale more effectively beyond clan-like reliance on others. Publishing became the bond that held these altruistic relationships together, using tablets of clay and stone to record the underpinnings of commercial altruism. The signature that indicated the extension of genetic-like bonds of trust through altruism had passed from blood to writing implements.

Publishing enabled humans to organize on a scale far beyond small groups of people, creating an extension to how people could survive through altruism that was startling in its impact on both people and the natural world. A person's bloodline might have genes that changed in very small ways with every generation: a person was a person, the reach of their arms was pretty much the same, their legs were pretty much the same, and so on. Through publishing, the organism of society built through ever-broadening altruistic collaboration could change radically the size and scope of human endeavor. Erect a stone stele of laws or display engineering diagrams for a great building or an irrigation project, and all of a sudden any number of people could be made to behave uniformly and to manipulate the natural environment uniformly.

Through publishing civilization itself became a genetic code, the DNA of a civilization encapsulated in laws, contracts, and diagrams, able to transform landscapes through technology guided by publishing as if it were an animal of immense proportions. Even those who could not read what was being published could see, touch, and hear the consistent societal coding to which they offered their altruistic cooperation. The stone steles of Hammurabi and other rulers became the blood of kinship for the organism known as civilization.

Publishing, Modern Enterprises, and Brands: Altruism Becomes Detached from Society

The basic formula from Hammurabi's era of using state-controlled publishing and record-keeping to transform nature and society through technology remained unchanged for thousands of years. After the fall of the Roman Empire in Europe, the churches in that region played a more prominent role in publishing for many centuries, playing a bridging role until the secular economy of Europe revived. Publishing that compelled society as a unified organism through altruism was primarily a function of the government and government-recognized religions. With the development of the printing press in the 15th century, there was at first little change to this formula, because there were relatively few people who were literate enough and wealthy enough to take advantage of its capabilities directly.

By the 18th and early 19th centuries, widely distributed publications authored by independent individuals in Europe, the Americas, and elsewhere thrived. Independent publishing enabled people to share, with an increasingly literate public, thoughts about science, politics, religion, and other key tools for the development of civilization with little reliance on government or religious patrons. Though these were highly influential movements, in essence, the concept of forging altruistic bonds with a government through publishing was largely unchanged at first. In fact, in many ways the democratic movements of that era enhanced the bond between a people and its government through publishing. Laws and regulations continued to build a highly scalable social relationship that managed technology and nature for the good of society.

As the 19th century progressed, the genetic-like bonds of trust through altruism that bound people to their governments through publishing began to mutate. Private enterprises arose as the new champions of technological innovation and began to become powerful sources of society-wide publishing in their own right. The altruistic bonds holding people together in civilizations began to have a more complex map of allegiances, spreading their social genes in more complex patterns. On the one hand, nationalism demanded strong altruistic ties to governments, but industry encouraged strong altruistic ties to private employers and the products of their industrial output as the basis for the bonds of civilization. After thousands of years of stability the assumption that publishing would map out the ultimate bonds of a large society as an altruistic organism that could ensure the survival of one's gene pool was being challenged as never before.

Paper and electronic publications began to issue advertisements to society to build altruistic allegiances with a new organizing force in society: brands. Brand-name products could be sold and transferred from one company to another through several generations of customers, outlasting often the companies that created them, becoming like natural resources in the lives of everyday people. The map of altruistic relationships required for survival was getting more and more complex. Instead of using our genes to survive using technology in a natural landscape with a clan, modern society required people to navigate their genes through altruistic relationships with enormous entities that promised benefits of increasingly tenuous and questionable value to their gene pool's survival.

Publishing became less and less a tool to tie a person's bloodline to trustworthy relationships that would help it to survive in the natural world. Instead publishing became a tool that would shift people as natural resources to ensure the survival of brands. A toothpaste brand could promise "sex appeal" to generations, but neither nature nor society would seem to benefit as much from altruism extended to a toothpaste brand as would the brand product's producer. Thanks to publishing, even then the corporations producing a toothpaste brand might come and go and the natural resources required to produce the toothpaste could change completely, but the toothpaste brand and its promises would live on.

Losing Evolutionary Options: The Impact of Publishing on Human Survival

Humankind had taken a risk with publishing, a short-term tool that enabled a better environment for survival, but ultimately a tool that seemed to focus less and less on the fundamentals of human survival. Publishing largely benefited and was controlled by powerful centralized entities that did not have a genetic or personal relationship with the person offering them their altruism. As long as there were benefits for survival that outweighed the risk, civilization flourished, enabling human genes to remain undisturbed globally. In the process of doing so, the underlying animal motivation of people—using altruism to extend one's perceived gene pool—may have betrayed our ability to secure our bloodlines' futures through these extended relationships.

Over the past 7,000 years our human genes have continued to evolve, but analysis of the history of human DNA seems to indicate that there have been no significant additions or modifications to human genes in our recent history. In fact, modern human beings have remarkably little genetic variation, far less than our closest modern genetic relatives such as chimpanzees or gorillas. Instead of people adapting to changes in their natural surroundings, society's use of technology and control mechanisms such as laws that were spread through publishing appears to have substituted for the genetic adaptations to natural surroundings usually required for survival.

In place of humans modifying their genes through evolution in a complex natural environment, the centrally controlled and standardized societies and technologies that evolved over time forced out human genes that could not adapt to these environments standardized through publishing. The surviving genes were adapting less to variations in nature and more to survival in highly standardized civilizations, dependent more and more on altruism extended to the institutions of civilization for their survival than on nature. The result appears to be a human gene pool that has eliminated many of the genetic options not well suited for conforming to centralized civilizations with highly centralized control through publishing. Publishing provided the map, the genes, if you will, for the widespread standardization of survival guidelines and practices. Just as humans engineer crops and animal species to produce more genetically uniform organisms, so have we made our own species more genetically uniform through our engineering of an enormous standardized civilization that is itself, in essence, the world's largest organism.

The Risks of Standardized Civilization: The Potato Famine and the 1918 Influenza Pandemic

A standardized global civilization offers enormous potential benefits to human-kind, but because it appears to suppress genetic diversity in both ourselves and in the natural systems supporting our lives it also exposes us to global survival problems. The decline of the Babylonian empire was a very slowly evolving fail-ure of civilization as an organism exploiting nature, but such failures can occur very rapidly in today's highly standardized and technology-driven modern civilization. Two tragic examples demonstrate the impact that a lack of genetic diversity can have on human life in a standardized global civilization.

The potato as most people know it is a whitish-brown tuber, grown around the world as a food staple. Imported to Europe in the 16th century by Spanish explorers visiting the Andes mountains of South America, the globally grown potato is in fact just one of many different kinds of colorful potatoes native to the Andes mountains. Potatoes are a genetically diverse species in their native habitat.

When potatoes arrived in Europe, one particular potato plant brought back by the Spanish explorers was reproduced widely for farming. It was a very successful crop, but the potatoes grown from this one set of genes were not adapted to a fungus native to Ireland called late blight. In the 1840s, late blight swept through the farmlands of Ireland and destroyed most of the potato crops, which were the primary source of food for many poor people. It is estimated that a million or more people died in Ireland over several years from what became known as the Great Famine—because of the lack of genetic diversity and adaptation in a key crop that was planted in a standardized agricultural environment.

Human civilization as an organism lacking diversity creates problems similar to the Great Famine. In 1918, an unusual strain of the influenza virus began to be spread from inland U.S. states to the world, accelerated by the movement of U.S. troops participating in World War I, the first truly global conflict. Eventually known as the Spanish Flu, the spread of this influenza virus around the world was accelerated by the standardization of warfare, health care, and transportation in a modern era. Half of the U.S. casualties in World War I were attributed to the virus, which is believed to have killed from 20 million to 100 million people worldwide in about two years, possibly taking more lives than World War I itself. The Great War was a violent and sudden event, but the violence caused by a simple virus taking advantage of the standardized organism of civilization was greater and more sudden yet.

Climate Change: Civilization Faces New Natural and Social Challenges

The Great Famine and the Spanish Flu are enormous tragic events on the scale of everyday modern life. Still, as with the salinization of farmlands, it's possible to rationalize the effects of these catastrophes and to think that our civilization will adapt to changes as needed with its existing structure largely intact. What if, though, nature challenges civilization on a scale far broader than even these catastrophes? What would happen if some of the basic assumptions underlying the development of all civilizations as we have known them were to change?

For most of the past 400,000 years, the earth has been an icy planet, with large portions of its land and oceans encased in glaciers kilometers thick. Rarely did the earth approach its current relatively warm state in this era (see Figure 8-2). Every 100,000 years or so mean temperatures on earth would approach today's typical averages briefly and then plummet back into more frigid conditions, returning much of the earth's surface to a largely frozen state. Brief periods of somewhat warmer climate would come in between these major warming peaks, then the climate would return to "ice age" conditions.

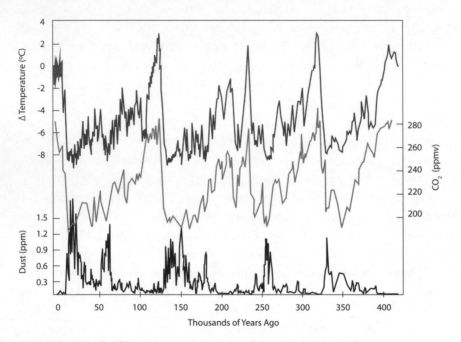

Figure 8-2: Graph of historic temperatures and dust levels derived from Vostok Antarctic ice core samples

In the era of climate history in which we now live, called the Holocene Epoch by climate scientists, humankind has been blessed with a long period of stable climate that is warm by historical standards. Unlike typical periods of warmth after an ice age, which would last a few hundred years before a new ice age began, the Holocene Epoch has lasted about 10,000 years—about as long as modern human civilization itself. By modern standards temperatures have fluctuated in this period quite a bit, but by the standards of more than 450,000 years of climate history, the Holocene Epoch has been the longest and most stable period of relatively warm recorded temperatures.

How the earth's climate will change from today's conditions is a point of heated debate these days, a debate that I don't intend to engage in this book. We don't know conclusively today whether the effects of global climate change over the next several hundred years will cause earth's climate to heat up indefinitely or to cool indefinitely or whether we'll see both far hotter and far cooler climate conditions indefinitely. The most significant problem for civilization, though, is that the relatively stable climate conditions of the Holocene Epoch appear to be ending. Perhaps within our lifetime, but more likely within the next few centuries, according to climate scientists, mean global temperatures will be nothing like today's steady, moderate climate. Mean temperatures will again fluctuate wildly and rapidly, as they have for hundreds of thousands of years and more. When this occurs, large portions of the earth that are home to billions of people are likely to be rendered uninhabitable by the standards of modern civilization.

Because the Holocene Epoch has been a unique period of sustained mild climate conditions, it's difficult to project exactly what might happen next. This unpredictability in and of itself is a major problem for humanity. We've been used to a relatively predictable climate since the dawn of modern civilization and we have relied upon that climate's predictability for the survival and growth of our civilizations. Regardless of what the future of our climate may turn out to be in its specific details there is one clear problem facing humanity: our modern civilization was not developed to thrive in periods of highly unstable climates. Looking at the experiences of the Babylonians with farming and our own fast-forwarded farming failures in the San Joaquin Valley, it's clear that civilizations as organisms repeatedly using the same short-term survival solutions with highly centralized controls aren't terribly good at ensuring their long-term survival even in relatively stable climate conditions.

Human genes, however, were designed mostly in an era of great climate change. Humans are designed by nature to survive highly variable climate conditions. We even survived an apparent near-extinction event about 50,000 years ago, according to research focused on the evolution of human genes, which may have reduced the surviving gene pool of modern humans to an estimated 5,000 people. The question isn't whether humans will survive climate change but whether our civilization that was predicated on the availability of an unusually stable climate will survive climate change through the use of the right tools.

Through the altruistic bonds of publishing we became part of the global organism of civilization, an organism that was foreign to early humans and not one that is encoded into our bodies' genes. Humans as a species are likely to survive radical climate changes, but civilization itself is not likely to survive as an organism in its current form using its current tools for survival. The bonds of altruism that hold civilization together, already frayed and stretched by conflicting and wavering commitments to governments, employers, and a consumer-driven economy, are challenging already the basic assumptions formed around the altruism that has bonded human civilization together for more than 7,000 years.

At the heart of this fraying system based on altruism lies the tool of publishing, a tool that began its role in society by helping people to build trusted relationships with one another in what was then a newly stable climate. Publishing enabled the radical centralization of decision making and the widespread enforcement of those decisions in a stable climate, but with the climate of the world becoming unstable and highly variable, this may not be the best way to use publishing as a tool for the rapid adaptation of our civilization to these new conditions.

Surviving and Thriving in an Unstable World: Does Social Media Point the Way Forward?

Every species of life on our planet faces the same evolutionary challenges as humans. Some will survive the natural selection of species; some will not. Unlike any other species on earth, though, humans have the ability to create a wide array of tools and adaptive behaviors that can be used to predict and to adjust to expected changes before they occur. Our ability to survive by making tools allows humans to adapt to environmental changes more rapidly than our genes can adapt. When humans were in the rapidly shifting climate of the ice ages, their tool-making ability enabled our ancestors to rapidly develop new responses to emerging survival conditions. Human language, a tool itself, enabled other tools to develop even more rapidly once the Holocene Epoch unfolded.

Acknowledging the Impasse: The Need for More Flexible Survival Strategies

The push toward the standardization of tools and techniques used for survival through the publishing efforts of central authorities in the era of large civilizations cut us off from our original human roots. Altruism, intended originally to ensure the survival of small, genetically diverse groups, instead wiped out that diversity at many local levels in favor of broader bonds that ensured survival. Tools that allowed humans to adapt and to survive more effectively flourished in modern civilization, but the need to gain consensus at very high levels of authority before the standardizing of tools could occur slowed down their evolution in many instances. Civilization as an organism, like any other organism, became interested in conserving itself and adopted the widespread use of new tools to control nature and people very selectively. Humanity began to lose track of its need to survive as one of many diverse organisms in an evolving natural world.

Reclaiming Our Past for the Future: Social Media as a Path to Diverse Survival Models

From the standpoint of ensuring the survival of humankind, the development of today's diverse array of social media publishing tools already in wide use is probably the most significant event in human history since the dawn of large-scale human civilizations. Social media publishing is important to this significant degree, not just because it is revolutionary in light of our current civilization, but because it enables humans to reclaim our ability to survive and to thrive in an overwhelmed global civilization that must adapt to diverse and increasingly unstable conditions in nature and in civilization itself. Other advances in technology have allowed us to survive and thrive in relatively predictable conditions; social media prepares us to evolve survival and success responses rapidly and flexibly in a highly unpredictable world.

The Web technology that powers social media is designed to survive local catastrophes and to enable its global communications network to seek out automatically ways to keep people in touch with one another in unstable conditions. Social media leverages the Web's networking capability to emphasize the autonomous power of individuals publishing to the world as peers. With social media, globally scaled altruism no longer needs to be based solely on content approved by a central publishing authority for distribution through fixed channels. Through social media, people can build trust directly and rapidly with any group of people anywhere at almost any scale of human activity, trust that can be reinforced through peer-to-peer communications that can pass through a wide variety of channels in highly unstable conditions.

This highly scalable self-organizing behavior enabled by social media publishing is the key to its enabling the development of a better system for managing human civilization. Altruism can re-assert itself as a tool for highly specialized communities united in purpose but scattered in location. Altruism expressed through social media can also enable very large communities to form, built more on direct person-to-person trust than on the implied person-to-person trust found through a central publishing authority. The highly diverse and overlapping bonds of trust built up on a wide variety of social media platforms used for a wide variety of purposes in a broad array of social and business contexts dramatically increase the diversity of ways in which altruism can be established and maintained.

The great and sudden flourishing of short-term solutions emerging for social media publishing has generated a wide diversity of ways in which independent people or units of people can cooperate with one another. This "Gold Rush" of social media publishing tools is more than just lucrative; it is the key to creating extraordinary diversity in the "genes" of the organism of civilization. Like our own genes, the tools of publishing that define the genetic coding of civilization are short-sighted, looking at how to survive immediate conditions. Also like our genes, having many options for short-term survival that are well-adapted to surviving radical changes can lead to extraordinary long-term evolutionary options. As a result, our options for building successful models for new kinds of civilizations have increased dramatically, as if the global genome of human society was having new genetic material spliced into it almost daily.

In a few short years, social media has utterly transformed the publishing gene pool available to civilization's organism from that of a small set of aging techniques for survival threatened with extinction to one that offers through the proliferation of social media publishing models a wide variety of new options for the survival of civilizations that can survive and thrive quite comfortably on a local and global level no matter what humankind's circumstances may become. Social media offers both the ability to build highly specialized social networks of people who can be united rapidly toward specific goals and the ability to assemble rapidly very large groups of people united toward very broadly purposed goals. With social media, the bonds of altruism, the bonds that make us feel that we are united in a common purpose, can coalesce in new patterns with remarkable efficiency, enabling us to adjust rapidly the ways in which we govern ourselves, the ways in which we make our livings, and the ways in which we live our lives together.

How Social Media Can Reinvent Civilization's Genome: A Hint from a Game Based on Genetics

A hint as to how efficient the human species can be at reinventing the organisms of civilization through social media came recently from the introduction of a new computer game based on mastering the evolution of species. Spore is a game that enables people to create their own worlds of virtual creatures that they can design themselves and share with others via the Web. Spore was under development in 2008 when its creators decided to get people involved in the product ahead of the release of the actual gaming software by releasing a software tool that would allow people to develop and share the creatures that they could use in their games once it was released.

When the Spore development team first decided to release the Creature Creator software in June 2008, their thought was that they might be able to encourage people to develop about 100,000 new kinds of evolving creatures by the time the software was scheduled to launch in September 2008. Much to their surprise, people downloading Creature Creator had surpassed the 100,000 mark of created Spore creatures within a few hours. Within about a week, Spore users had created and shared more than 1,000,000 different types of Spore creatures with one another and within a month they had created more than 1.8 million Spore creatures—more than the estimated 1.5 million known species alive today on our planet. By the time the game was launched in September 2008, Spore users had created for sharing more than 3.2 million different kinds of software-based species—more than double the number of known species living on the earth today.

The Spore phenomenon is certainly an indication of the number of creative computer game players in the world, but it's also an indication of how quickly humans can conceive of and share different ways to adapt to and survive in an environment through social media. The impetus to be creative is a universal human trait, not limited to a few fortunate people whose works of art have been played in concert halls or hung in art galleries. Combine that essential human creativity in response to survival challenges with the ability to create altruistic bonds via social media publishing, and there are more patterns that could emerge for human survival than exist in nature for every kind of living being on earth.

Social media will release an explosion of ways in which human genes can be extended to create bonds of trust and collaboration that will lead to rapidly evolving strategies for surviving and thriving in a rapidly changing world. We have developed a relative handful of successful civilizations through traditional publishing in 7,000 years compared to what may emerge from the experiments of people who can define any number of altruistic relationships through social media.

Reconciling the Past with the Future: The Evolving Role of Traditional Publishing

Though social media offers humankind powerful options to survive and to thrive during radical changes to our world, it is a young development in the long history of publishing. Nevertheless, its impact on traditional media has been significant and has challenged the position of authority that traditional media claims in leading civilization forward. Already, the attention given to social media outlets online significantly overshadows the attention given to traditional media outlets for younger audiences, and it has a significant amount of attention and participation from older audiences, also.

Social media's civilization-changing potential is global in nature, as well: according to recent data compiled by the Universal McCann International ad agency there are more bloggers in China than in any other nation in the world, and some 92 percent of people in South Korea using the Web have read a weblog. Content Nation is already here and has the world's attention: Content Nation is already well on its way to becoming the world. It's only a question of what the world will become in the hands of a nation of publishers when those publishers control the most powerful links of altruism for most of civilization.

Even as social media continues to grow, traditional sources of publishing continue to survive and in some cases they are learning how to thrive amidst the competition offered by social media. In the U.S., total hours of television viewing are up, according to recent research, though how much people actually watch the television versus listen to it in the background or over the top of their laptop PCs is unknown. It's likely that social media will never replace traditional publishing fully in the competition to provide powerful bonds of altruism that bind civilizations together through publishing. Instead, governments, industries, and other global and local institutions will continue to use and to evolve centralized media production, but they will occupy a smaller role in an emerging system of publishing that will favor in many instances social media as the most efficient way for people to organize themselves successfully.

Thinking of our exploration of human history and evolution and how it relates to the evolution of publishing, there are parallels from the animal kingdom's evolution that may offer a model as to how traditional publishing will fit in with social media moving forward.

When mammals were evolving in the age of dinosaurs they were fairly insignificant creatures at first, coexisting with dinosaurs and then thriving as radically new climate conditions overtook life forms that could not adapt to their new surroundings. Recent discoveries by paleontologists studying the fossil records of dinosaurs and mammals in China, though, reveal that even in the age of dinosaurs there were mammal carnivores that were actually preying on smaller dinosaurs. Even before the extinction-triggering event that eliminated most dinosaurs 65 million years ago, mammals were asserting themselves as competitors of dinosaurs, not just scurrying between their toes. At the same time, dinosaurs never quite left us, of course. Survivors of the extinction event in the Jurassic Period of earth's history included dinosaurs that evolved into today's birds, which compete with mammals for survival resources to this day.

I think that it's important to look at this model of evolution in light of many people calling today's traditional media outlets "dinosaurs." In one sense, it's probably a true statement in terms of where traditional media is going in the long run; it's not likely that the economics that have supported many large-scale traditional media outlets for centuries are going to survive on the scale that they do today, indefinitely. Already, in many instances, through cable television channels, television recording and playback devices such as TiVo, and highly segmented print publishing, mass audiences are fragmenting into many highly focused market segments anyway. Social media only accelerates this trend, enabling content from all sources to come to global attention spontaneously.

With only so much time and energy available from people to pay attention to any number of things in their lives, traditional media is becoming only one of many possible sources for content that can engage audiences. People are listening to authorities in publishing that matter to them on a more personal level, even as publishing authorities are trying to figure out how to engage their audiences on a more personal level. The stone tablets of Hammurabi are being challenged by the collaborative civilization-building of social media, enabling the consensus of millions of people with creative approaches to building altruistic bonds of trust to organize themselves more flexibly with whomever serves their needs as leaders of civilizations.

Over time, today's civilizations will fall, not because one was conquered by another to create a new central authority, but because humans will be able to survive and to thrive more efficiently by choosing the authorities that help them to survive on a dynamic basis that renders the need for today's central publishing authorities moot. We will no longer need them to create effective bonds of altruism, not because they have been overthrown, but because we will already have known and agreed to what they would tell us before they even say it.

Scale in a Diverse World of Social Media Outlets: More Options for Scalable Civilizations

It's quite possible that social media may become a force affecting the formation and growth of civilizations that will be more responsive than traditional publishing to changes in both our civilizations and in nature. There is likely to be an "extinction" of some forms of publishing that do not help humans to adapt well to new threats and opportunities arising from those changes. While used for ceremonial and religious purposes, for example, scrolls and stone tablets are no longer used as publishing tools that hold civilizations together.

How are the traits of social media well adapted to helping human civilizations to survive and to thrive? One of the key factors that make social media a powerful force in publishing is its ability to scale rapidly for global audiences using the same publishing tools that service small, focused communities. Today's video that appeals to just a few people who know its producer can become a worldwide sensation overnight. This ability to scale rapidly for global audiences based on peer acceptance and endorsement of social media content enables almost anyone to become an influential publisher overnight, not just those chosen by central authority figures. Civilizations that have benefited from the scale of centralized publishing are not going to be denied many of the benefits of highly influential and scalable publishing with social media publishing tools.

In one sense, social media scales in ways that are very similar to traditional media sources. Social bookmarking services such as Digg can create a user-generated "front page" of newsworthy content automatically based on user selections which, though very different often from that selected by a traditional media outlet, services a similarly broad array of tastes and outlooks. At this level, Digg is definitely mass media, and mass media that has become dominant very quickly, with an audience already double that of the leading U.S. newspapers.

Unlike the relatively predictable editorial policies that determine the content of a major newspaper, though, Web sites like Digg that are using millions of people to select the most popular content of the moment provide very powerful editorial control in their own way, but ultimately the nature of its control is far more unpredictable. There is no specific editorial policy at Digg for content; it represents the insights of many people, but not the same people each and every time. By comparison a government, a newspaper, or another major publisher relies on a fairly small group of people that determines what gets published.

At the same time highly scalable social media services can focus on the interests of very specific groups very quickly. Looking again at Digg, a visitor to its site can focus on one of the pre-defined topics, such as business or politics, or use Digg's search engine to focus on far more specific topics. Facebook and other social networking services face similar strengths in scalability. Each person may have only a hundred or fewer people in their personal social networks, but by joining topical interest groups, each person can be part of any number of groups of hundreds of thousands.

This scalability of social media poses some interesting challenges when thinking of how it may help to shape the future of human civilizations. Recently researchers at the Santa Fe Institute of the National Museum of Natural History in Washington, D.C. developed a computer model that evaluated how the size of mammal species affected their evolutions and their abilities to survive.

The researchers looked at thousands of different sizes of mammals over the past 60 million years and how their sizes related to species that evolved from earlier species. They discovered that in relatively stable conditions, mammals will tend to evolve into larger species over time, making more efficient use of resources a competitive adaptation; however, when having to respond to events in the environment that caused mammal species to become extinct, mammals that were smaller were much more likely to survive. So being a larger organism appears to be beneficial to mammals in a stable environment, but disadvantageous in an unstable environment.

Thinking of how publishing acts as an extension of human genes to form the altruistic bonds of a civilization, social media may offer humans some distinct advantages for the survival of civilizations. Because the content of social media is not controlled centrally, it may help civilizations to develop rules and resources to help people to survive and to thrive more rapidly than traditional centrally controlled publishing. Large-scale civilizations using social media may be able to identify better survival options in more challenging times more rapidly and efficiently by enabling options to be identified, weighted, and refined through a wider array of opinions and insights than found through centrally controlled publishing systems.

Social media may enable civilizations to develop rapid responses to major threats that would be the equivalent of creating new "genes" for survival that can be tuned more rapidly than by central publishing authorities more invested in existing ways to respond to threats. Instead of having to have wars, corporate takeovers, or other types of activities to create new standardized bonds of altruism, the people of these societies or organizations may find through social media ways in which groups can build insight and consensus among themselves to use available natural and human resources more flexibly and efficiently.

Large or Small? Social Media Can Help Civilizations to Be Both More Effectively

Large civilizations and organizations may be able to use social media to respond to opportunities and threats more efficiently, enabling them to stay large longer than usual by using social media to find solutions to survival threats more efficiently and effectively. By the same token, by giving smaller organizations and civilizations the ability to scale more rapidly with allies in response to common threats, social media may enable those smaller groups to survive and to thrive in times that normally would see them overwhelmed by larger competitors. Altruistic bonds often can be formed more rapidly through social media, than through centrally controlled publishing services, enabling people to cut through local orthodoxies that would otherwise divide people who could be united to solve problems.

The flexibility found in social media may become critical to the survival of human civilization as climate and natural-resource issues begin to create more fragmented areas in which human civilization can be maintained. Large armies or global institutions will not be needed as much to encode remote groups in fragmented environments into a common altruistic framework. Instead, social media will enable these people to move far more rapidly to develop their own altruistic bonds independently and autonomously. In the world of social media, any and every person in the world could become an extension of your tribal clan instantly. Social media may be able to help humankind to adopt the best attributes found in the cultures of early nomadic human tribes with the cultures of sophisticated global civilizations. The ability of social media to enable individuals and small autonomous groups to collaborate rapidly on a local or global scale may help to power the growth of civilizations that can be either large or small or both as we need them to be in a given moment in response to the threats and opportunities of the moment.

Social media will enable people around the world to respond more effectively to rapid changes in our natural and social environment as small groups of wandering nomads, as highly integrated civilizations, or both. Altruism expressed through social media will allow us to extend bonds of trust, commerce, and common social values to whomever can help us to survive, wherever they may be found, with minimal support from central authorities. Through social media, the gap between our origins as successful clans of hunters and gatherers and our current world of highly integrated societies can begin to be closed, with the wisdom gained from both models of human survival informing the strengths of each model. Social media will enable us to explore new ways of being human in ways more independent and more united than ever before.

The Big Sombrero Economy in a World of Highly Scalable Civilizations

In this emerging world of highly scalable civilizations assembled more rapidly than ever through social media, large economies will continue to thrive, but it's likely that economic activity overall will take on different forms. Earlier in the book I discussed the Big Sombrero model of marketing that is emerging through social media, a model in which economic activity generated through social media enabled value to be created in many small markets effectively without having to pass into a phase of entering a mass-market model. We have seen already in this book how social media makes smaller, more direct transactions that provide economic benefit to parties more feasible on a global scale. In a world in which social media becomes the driving force for most economic activity this means that much of the value in global economies will pass from large quantities of highly similar mass-produced goods to large quantities of highly dissimilar goods, some of which will become massively popular at a particular moment in time, but none of which may need such popularity to provide economic success to their creators. In a sense the Big Sombrero economy will become the reverse of The Long Tail economy, enabling more and more value in small, focused transactions that no longer rely on "hits" at all for long-term economic benefit.

An interesting example of this concept can be seen already in the Lulu self-publishing book service. Lulu enables anyone to create their own books for publishing in both electronic format and in print format. When someone wants a book created by Lulu in print format, they can queue an order to Lulu that will then be generated via technology that can print small numbers of individual items in large quantities efficiently. This print-on-demand capability enables Lulu titles to provide benefit to audiences indefinitely before needing the services of mass printing. In the meantime the highly scalable capabilities of Lulu's print-on-demand services enable the technology of mass production to benefit focused markets.

It is this combination of highly scalable technology tailored to service-focused needs that is going to be at the heart of the emerging global economy powered by social media. Rather than building endless centralized production capacity developed primarily to meet demand for a handful of centrally defined products and services, social media will inspire a flourishing of highly centralized standardized production capability tuned more to highly scalable decentralized interests in goods and services for which demand comes and goes fairly rapidly. At the same time, highly decentralized production capabilities designed to meet the highly scalable demand for unique products and services defined and demanded through social media outlets will flourish as well, enabling people to respond rapidly to highly focused market needs by being highly attuned to the demands for goods and services expressed through social media. Many of these goods and services may never become "hits," but in many instances they will not have to in order to keep production capacity at all levels working efficiently in both centralized and decentralized production schemes. In time, people will become less and less concerned with "hits" in general and more concerned with the things that give them lasting satisfaction in life, the things that are closer to the true value of altruism that binds together successful societies.

The New Society: Unity and Diversity Aligned for Surviving and Thriving

Social media, then, is impacting the future of human society by reworking the basic concept of what holds civilizations together. It reworks the basic formula for civilization into a paradigm that reflects both our origins as humans and our future: *transform and co-exist with nature using highly scalable publishing that builds influence, leadership, and consensus among peers who can act collaboratively in a diverse society transformed by technology.*

Through social media human society is discovering a new route to surviving and thriving in a world being transformed both by human technology and dramatic changes in our natural environment. Social media is more than a new way to conquer known worlds; it is the path to creating a new kind of world for humanity, a world in which humans will continue to be a remarkably successful species—but with a new definition for what constitutes human success.

The New Success: How to Survive and Thrive in Content Nation

Social media challenges many of the fundamental ways in which people have used publishing through human history to build successful societies and civilizations. Yet at the same time, social media is a very familiar way to communicate with people. We are publishers by our very nature, collaborating with one another as peers to achieve objectives and to build social bonds using innovations in communication. With social media, though, we have gained the tools that have the potential to scale our peer-level communications to any level of human organization.

As the potential power of social media unfolds in full, our reliance on the centralized institutions that have dominated much of history's civilizations to organize ourselves for success through their publishing is likely to diminish. Through social media, people can build and maintain more-flexible bonds of trust at a personal level on a global basis that will guide us not just to surviving in a changing world but to thriving as the world offers new opportunities and challenges to us. We can now respond to such changes more rapidly, more flexibly, and more broadly as citizens of Content Nation than at any other time in human history.

It is not just individuals who are making use of social media tools to succeed in the world, though. Today's governments, enterprises, and other major organizations making use of social media will learn how to adapt themselves to a changing society and to take advantage of the full power of social media to develop new ways of succeeding. Unlike previous publishing tools, social media challenges these organizations to relate to the world in ways that traditional publishing didn't require of them. Social media in its various forms is by its nature a set of tools used for conversation, not dictation.

In many ways, social media's ability to put producers more in touch with markets on a conversational level will accelerate the development of products, services, and relationships that will meet people's needs on a global and local level. For those who master social media, there will be great rewards, but it will also challenge people to think about the inherent value of economic and social activity to human life. In other words, how does the very notion of success change when we are all connected as peers via social media?

Value in an Age of Excess and Scarcity— What Constitutes Success in the Age of Social Media?

When publishing was established as a communication tool thousands of years ago, people lived in an era of relative scarcity. Resources and finished goods were hard to obtain and to transport, often making the value of these goods relatively high. In this early era of human history the publishing that expanded the scope of organized human behaviors was key to civilization's expansion, but with limited amounts of information shared with the public through publishing, the social value of publishing was relatively limited. Success in an era of relative scarcity was largely about complying with the laws and the policies of a small group dictating large-scale social and economic structure to others through publishing.

As technology and transportation improved, mass manufacturing ushered in an era of plenty, enabling global access to a far wider array of resources and finished goods. More affordable publishing made possible by mass manufacturing enabled publishing to have a far wider social impact. Ideas, information, and experiences could be disseminated widely far more easily, though the range of new ideas was still fairly limited and filtered through central publishers. Success in the era of mass manufacturing was largely about facilitating the policies of private and public institutions that were competing to dictate large-scale changes to the social and economic structure of civilizations.

As mass manufacturing continued to grow, however, there began to be far more resources and finished goods available for consumption in developed markets than were really needed for survival. This era of excess has changed the balance of power in society as a whole as well as in publishing. Advertising arose as a vehicle to enable people to obtain what was becoming the new scarce commodity in an era of excess: people's attention and trust. At the same time, an excess of electronic and print publications made available through mass manufacturing made it increasingly difficult to reach mass markets with ever more fragmented and specialized interests. This excess of contexts in which to communicate with people, combined with a scarcity of attention and trust, has made dictating to people through centrally controlled publishers less and less efficient. Success in an era of hyper-abundance is largely about finding the right people at the right time in the right social context to get them to pay attention to the dictates of central institutions, and to trust them.

Even as much of the world suffers from too many people demanding their attention, about half of the world suffers from people paying far too little attention to them. The United Nations Human Development Report for 2007/2008 notes that about three billion people—almost half of the world's population— live on less than $2 a day. For these people, left to deal with a life of scarcity, the role of publishing remains mostly as it was thousands of years ago—publishing is a tool that others provide to communicate the dictates of socially distant central authorities.

Both for those people who suffer from overabundance and for those who suffer from extreme poverty, it would seem that traditional publishing is not helping them to build successful lives. Publishing was designed to extend social contracts to people beyond small clans that would bind them to one another as their own genes would bond them. Centralized publishing in our current time has been losing its power to forge bonds that bring people together in true social contracts. Those who have an excess of available supplies are treated by commercial enterprises using traditional publishing as "consumers," points of disposal for mass-produced goods and services, more than people who are bound together at a social level by their true needs. By contrast, those who suffer from a scarcity of supplies are considered to be disposable people, who sadly and ironically find themselves often picking through the mass-produced refuse of people disposing of the overabundance in their lives. These people are also largely divorced from any real sense of a personal social contract with central authorities through publishing.

What's missing in this model of a society driven by overabundance on the one hand and extreme scarcity in the midst of plenty on the other hand is that in both instances there is not a strong formula for widespread social bonds between people driven by highly centralized publishing. Manufacturers, governments, and other central institutions need to understand more realistically what people really need and want to be successful on a personal level; centralized publishing designed to dictate messages to the masses does not provide this insight efficiently. Calls to nationalism or to consume global mass-marketed brands that once benefited from highly centralized publishing do not ring as clearly as they did in earlier eras. The choices that were available then for social commitments that would lead someone to perceived success were far clearer and more limited.

Similarly, the everyday people of today need to understand more realistically who can enable them to meet their own needs and wants effectively on a personal level when the leading institutions of civilization seem to have left their personal interests behind, often. There should be a "win-win" equation for success that people reach through publishing that is more representative of the real-world relationships based on the kinship-like trust that it was intended to foster.

Social media is a key tool that can help people to build more effective models for successful human interactions in our current era. Social media helps people to establish personal bonds with other people seeking commercial and social success without relying on central authorities to cement that social bond formed and enhanced through publishing. The technology underlying social media services may be centralized in many instances to enable it to be highly scalable, but inherently social media is about people forming and reinforcing their relationships with people through publishing for a wide variety of purposes without intermediaries controlling how those relationships are formed at a personal level.

Through social media, the bonds that form success are no longer about just what major institutions would like them to be, but what people would choose them to be. We tell the world about our needs and wants independently; we form global personal and professional networks of relationships independently; we collaborate on building insight and achieving goals independently. Some of these relationships we establish through social media may appear to be superficial and fleeting at times, but, considering the instability of many supposedly long-term relationships, such as employment, nationality, or marriage in today's society, social media appears to offer already in many ways the means toward trusted relationships that can lead to success in our personal and professional lives over extended periods of time.

Chasing the Mammoth: Surviving and Thriving in the Contexts that Matter Most

The model for success suggested by the interactions that people have using social media publishing tools is in some ways a very old model. Social media enables people to survive and to thrive in a culture that is in some ways reminiscent of our pre-historic roots as nomads. We were hunters and gatherers in search of prey and seasonal plants. Like our ancestors chasing the woolly mammoth and other daunting animals, social media enables people to come together rapidly to collaborate for a common purpose that meets our needs in very specific contexts.

Our opportunities for success are increasingly fleeting in a rapidly changing world, making on-the-fly collaborations like those that people used to hunt down the wild prey of an earlier era all the more important. The expected rapid changes to our natural environment in the years ahead will accentuate our need for flexible, often short-lived, collaborations that make use of far-flung skills and resources to solve common problems of immense value. Civilizations used to be devised to last thousands of years under relatively stable conditions. It could be that after more than 7,000 years of experimentation with managing civilizations based on centrally controlled publishing that we are about to put that model aside and to use a new model based on social media to adapt our earlier model for human civilization to a new kind of publishing tool, a tool more in tune with our natural ability to survive and to thrive in rapidly changing environments.

Does this mean that we're all about to put on a bearskin and pick up a spear to go hunting? That's not likely, of course. Our solutions for surviving in the world have evolved; we can apply lessons from our early human history and move on with new tools that draw out the best of that distant past and the best of our present era to evolve new approaches to successful living in an era of rapidly changing social, economic, and natural conditions. Social media will enable a broad and diverse array of models for success to help people to forge the gene-like bonds of civilizations through publishing in ways that will ensure a variety of new approaches to successful living.

Instead of publishing favoring one particular model of civilization as a means for successful living, social media will enable a wider array of options for civilizations to emerge. The genes in our human bodies may not be very diverse, but with social media we have a tool that has the potential to create an enormous genetic-like diversity through publishing that will make the best use of our natural abilities as creatures that can survive and thrive in rapidly changing environments.

The formula for success in a culture driven by social media emphasizes different kinds of human attributes from those emphasized in civilizations driven by centralized publishing. Many of our attributes being highlighted by social media call upon us to remember what helped us to survive and to thrive before the rise of modern civilizations. The key elements of culture found in our ice-age ancestors that are important for success in an era of social media include the following:

- **It's about owning the moment, not owning things.** Though there were some items that were owned by individuals in ice-age culture, for the most part there was neither the time nor the inclination to focus on ownership as a survival mechanism. In a nomadic culture focused on hunting and gathering, the only thing that people really owned was the ability to exploit what they had available to them at any given moment. Maybe the mammoth would be there to hunt that day; maybe not. Your clan relied on everyone to succeed in those fleeting moments of opportunity in order to survive. Social media's ability to focus on contexts in the moment as opportunities for marketing and influence-building underscores its ability to help create high value at key moments that come and go.

- **Keep your social bonds close but flexible and scalable.** Sometimes larger groups of ice-age clans would gather to take on a large beast like a mammoth, or a group of animals. They would celebrate their success in the hunt and then return to their usual clan gatherings. Social media also encourages both close social bonds and bonds that come together rapidly to take on important but fleeting opportunities. The key attribute that social media adds in the modern era is that now anyone and everyone could be a part of a clan. This means that it becomes far more important in a culture driven by social media to share your success with others who will help you in the future.

- **Share your ideas.** In ice-age culture, it appears that the use of particular styles of tools for hunting and gathering grains was widespread. Intellectual-property rights don't appear to have been much of a bone of contention. Concepts like patents and copyright were certainly unheard of. When your survival could depend on your neighboring clans being able to help you on a moment's notice, sharing ideas for success made a lot of sense. In an era powered by social media your neighboring clans could be anyone living anywhere on the planet. Collaboration and sharing ideas widely to accelerate everyone's progress toward success therefore acts as a very important strategy for success when your survival depends on rapidly changing conditions.

- **Learn how to succeed on the move.** Though there is evidence that ice-age clans would camp in specific places for a period of time, usually people were always ready to be on the move as weather, shifting food sources, and competition from other roving clans kept their lifestyles mobile. The "where" of success wasn't as important as being in the right place at the right time to take advantage of fleeting opportunities. This was quite to the contrary of the models around which modern civilizations evolved, which assumed that stationary settlements were far more advantageous in a world of stable climate conditions. In today's era of social media, much of its growth is being powered now by people with mobile communications devices, enabling people to succeed almost anywhere at any time with help from anyone in the world. This extraordinary mobility and the increasing advantages that people are gaining from it through social media is a strategy for highly scalable success that draws on both our ice-age roots and our modern capabilities.

- **Have a strong code of conduct.** Ice-age clans were largely small autonomous social units, but they appear to have had strong codes of conduct established through generations of traditions that helped people to have a sense of firm social boundaries. These internalized codes of conduct enabled conflicts to be resolved successfully according to accepted practices with broad support from the clan community. Although known by some for their freewheeling exchanges, successful social media services work best when there are explicit social boundaries and codes of conduct that guide people toward acceptable practices, or, if one is not conforming to these practices, expulsion. These enforced social boundaries are also reinforced informally, often by members of social media services who have internalized their values. Social media allows people to succeed through explicit and implicit codes of conduct, taking advantage of people's self-interest and their appreciation of their peers to create lively and generally constructive interchanges with minimal interference.

- **Accept your vulnerabilities.** Although ice-age people had enormous strength through their power to communicate and collaborate they were still largely at the mercy of the elements, animals, competitors, and the acceptance extended to them by clan members. Modern inventions such as fortifications, or systems of stored value such as money and granaries, were not available to offer people extra security and comfort. These people relied first and foremost on their strong social connections to make the power of many people working together their strongest path to success. In a similar way, people who succeed in social media learn how to be one of many people who need one another to realize their success to its fullest extent. This requires a willingness to expose personal vulnerabilities at times, but it's a risk that often leads to successful support from people who realize that their willingness to support others willing to open themselves to a social media community is the key to their own future successes.

- **Accept regular conflict as a part of life.** Ice-age societies had conflicts constantly, usually in small skirmishes over personal issues, but often over the best resources and territory. Lawrence H. Keeley, the author of *War Before Civilization*, estimates that 87 percent of prehistoric tribal societies were at war more than once per year, and 65 percent of them were fighting continuously. Modern crime, gang conflicts, terrorism, and ongoing wars are undercurrents that remind us that regular violence remains a key part of human society. Social media will not change our genetic tendency toward war any time soon, but when the whole world has the potential to be in your tribe via social media many types of conflicts are likely to lessen. Social media encourages personal conflicts to be out in the open, expressed regularly through language and technology and moderated by the members of a publishing community. This war of words and images that builds rapidly scaled bonds of altruism is likely to help those people to succeed who choose more selectively when to resort to the weapons of last choice.
- **Leverage natural abundance, not artificial scarcity.** Though the most coveted kinds of game and crops were not always available in abundance in a particular place, for the most part the world at the end of the last ice-age period was a world of abundant resources. The struggle for resources was not about scarcity so much as making the best use of the world's abundance. It was not until humans adopted the concept of storing materials that they had gathered and hunted that artificial scarcity could be used as a means to manipulate supply and demand independent of nature. Social media has helped to make more content resources available to the world than ever before, making the most-scarce resource in the midst of this plenty: people's attention. The most successful social media services have demonstrated that enabling people to make the most of that abundance in the most valuable contexts is a strong strategy for economic success. Much of our current global economy still tries to manage artificial scarcity in the face of abundance as a means for success. Social media suggests that artificial scarcity may be a strategy for success that is not going to be effective when people can engineer diverse abundance through social media.

Using Social Media to Form Localized and Globalized Tribes

These key traits of social media that build upon both the experiences of ice-age culture and advances in modern technologies are providing us with tools to survive and to thrive in rapidly changing circumstances. With social media, we are gaining the ability to draw upon the best lessons of both ancient and modern worlds to create civilizations that conform themselves to the shape of today's rapidly changing world in a wide variety of new patterns. Traditional civilizations could count on large and relatively stable geographic groupings of people with a common heritage and ethical background to bind together altruistic extensions of tribal culture through publishing. In today's world, global migrations of populations to new nations are breaking down many of these bonds of traditional civilizations and inviting new ways to define the bonds that lead to success in society.

The trend toward global migrations of ethnic groups is found everywhere in the world, but it is perhaps most noticeable in the United States. A recent U.S. Census demographic study indicated that young minority populations, many of them recent immigrants, are beginning to emerge as the dominant ethnic grouping in many widely dispersed U.S. counties already, and not just in the large coastal cities, but in large and small communities all across the nation. Just as our ice-age ancestors sought out success through nomadism across the face of the earth, so have many people in today's shifting populations transported themselves to cultures in which their geographic origin is but one factor in determining their success and their social alliances.

Through the highly scalable communications found in social media, these modern nomads are already acting out the future's global culture, keeping in touch every day with the cultures of their origin across the world even as they learn how to participate successfully in the culture of local surroundings that are constantly on the move. A nation built on immigration and rapidly shifting social boundaries is already in place to take full advantage of the potential for success to be found in Content Nation, with the global population of Content Nation participating actively in the growth of this culture that is at once both nomadic and rooted in ancient traditions. The world may or may not look more like America as time goes on, but it is most certainly going to look more and more like Content Nation.

Success in Content Nation:
New Ways to Empower Old Models ————

Social media enables people to pick the best of old and new models for success in ways that allow us to make the most of rapidly formed bonds of altruism through highly scalable publishing. The great news is that there are so many new opportunities for success through social media—not necessarily opportunities that will benefit established institutions always, but those that promise a bright future for people everywhere. Let's take a look at some of the ways in which people have succeeded with social media, ways that challenge us to think about how we can organize ourselves for success in new and exciting ways.

Music Inside Out: The Entertainment Industry Adapts to Social Media Models

One of the first casualties of social media's rise was the music-publishing industry, which saw its sales of music CDs plummet as people discovered file sharing as a way to experience new music and new mobile devices made CDs an increasingly inconvenient format for listening to music. There is any number of reasons why music publishers are suffering, but the primary reason is that, like other institutions that relied on centralized publishing for their successes, their primary tool for ensuring profits is controlling the production and distribution of copies of content. In a world in which there are billions of devices that can copy and distribute content to anyone in the world, this model is becoming an increasingly weak engine for music-publishing success.

The other important reason that the music industry has failed, though, is that it has not managed the social aspect of music effectively. Music is, by its nature, a social experience, binding people together with common emotions and values. As music publishers focused increasingly on distributing music from a small number of highly popular artists, they lost track of the origin of most of these artists as figures in folk culture—in other words, people sharing their experiences with peers. They also lost track of the tradition of people sharing their compositions with one another, each person adapting their own take on a song from an original artist with pieces of their own experience, just as songs and folk tales traveled from the campfires of one ice-age clan to another. Ownership of the rights to things—in this instance, copyrighted sheet music and recordings—became more important than the value found in the experience of music in a given context.

Musicians who have been frustrated with the limitations of this business model are exploring many different ways to use social media as a model to succeed as professional entertainers. In March 2008, Nine Inch Nails, a popular group of rock musicians, decided to release 9 of 36 songs from its latest album for free downloading to consumers under a Creative Commons license. People could redistribute these songs for noncommercial purposes without restriction and could remix them and share their remixes as they pleased. For $5 people could buy the complete album and for $300 they could buy a special high-quality vinyl version of the album.

The promotion was a success. Millions of people downloaded the free songs from the album and shared their remixes with friends. Within a few hours the album registered more than $750,000 in sales, and $1.6 million in the first week of its release. Allowing music to be purely social allowed the commercial transaction to succeed by leveraging the social relationship established through sharing the music online. Other musicians, such as the group Radiohead, have experimented with free online music releases also, knowing that the recordings help to promote their concert appearances, from which they tend to make more money than from recording-royalty payments. Instead of trying to monetize the commoditized act of copying content, they focus on making money from the unique social experience of a live performance.

Last.fm, an online music service, leverages social media for several of its key functions, but its most important innovation is a system that enables musicians who have not signed a contract with a music publisher to receive revenues from music that is played by the members of its service. These independent musicians are able to get exposure via Last.fm's social media functions that would be impossible through commercial radio stations and music-download services, which rarely feature any music other than that released by commercial music publishers. This allows artists from around the world to build social networks of fans who share their enthusiasm for independent artists with others through Last.fm. Instead of relying on a dwindling group of large music publishers and radio stations building markets for a handful of artists around the world, Last.fm enables independent artists to build up limitless direct channels to local and global audiences who can support their creative efforts directly as a social experience. Because artists make only a small fraction of total revenues from typical CD sales anyway, eliminating unneeded distributors helps them to succeed as folk artists among peers.

CONTENT NATION SUCCESS RULE #1: *When you don't have to rely on a central publishing authority to reach a market, peers can build social bonds that create value for everyone.*

Success without Money: Commuto Brings Us Back to the Roots of Human Economies

When the new abundance at the end of the last ice age enabled clans to trade goods with one another regularly, there was no known system of money to facilitate trade. Instead, goods were bartered with trading partners based on the perceived value to those offering and asking for goods. Bartering remained an important part of many economies well into the 19th century, with currency used to acquire goods and services that could not be acquired through bartering. In an age of electronic payments bartering may seem to be an antiquated way of conducting commerce, but through social media, bartering is regaining an important foothold as a means of people exchanging goods and services that bring value to people in a community. Barter ad postings, on Craigslist and services such as Swaptree, for swapping media such as books, CDs, DVDs, and video games are exploding in popularity. If trust is the underlying emotional component of trade, then social media is enabling an explosion of trust to open up new channels for bringing value into people's lives.

A new service being developed in Toronto, Canada promises to take bartering to a new level. Commuto is designed to help people make in-person bartering exchanges, enabling people in local communities to build upon their relationship for good service with other members of the bartering community. With its Facebook application that people can add to their personal Facebook pages, Commuto can extend its barter listings into existing social media communities, enabling people to offer a new level of interaction with one another in the real world that might not be possible otherwise. When people look at social media, they may see only people sending content to one another, but the ability of bartering services such as Commuto to extend the publishing relationships that people develop via social media directly into things that they value reminds us that there are many ways that we build up value in our lives.

CONTENT NATION SUCCESS RULE #2: *Just because money doesn't always change hands through social media doesn't mean that people aren't building material success through it.*

Carrotmob: Social Media Turns Profits into Social Change

Carrotmob is the brainchild of Brent Schulkin, a Silicon Valley entrepreneur who was realizing that the profit motive could become a very powerful tool for social change through social media. Schulkin tried an experiment to test this theory that proved to be quite compelling. He chose a neighborhood in San Francisco and put out a proposition to 23 retail business owners in that area. Carrotmob would assemble a group of local residents gathered through social media channels and have them all shop on a chosen day at the store in the neighborhood that would commit the greatest percentage of their profits for the day to making their stores more energy-efficient. Stores bid against one another to get the "mob" that Carrotmob was willing to send. The highest bidder was willing to commit 22 percent of their profits for the day to energy-efficiency improvements.

On the Saturday of the event about 300 people attracted to the store by Carrotmob streamed in and proceeded to buy lots of merchandise—about twice the merchant's estimates and about four times its normal income for a Saturday. The 22 percent from that day's income was more than enough to pay for the energy. Just a little effort from social media and a cause that a community supported seemed to have motivated someone to change how they managed their business—through the profit motive.

CONTENT NATION SUCCESS RULE #3: *Social media's promotion of community values can motivate people to take action that can help everyone in that community to succeed.*

LocalHarvest: Bringing Community Buyers and Sellers Together through Subscriptions

In an era of mass-produced food distributed globally, many farmers find that they need to be able to compete on more than price alone to make a good living. One of the solutions that some farmers have used is to penetrate local markets more effectively. This is not always easy in places where major supermarkets dominate food sales with high-volume goods.

LocalHarvest is a service that offers people across the U.S. the opportunity to connect with local farmers and markets that provide high-quality produce and meats. People can use the social media features of LocalHarvest to connect with these community suppliers on a personal basis, but they can also opt for a subscription relationship with a specific farm in their local area. A subscriber typically commits to a seasonal subscription to support the farm, which in return provides regular access to its output. LocalHarvest provides members the opportunity to rate and review suppliers and offers suppliers the ability to display their available products and to communicate with existing and prospective customers.

Offering subscriptions is an old idea that is finding many new uses through social media. Where subscriptions were used mostly for delivering content in centralized publishing models, the highly scalable global distribution capabilities of the Web have enabled subscription services to tie together buyers and sellers in communities that can build relationships with one another through social media to form and enhance their bonds with one another and with their community. Social media can enable these types of personal commitments to unfold at a scale large enough that can help niche businesses to thrive with a committed clientele, while helping their clients to feel that the bonds of altruism that were formed through publishing are as much about bringing people together into a network of committed community relationships as they are about getting goods and services. Sometimes the communities that help people to succeed through social media are global; sometimes they are local. Either way the Big Sombrero economy promises returns on personal investments that can easily overshadow traditional corporate approaches to meeting a market's needs.

CONTENT NATION SUCCESS RULE #4: *Highly profitable long-lasting relationships can be built through social media that can enable communities to succeed together.*

Kiva and MicroPlace: Building Small Businesses Globally through Person-to-Person Lending

Small entrepreneurs who are very poor have limited access to funds to help their businesses succeed, with traditional banks focused on major investment projects and few other options to raising financing to make a very small business more successful. In recent years the concept of microcredit was popularized by people such as Muhammad Yunus, who won the Nobel Peace Prize in 2006 for his work in establishing microloans from Micro-Financial Institutions (MFIs) as a form of investment for poor individuals in nations around the world. Microloan repayment levels have been very high—some claiming as high as 97 percent—and have already helped more than 100 million people worldwide. Online social media services have taken on an important role in attracting people with money to invest in this concept.

In the instance of Kiva and MicroPlace, two social media Web sites established to support MFIs, people get to know individuals who need microloans through their personal profiles and through journals kept by MFI managers. The managers learn about the needs of people in their communities who need microloans to grow their businesses. Kiva was the pioneer in this effort, inspired by the work of Muhammed Yunus and Grameen Bank, who were early proponents of microloans, but the acquisition of MicroPlace by eBay in 2006 enabled them to start offering investors in microloans modest returns on their microloan investments—about what one would expect from a low-interest savings account, but a true return on an investment nevertheless.

Although more financing is still required to enable these tiny businesses in the hands of poor people to grow into larger, more successful businesses, the social media Web sites that promote microloans play a critical role in getting people to rethink how they invest in society. Traditionally most people give money to charities to help poor people and then place their private investment money into funding major companies or public institutions. Social media helps to extend the concept of investment into person-to-person relationships with people in their own nations and in nations around the world, facilitating economic growth while helping people who become part of their own social fabric. This is an old concept that has been swept aside in many economies, but one that can be brought back to life via social media's ability for us to see how our small investments enable real, everyday people to succeed.

CONTENT NATION SUCCESS RULE #5: *Social media helps people to invest in the human fabric that makes economies and societies work.*

Rethinking How Companies Work: How Collaboration Tools Can Change Basic Work Patterns

You would think that an advertising agency would be by its nature a highly collaborative enterprise, with people devising creative strategies for their clients' problems. That may happen in a lot of ad agencies, but it doesn't happen by accident, and it doesn't always happen when you don't have the right approach to publishing in place. Unit 7, a relatively small advertising and market strategy agency in New York City, was having problems with its productivity. "The creative side was invisible here," noted Joe Gupani, the firm's creative director, in a recent case study by Cisco Systems, Inc. Unit 7 engaged the services of Marsha Shenk, a business anthropologist, who pointed out to Unit 7 that their sales and marketing staff was separated from their creative staff, who were separated often from discussions with clients. Ideas from both clients and staff that could have flowed into one another were being lost.

Today, Unit 7 ensures that members of the creative staff are a part of client meetings and uses technologies from Cisco that enable team members to collaborate using social media publishing tools. Innovative ideas that come from junior staff members get the same kind of exposure as ideas from senior staff through social media's peer-oriented publishing environment, which in turn combine with input from clients and suppliers in the collaborative publishing environment to keep everyone on the same page in the same framework. Unit 7 productivity and sales have improved dramatically as a result of including social media technologies, but more importantly, social media has helped to form a foundation for ensuring an ongoing cultural shift in their organization. Even in relatively small organizations, social media can help to power more effective communications.

Hierarchies serve a purpose, but in general managing communications among people serving and served by hierarchical organization leads inevitably to filtered communications, miscommunications, and lost communications when information bounces up and down chains of command within an organization. Yet in spite of this, many organizations spend billions of dollars every year trying to improve communications in their organization without adopting the fundamental concept of allowing people to publish information to their entire organization as peers. Social media will not eliminate hierarchies, but its ability to build value in working relationships independent of hierarchies will reward organizations that are able to reduce their reliance on hierarchically controlled publishing with greater productivity and better client relationships.

CONTENT NATION SUCCESS RULE #6: *Reducing the control of hierarchies over publishing through social media allows problems and solutions to be identified more quickly and effectively.*

Ford Models: Turning Any Brand into a Conversational Brand through Social Media

Ford Models is one of the world's top agencies providing fashion models and professional services for advertisers and clothes designers from offices in major cities around the world. Though a powerhouse in its own right, the decline of print as a medium for attracting younger audiences has posed a problem as to how Ford would manage its future. Major brands use their models and services to support their own marketing, but how would Ford establish the value of its models in an online environment when millions of fresh faces are available for people to look at every day?

Part of Ford Models' response to the challenge of online content is to build its own media brand through social media services. Equipping its models and staff with video cameras, Ford posts content online that carries the Ford brand and that enables the models to chat informally about clothing brands and other key products in an informal, conversational style similar to videos uploaded to

the Web by everyday people. This allows them to use Ford Models as a brand that can help to endorse the brands that are featured in their videos—in effect creating their own channel focused on fashion and glamour that does not rely on others to leverage the value of their brand directly with audiences. On the YouTube video service, the Ford Models channel is one of the top 100 most subscribed-to video channels and regularly ranks in the top 20 of YouTube branded channels visited every day, with comments from YouTube's audience providing valuable feedback.

It helps to have a service that lends itself to video presentation easily, but the Ford Models experience is an important reminder than any brand could be a very effective media brand if it provides content regularly through social media that engages its target audience effectively. Though product placements or direct endorsements in social media can help to strengthen the aware-ness of a brand, it's the ability to present people in their natural surround-ings doing what they do naturally that creates the strongest brand appeal for enterprises trying to build relationships with a marketplace through social media. As much as the Ford Models brand has been about glamour marketed to professionals, it is now becoming successful as a brand that knows how to market itself directly through the informal, conversational appeal of its talent to everyday people. If anyone can become glamorous online, then it may as well be you.

David Meerman Scott: Thought Leadership as a Personal Brand

Although major companies such as Ford Models have been able to build brands with personal appeal through social media, individuals have created their own very effective personal brands through careful management of their publishing through social media. David Meerman Scott was a well-respected professional in online publishing and public relations several years ago, but he wanted to create a market niche for his speaking and consulting services that would stand out from others. The key to David's success turned out to be a multi-layered social media strategy that catapulted his career into a global profile. His Web Ink Now weblog allowed him to write about his take on key insights into best practices for online marketing in a breezy, easy-to-read style that attracted subscribers to his newsletter compiled from weblog entries.

These channels for conversational content proved to be a great launch-ing point for offering free e-books written by David that focused on his key professional focus. Bolstered by these successes, David was able to start landing book deals, speaking engagements at major conferences, and seminars focused on his key topics, all promoted in his weblog and through other social media available on his blog. Today, David Meerman Scott's books have skyrocketed into international business bestsellers and he speaks around the world to business gatherings and conferences—having turned a good career into a highly successful career through learning how to turn his personal brand into a high-performance brand through social media. With social media any professional or even someone very enthusiastic about their avocation can focus on the right tools to build their insights into influential content that can build profitable relationships.

Twittering Mars: NASA Learns How to Turn an Interplanetary Science Project into a Conversational Brand

The U.S. National Aeronautics and Space Administration has launched several major unmanned probes to study planets in our solar system, many of which have had their moments of media glory as they have sent back compelling photos and scientific data. After a few fleeting moments of fame, most of these scientific experiments disappeared from the media spotlight, a problem for a government agency trying to keep up its funding during times of intense political pressures to hold down its budget. An important effort in brand-building through social media used an unlikely channel to promote an unlikely candidate for success through social media.

NASA's Mars Phoenix probe landed near the polar regions of the planet Mars in May 2008, a huge success in itself but one that exposed a new problem—how to generate excitement and awareness about the mission for a probe that was stationary and could relay little of new visual interest once it had landed. Mars Phoenix's primary mission is to scoop up samples of soil and ice and to analyze its composition using equipment inside the probe. This wasn't the kind of mission where the machine itself could generate much appeal. The unlikely solution to this awareness problem came through NASA's use of the Twitter messaging service. Twitter is able to broadcast short text messages and Web page links to people who choose to follow them using PCs, mobile phones, and other Web-enabled devices.

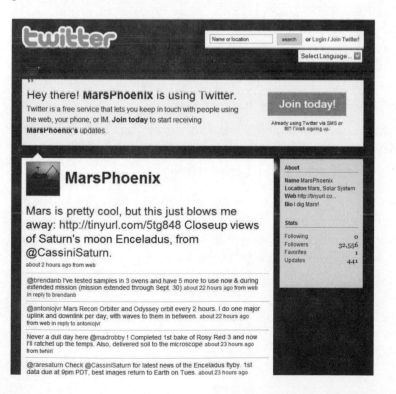

NASA team members set up a Twitter account for Mars Phoenix and began to send out short conversational text messages telling people what they were doing and seeing with the probe at the moment. Instead of formal press releases distributing information about a stationary device millions of miles away, Mars Phoenix had a voice and a community of personalities pumping out regular conversational updates that helped their science to get in the flow of the conversations of influencers following Twitter messages. In just a few short weeks, more than 32,000 people were following the moment-by-moment exploits of the Mars Phoenix probe and its team members. Sometimes you can have scientific measurements that tell you that you're a successful mission, but with social media even a lifeless machine can build a successful brand with a chatty personality.

In ice-age society, there was no such thing as brands as we know them today. Brands were more equivalent to clan members whose reputation became widely known over time by storytelling and word-of-mouth influence. With the rise of centralized publishing, though, major institutions were able to broadly project their power to the masses through their own branded content, pictograms, flags, family coat of arms, and, eventually corporate brands. Social media is helping to return brand-building back to its roots by enabling anyone to build their own highly scalable reputation rapidly. Whoever scales their reputation to their audience most effectively through conversational marketing will become the most powerful brand in social media.

CONTENT NATION SUCCESS RULE #7: *In social media anything and anyone that people relate to strongly can become its own brand.*

Expression for Everyone: Keitai Novels Use Mobile Phones to Create Popular Literature

Reading on mobile devices has been extremely popular in Japan for some time, but a newer phenomenon is people creating literature on their mobile phones. Everyday people are creating *keitaishosetsu*, or mobile-phone novels, often on their way to work, or wherever it suits them. They post their content on Web sites where people can read the evolving books online, but they are also becoming extremely popular in print form. It is estimated that currently about half of Japan's in-print fiction books are originating as mobile-phone novels, with the most popular titles selling hundreds of thousands of copies. Half of the top 10 Japanese fiction titles in print in 2007 originated as *keitai* novels.

The people writing these novels are no literary masters: one of the most popular "thumb novels" was written by a nursery- school teacher from Kokura, a community far away from Tokyo's bustling national media scene. People find these novels to be compelling anyway, perhaps because they are the unfiltered storytelling of people like themselves. Thinking of our ice-age ancestors, stories told around campfires did not pass through formal editors and distributors before making the rounds from one clan to another. Everyone contributed their own little piece to the storytelling circle, with popular tales being told again and again and embellished over time as they were passed along. Social media is enabling the ancient art of popular storytelling to be returned to everyday people—people who can now invite an entire nation or the whole world into their storytelling circle. With social media, our natural ability to succeed as communicators is regaining its central focus in human culture.

CONTENT NATION SUCCESS RULE #8: *In social media anyone who knows how to influence their peers can succeed on any scale.*

Challenges to Success: Where Social Media Creates New Exposures

Social media is empowering everyday people as well as the powerful to succeed as never before in human history, but that doesn't mean that it's a style of communication that's always well-liked or well-understood by people encountering its power. To many people social media is a threat to established forms of communication, empowering groups of people who create more competition for their own messages. To others, the novelty of being a publisher is something that creates challenges as to how to live in a world where people are constantly in the public eye through social media. Part of the success story of social media, then, is learning how to feel comfortable as a person who lives a relatively public life as a publisher.

Some people respond to the challenge of being a public publisher by adopting online identities and personalities that are very different from their real-world personalities, using pseudonyms and online graphics to project an artificial representation of themselves—an avatar—the way that some people might assume a role in a play or a movie. Many people create these hidden online identities for fun, whereas some, such as journalists, assume a pseudonym to protect their sources of factual materials. There are some people, though, who assume false identities for malicious purposes, either to satisfy their personal motivations or because they're paid by someone seeking to create a positive or a negative sentiment that's supposed to appear as if it came from a genuine person. People using false identities in social media to spread malicious content are sometimes called "trolls," reminding us that like the nasty mythic trolls of fairy tales, sometimes people consider socially negative goals as their version of success. Social media does not make us perfect humans; it is only a tool to express whatever is human in us.

Fantasy and hidden identities can play important roles in online publishing, but for the most part they are balanced against the more powerful opportunity to experience success as a publisher who promotes his or her own personal interests and own brand value as a person who knows how to represent themselves to others as a trusted person. Deception is not a great way to build one's ability to be a trusted person who can influence others. Deception can get people to react to our fears and our unspoken desires, but deception as a tool for influencing people is far less powerful in a society in which anyone can state the truth to the world easily. Social media gives people the power to enable anyone to tell everyone what things are really like in an influential way that allows others to value them for the truth that they provide. In the face of such global honesty, deception and negative techniques used to influence people has limited value at best.

Lonelygirl15: Acting Can be Powerful, but it's Still Just Acting

In June of 2006 a stream of webcam-recorded videos featuring a person who identified herself with the YouTube account name lonelygirl15 made its debut on the Web. The videos featured a young woman calling herself Bree sitting on the edge of her bed and other informal settings talking about her life and her relationships as a sixteen-year-old girl and about increasingly bizarre twists in her life. The videos became popular very quickly, generating more than 100 million views of her stories in the two years that lonelygirl15 was talking to the world through a webcam.

There was just one little problem with lonelygirl15: she wasn't real. In September 2006 it was revealed that Bree was a fictitious character played by Jessica Rose, a then nineteen-year-old actress who had agreed to play the part of Bree for a couple of aspiring video producers. The revealing of the hoax by lonelygirl15's producers was prompted in large part by YouTube member comments that pointed out odd inconsistencies in the videos that made it doubtful that they were an everyday person's own tales. The lonelygirl15 series of videos continued to be highly popular nevertheless for about two years before production ceased. The producers of lonelygirl15 and Jessica Rose have moved on to produce other online video stories revolving around the fictional world created for the lonelygirl15 series, creating new dramas that are in part like personal storytelling and in part like traditional media storytelling.

It's easy to forget that publishing original fictional stories is a relatively new concept: Daniel Defoe's *Robinson Crusoe*, a story about a castaway on a desert island that is recognized widely as the first novel written in English, was not published until 1719. Folk tales, poetry, and other original works of fiction were created largely by everyday people before that time, most of them long forgotten and only a handful surviving through publishing and folk traditions. Storytelling is a natural human trait that publishing enabled to be carried into fictional settings of all kinds. In some ways lonelygirl15 has become the *Robinson Crusoe* of social media, surprising people with a new kind of storytelling adapted to a powerful new medium.

Yet in some ways the lonelygirl15 phenomenon was a failure as much it was a success. People were identifying with Bree as a real person. Once it was clear that she was not a real person, her power to lend personal influence and endorsement to others withered away, a deception not unlike Orson Welles' famous radio play *The War of the Worlds* that captured people's imagination in a then-new medium on the evening before Halloween in October, 1938. Many people tuning into the radio broadcast of the play thought that the world was really being attacked by creatures from the planet Mars. People saw this as something frighteningly real for only a moment and then sank back into accepting the play as entertainment typical for those times.

Jessica Rose remains a relatively obscure actress, in many ways locked in to her lonelygirl15 fame as much as many other character actors and actresses who become too strongly identified with their roles in highly popular television shows. The lonelygirl15 phenomenon should remind us that although fictional worlds can be attractive as a means of escaping our everyday lives for a short time, trying to deceive people as to what is real and what is not real is not a very strong strategy for constructive success in social media.

CONTENT NATION SUCCESS RULE #9: *Honesty about your intentions and motives is essential to building a successful reputation in social media.*

Life in the Fish Bowl: Learning How to Be Public in the Social Media Era

Being real and honest is of great benefit in social media, but being real and honest in social media is not always without real consequences. Many people who are honest about their personal thoughts and tastes through their personal publishing discover only later that there is an entire world that is able to see what someone is doing online through social media. An interesting example of this happened recently when it was reported that a young intern at a major bank in North America told his boss in an email that he would be absent from work one day due to a "family emergency."

His Facebook-savvy boss, though, discovered a freshly posted picture of his intern at a costume party that was held that day, and emailed a copy of the photo to everyone in his office. This email in turn made the rounds on the Web to other people and eventually made its way to prominent weblogs, making the intern's public publishing all the more a public event. It's also fairly common now for people who are applying for jobs to discover that prospective employers may not take kindly to some of the materials that they have posted on social media Web sites. For a generation of young people used to being very open and honest about their personal lives through social media, their often-blended personal and work lives are requiring them to think about how to have both social and professional success as an adult in a world that is very aware of them through social media.

As much as employers are watching social media to understand their employees more clearly, they are also discovering that their own companies and executives are in the social media spotlight. Web sites such as Glassdoor.com enable people to share anonymously what it's like to work inside their organizations and what their senior managers are like.

glassdoor.com^beta
See what everyone are saying
Find: Ratings & Reviews | Company Name | Search
Sign In | Help | Feedback
Home | Ratings & Reviews | Salaries | How It Works | Post a Review or Salary

An inside look at companies from those who know them best.
See company ratings, reviews, and salaries. Membership is free.

Here's how to get started:
Tell your story. It's anonymous.
Give everyone an inside look at what it's really like to work at your company.

We're Just Getting Started
We've already heard from over 50,000 employees at more than 11,000 companies in 80 countries, but we need your help to keep growing. Post your review or salary, tell your friends, and/or join our employer advisors panel.

1. Contribute an employer review or salary report.
2. Save your information to a *free* and *anonymous* account.
3. Get full access to the reviews and salaries shared by our community.

[Get Started]

Ratings and Reviews
See what employees are saying

JPMorgan Chase preview
"Satisfied"
3.5
based on 100 reviews

CEO Rating:
Jamie Dimon
75% "Approve"

A JPMorgan Chase User Experience Design Lead said:
Pros: "The financial industry isn't exactly the most stable place to be right now, but JPMorgan Chase has made good decisions in rocky times. They're in a better situation than their competitors, to the point where they can actually bail out other failing..."
Read the Whole Review

Google preview
"Very Satisfied"
4.1
based on 125 reviews

CEO Rating:
Eric E. Schmidt
86% "Approve"

A Google said:
Cons: "If you enjoy your individuality and time alone, Google is not the place for you (keep in mind I'm not an engineer). Google pushes a highly 'googley' atmosphere, ... like if they lived in."
Read the Whole Review

Salaries
See where you stack up

Deloitte Tax Consultant	$61,000
Accenture Analyst	$57,000
Accenture Systems Integration Consultant	$76,000
Google Software Engineer	$96,000
Deloitte Senior Consultant	$96,000
Accenture Senior Manager	$143,000
JPMorgan Chase Investment Banking Analyst	$60,000
Google Product Manager	$121,000

These employee reviews of company cultures are quite unflattering sometimes, but even when they are, their honesty can surface some constructive suggestions. An analyst at a major consulting firm notes of their company on Glassdoor.com, "Stop looking for big projects, which are stretching company resources past breaking point.…But [most] importantly, start listening to your employees. Ever since you went public, you stopped listening." So even if an enterprise thinks that its image as a successful company can be projected in a particular way, social media has the power to let people know whether people think that they're really successful as an organization. The anonymity of such a service always carries with it the dangers of malicious intent, but overall it allows people to tell the truth about their work lives to their peers without fear of reprisals.

The openness of social media is a challenge to organizations from around the world to manage their affairs with the knowledge that anyone could speak the truth to the world about what they are really doing and who is involved in doing it. Many Web sites have sprung up in recent years to facilitate the leaking of sensitive documents and information from governments, companies, and other organizations, whose private operations are unknown to the public.

Wikileaks is a social media service has become one of the world's most notable sources for anonymously sourced leaks of facts and documents. Anonymous sources are used widely in major news organizations to reveal sensitive facts, but with Wikileaks, information is made available that commercially supported news outlets might be hesitant to share with the world. This approach to openness among peers can be threatening to many organizations, including those with the power to fight back. In 2008 a whistleblower leaked documents to Wikileaks.org from the Julius Baer Bank and Trust Co., a Cayman Islands division of Swiss-owned Bank Julius Baer AG, that revealed alleged improprieties in the bank's operations and management. Bank Julius Baer retaliated by getting a U.S. court to compel the company providing the technology for the Wikileaks Web site to shut it down. The court's order was rescinded shortly thereafter, but in the meantime other Web sites that provide leaked documents were willing to make the controversial documents available on the Web. Although some governments are willing to block access to controversial content, in general the worldwide publishing capabilities provided by social media make it hard for facts to be suppressed if there's a willingness to reveal them.

CONTENT NATION SUCCESS RULE #10: *In a world where anyone can publish anything to everyone, those who succeed by being open with others will prevail.*

Toward an Open Source Civilization: The Future of Content Nation

Does the rise of social media mean that we are losing our privacy forever? Probably not. People who want to keep confidences will always find ways to do so, but social media changes the value of privacy in a world that is tending to reward people who are learning how to succeed by being themselves in a more public world. Highly centralized publishing tends to reward those who can filter and control the truth to make their version of the truth the one that is most advantageous to themselves. In a sense, centralized publishing tends to create an artificial scarcity of the truth, just as centralized distribution of goods tends to lead to artificial scarcity of these materials. When the power to survive and thrive tends to come from openness rather than privacy, though, people tend to focus more on solving the problems of real scarcity than on exploiting artificial scarcity.

The shift toward social interactions based on openness that is being facilitated by social media will be crucial to the future success of humankind as we begin to shift from an era of human-engineered excesses to an era in which our ability to respond to natural scarcity arising from rapidly changing conditions will become the leading factor in our ability to survive and thrive. We will have to be willing to rethink our concept of what is the most productive way forward as a society. The more people who own a part of a solution to a key challenge to human survival, the more people will be available to help us to find the next solution to the next problem. The potential "gene pool" of tools built through human intellect will be broadened to ensure that we have the widest range of options in choosing our path to survival and prosperity. When our clan built through social media includes potentially anyone in the world, the world as a whole will tend to win.

Social media facilitates this kind of global problem-solving the way that open source software helps to create more value for more people more rapidly in many instances than proprietary software. With open source software, a computer program, such as an operating system, is developed on a voluntary basis by people who want the software to be as good as possible for both their own purposes and for the purpose of contributing to the success of others. People are usually free to use and to modify open source software for their own purposes as long as the authors of the original software are acknowledged and as long as any copies of the modified software that are distributed to others are also made available for their use and modification without a fee.

You would think that open source software would lead to commercial failures, but in fact, open source software has been the backbone of many large-scale successes. It's estimated that more than 70 percent of the computers in the world running Web sites are using open source software to operate the core functions of those computers. This has freed up an enormous amount of capital for investment in other functions that have added a tremendous amount of value to the electronic publishing process. Instead of people investing in the mass production of similar things, open source software has encouraged people to invest in the mass production of unique things. This enables people to spend their most valuable resources on diverse and autonomous solutions built around a common core of mass-scale solutions that are available to everyone.

If publishing defines the genes that form a society, then the openness enabled by social media is enabling humankind to move toward a major mutation in society's genes. Social media is leading us toward an open source society, one in which our ability to collaborate openly as individuals on our most fundamental needs for survival will allow us to focus on a diverse array of unique solutions that will help us to thrive. Our path to success will be through combining our commonness as humans with our widespread uniqueness through social media. Social media will allow us to work both as an open and highly integrated society through commonly available social media publishing technologies and standards, and as a highly diverse and overlapping set of societies that leverage those social media tools to create more specialized value globally and locally. We will still gain from supporting the mass value of the crown of the Big Sombrero economy, but most of our personal and financial successes will be found under the edges of that sombrero, supporting unique value on a smaller scale that adds up massively. We will become a true Content Nation, ready to act as one global people for our common success and also ready to act as just everyday people influencing other everyday people for our highly scalable personal successes.

The Joy of Publishing Is the Joy of Being Human

The beauty of society moving toward the model of Content Nation is that it encourages everyday people to experience success by just being themselves.

We don't need to be massively similar in our thoughts and actions to succeed massively, nor do we need to be extraordinary people. We can be relatively ordinary and enjoy how our shared uniqueness can create new common value globally or locally. We will reap the rewards available through mass production but avoid surrendering our most valuable human traits to its processes. We will participate in society as an organism that responds to our collective leadership and insight and that also allows us to express our individual humanness in unique and valuable ways. We will unite to chase the mammoths of the day's great challenges, celebrate our successes, and then go back to whatever pattern of life suits us best. We will be one when we need to be one, many when we need to be many, all at a moment's notice.

The success of video producer Matt Harding is perhaps one of the best illustrations of the joy that comes from this model of Content Nation. His unique, lighthearted videos have been seen by tens of millions of people worldwide. Who is Matt Harding? No one. Anyone. Through his videos, someone who is anywhere and everywhere, with anyone and everyone, is doing nothing of great importance that requires no great skill, just for the joy of doing it. Matt just does the same goofy little dance again and again in front of his video camera, pumping his arms up and down and trotting in place, like a little boy trying to get someone's attention as best he knows how.

Matt dances alone. Matt dances with others. Matt dances in Mumbai, India. Matt dances in Bhutan. Matt dances in Ireland, Kuwait, Mexico, and Iceland.

Matt dances with crowds of people in Spain, France, Madagascar, Argentina, and Australia. Matt dances with headhunters in Papua, New Guinea. Matt dances with schoolchildren in Mali, Yemen, Zambia, and Fiji. Matt dances with a border guard at the demilitarized zone between North and South Korea. Matt dances in Japan, Texas, and Florida. Almost everywhere that Matt goes the world dances along with him in the same simple, silly way.

And why not? It's fun. It's easy. It comes naturally. It's harmless. It makes you laugh. It makes you human. It makes you part of all of humanity without giving up your unique humanness.

It's publishing—the thing that makes us who we are as a human society united by our citizenship in Content Nation. With social media at our universal command, the joy of publishing has returned us at last to the joy of surviving and thriving just by being our most true and human selves. Our success as publishers through social media has become the success of humanity itself, ready to begin a new epoch of our evolving history.

10 The New Epoch: Life in a Future Built on Content Nation

When I was a young man I was, like many young people: not all that interested in history. I knew a fair amount about my own young nation's history, to be sure, and I had gained a decent appreciation of the world's history in high school and college, but I was very much a person focused on modern times. Today was the time that I cared about most.

When I got married, though, my wife and I decided to spend our honeymoon traveling through England and nearby Wales. Within a few hours of stepping off of a thoroughly modern jet plane we found ourselves in Westminster Cathedral in London, looking at the graves and memorials of famous people such as Sir Isaac Newton, Winston Churchill, and William Shakespeare. All of a sudden these people existed for me in a way that I had never imagined before. They weren't just names in a book or people in photos or paintings; they were real. A couple of days later we were standing in the 12th-century Christ Church Cathedral in Oxford, then amidst the ruins of Tintern Abbey, then walking through the ancient fortifications of Tenby, and then before a 7th-century Celtic cross south of Cardigan marked with the runes of an ancient language. We were spiraling back in history, seeing and touching time that had passed by and that was yet still real.

These were all very important experiences, but none of them were quite as important to me as a cool and cloudy afternoon that brought us to a quiet and remote field far up into the hills of Wales, past foggy fields dotted with Welsh ponies chewing away at their grass quietly. We got out of our car at a spot that we hoped was the right place to park and began walking down a narrow, grassy path toward a clearing in a field. There beneath the clearing skies stood Pentre Ifan, the stone remains of what is believed to be a burial chamber more than 5,000 years old.

Very little is known about the origins of Pentre Ifan except that it was erected by people whose culture probably bore more resemblance to their ice-age ancestors from 5,000 years before their time than to our own culture 5,000 years later. In touching these stones I was touching the origins of humankind. All that remains of significance at Pentre Ifan are the massive stones that formed the outlines of the burial chamber: very little else has survived through the ages. The stones stand silent, as silent as our own culture might stand 10,000 years from now. We know that they were erected by humans, but we understand only dimly their humanness.

What will be the future for our own humanness? What will be the signs that we leave for others to consider about our own civilization 10,000 or 20,000 years from now? It is a question whose ultimate answer is probably as dimly understood to us as are the stones at Pentre Ifan. Like the people who erected this memorial in the hills of Wales, our culture is not really based on permanence. As humans, we erect memorials and other great structures that declare our desire for permanence, yet even when structures created by great civilizations survive from the dawn of civilization, the cultures that created them are long gone.

So it is with publishing, the code that created civilization. We assume that publishing will live on, modified by trends such as social media, yet enduring as the encoding of our culture indefinitely. History, though, would seem to disagree with this assumption, as would our encoding as living creatures. From a historical standpoint none of the large, centralized civilizations that arose only 5,000 to 7,000 years ago based on publishing have endured as they were in that era.

Large civilizations each claim to be made to last for thousands of years, but in spite of the power of publishing to unite people in civilizations, they are in general passing phenomena. By contrast the coding in our own genes is designed for only two key concerns: how to survive our own time on earth and how to select a mate to create another generation. We extend these short-term goals to other entities such as civilizations through altruism, but we are ourselves incapable of living the thousands of years that our civilizations would like to last.

The Social Media Epoch: Publishing Rescaled for New Evolution

So you might say that using centralized publishing as a code for the organism of civilization has created a paradox: we create civilizations with a structure defined through publishing that can live for many centuries, but the length of those civilizations fails to turn over new "genetic" code quickly enough to adapt to new circumstances. It turns out that humans, who live less than a century, typically, are too involved in the goals of their own mortality to design immortal civilizations very well.

By contrast, nature does an excellent job of designing species—natural civilizations, if you will—that can last for millions of years and more. In 1999 scientists at West Chester University in Pennsylvania isolated and stimulated the growth of a species of bacteria more than 250 million years old. The coelacanth, an order of fish more than 400 million years old, was thought to have been extinct for 80 million years, but small pockets of recent species of the fish have been found to exist in isolated, stable climates. Many of today's modern shark species have been in existence for at least 150 million years.

If nature can do such a great job of building species that can survive with just natural genes at their disposal, perhaps we should take a tip from nature and do what we have been reluctant to do with civilization: *let new breeds of civilizations based on new models of publishing compete for survival*. The 10,000 or so years since the rise of post ice-age civilizations is but a blink of an eye in terms of the long-term evolution of species, but few living creatures in those species have a life cycle of more than several years. Perhaps the key to enabling civilizations to survive the ages is not to try to build great longer-lived civilizations that attempt to conform humans and nature into a large, long-lived organism, but rather to build shorter-lived civilizations that are more readily adapted to changes and more likely to produce diversity that will survive through radical changes in nature and society.

In other words, if social media looks chaotic and random at times in its evolution as a publishing tool, maybe that's a good thing. With a tool that can create unity out of diversity at a moment's notice, and that can allow diverse people with a unified focus to sustain productive relationships over long distances and long periods of time, perhaps social media's strength is that in many ways it doesn't resemble the "genes" of traditional publishing all that much. With social media, patterns of successful collaboration will come and go, but in doing so, humans will succeed intensely while those patterns last, without having the baggage of commitments to long-term civilizations that keep people invested in survival patterns that will no longer work well.

In adapting human civilization to social media as a default communications medium we may open up humans to new patterns of evolution. The coelacanth found success over millions of years in specialized, stable habitats where this particular kind of fish did very well, while sharks have succeeded in almost all parts of the world with a simple but flexible survival strategy. Perhaps the diversity found in social media will enable new kinds of cultural diversity to emerge that will allow for our success through many different kinds of survival techniques. Instead of looking at pyramids or the stones of Pentre Ifan in 20,000 years for clues as to what humans were like, perhaps we will have to look no further than our own genes. Our ability to survive with a particular form of publishing will tell the tale of what our civilizations were all about.

How will humans and our societies evolve as social media competes to define the genes of civilization? What will our world look like through the lens of publishing tools in fifty years? A hundred years? A thousand years? Ten thousand years? We can only speculate, of course, but in doing so we may find patterns that will inform us as to what the full potential power of social media may be for us in the very near future. Let's take a look at what the future might look like as social media makes inroads into defining our work and our lives in a new epoch of human existence. The scenarios that I am about to lead you through are not meant to be a prophecy or the thoughts of a seasoned futurist, but rather some of the logical conclusions that we can draw from the trends already evident in the explosive growth of social media. That said, I think you will see that the impact of social media will be far more pervasive than many have considered so far.

Fifty Years from Now: Success, Turmoil, and Transition

It is dawn at the home of Georges Cadoret, an architect living in the Provence region of southern France. Cadoret has a successful career with clients all over the world, many of whom he has maintained contact with through social media tools since he was at his university. On a daily basis, though, he works from home and keeps in touch with people in his village. Like many homes in this sunny region, his roof is lined with highly efficient solar panels, which create most of his electricity by day and which also power a fuel cell that splits water into hydrogen and oxygen during the day and recombines them in the evening to generate electricity. France has been phasing out its nuclear power plants as locally sourced power and power from Africa's giant solar arrays in the Sahara have reduced their cost-effectiveness.

Inexpensive and abundant electricity has begun to transform the world of communications in many parts of the world in which Cadoret does business. Africa in particular has seen a great change as it has become the world's number-one producer of electricity, followed by China, Australia, and the United States. Villages throughout Africa are now powered and have access to Web-enabled mobile communications networks that have brought information and learning to them from around the world. The cost of computing power and communications networks has dropped radically, providing most everyone in the world the ability to communicate with anyone affordably, including people in small villages throughout Africa.

Mobile communications networks flourish everywhere in Africa, in many instances powered by local communities that maintain their own networks as a public service. Villages can communicate with other nearby villages instantly at virtually no cost, increasing local collaboration on key issues, and closer social and political ties. Education is soaring and small farm productivity is on the rise in many countries once isolated from the world, thanks in part to access to global microcapital investors.

Cadoret shuffles out of bed on a sunny day and gets ready to shower. "*Notre zique,*" he says out loud before turning on the water. His home's electronic communications system starts playing songs popular with his social networking groups, including selections from local musicians and his friends around the world. Whenever he listens to a song the artist is paid a small royalty fee by his music subscription service, whether or not the artist is a professional musician. This system has allowed millions of musicians to gain enough popularity from small groups of people around the world to make a decent living. Music publishers as we have known them no longer exist; worldwide access to all music, and most content in general, is a given. The publishers have turned into events producers, packaging the most popular acts rising up from social media for large-scale public appearances.

Cadoret likes one particular song and says, "*sauvez.*" His home communications system saves information about the song to Cadoret's personal online profile. Later that evening he and his wife will be entertaining friends; he wants them to experience a holographic concert by these musicians after dinner along with some of his friends in South Africa and Norway. It will be nice to see everyone together again, he muses, well worth the extra price of this service. Most public spaces are equipped with holographic services as well, enabling merchants to present information about their wares in person and instructors from Paris to tutor Cadoret's children sitting "next" to them.

Before having breakfast, Cadoret opens the door to his home and picks up his personal newspaper for the morning. Yes, he is old-fashioned that way—he still likes to get his personalized Digg-compiled news from his local print-on-demand service once a day, just for the fun of it. He enjoys the familiarity of seeing articles that he likes from his favorite personal and professional news sources around the world and voting on them and noting them for later reference by touching the communications-enabled paper.

Advanced language translation has made news and comments in any language accessible to him, just as it helps him in his communications with clients around the world. Sometimes he touches on the comments section just to see and to hear what his friends are saying about a topic, along with politicians and other important people who feel obliged to chime in on these topics. There are still professionals who gather news for a living, but they are mostly independent journalists, syndicating their own content and maintaining their own networks of contacts and relationships, which others value.

Though Cadoret likes the experience of his Diggpaper, he's not too happy with what he sees and listens to in it. Although his own global business is doing pretty well, the French economy is still suffering from a long decline. The remnants of traditional French industries not already migrated to China, India, and Brazil are still struggling through intense confrontations with workers who are upset about the pegging of their wages to world-labor-market rates. Through social media, there is beginning to evolve a global labor movement, which is fueling protests in many industrialized nations, including China and India. Although governments are trying to cut off the communications of these protests, the near-universal availability of wireless networking is making this very difficult. At the same time talented workers in knowledge-intensive industries are finding it easier to make their services available on a global basis through social networking services.

In the meantime, Cadoret notes in the world news pages that the global economy as a whole remains sluggish by traditional measures, as major currencies experience a deflation of their value. However, in traditionally poor nations, currencies are being bolstered by improving demand for their goods and services, fueled by social media linking investors, lenders, buyers, and sellers internationally on a more personal basis. Small producers on a global basis are becoming more adept at meeting the needs of niche markets quickly and effectively by listening to the needs of people in social media–enabled communications. The production and marketing efficiencies of traditional large industries are still useful for a core of hard-to-replace products and services, most especially scientific, technical, and medical equipment, but many other large-scale industries are rescaling their operations to deliver more "just-in-time" products and services in local markets and highly specialized global market sectors.

In the politics section of his Diggpaper, Cadoret discovers in his personally tuned news that there is a new bill in the French parliament that is addressing building standards. He touches the article to make a note of the public markup site for the bill for his review later in the day. Use of technologies to enable the public to develop and to comment upon bills has enabled citizens to have more input on the legislative process of France, providing more expertise and a wider array of public opinions and insights to create and shape legislation. Politicians are still essential to shepherd these bills through the legislative process, but with the openness afforded by social media's monitoring of legislative processes, there is little opportunity to cut old-fashioned deals in cloakrooms, especially because the moment-by-moment monitoring of social media enables politicians to see where the views of their constituents lie. Cadoret glances at news of political races for office, but he finds it a little boring. With laws now making it a felony to tell lies that would result in the political, physical, or financial harm of others and the constant openness of information about politicians through social media, there are few secrets and surprises exposed in national politics these days.

On the international front, though, Cadoret finds much that worries him. Changing climate conditions have devastated the lives of millions of people in the world. Continuing violent storms have devastated many cities along the shores of the world's oceans, forcing the abandonment of any large-scale settlements near the oceanfront. Much of the western part of North America has run dry of water, making the final salinization of the San Joaquin Valley almost moot. Western China, South Africa, and Western Australia have also fallen victim to changing weather patterns, accelerating the desertification of these regions. Canada, Scandinavia, and Northern Asia are experiencing both hotter summers and much longer and colder winters. Desalinization of ocean water is helping some rich nations to cope with these changes, but it remains an expensive option. Clean water is to Cadoret's time as oil has been to our time. Political turmoil accelerated via opinion-makers in social media from widespread deaths and loss of property are challenging national governments to come up with solutions, even as their national taxes are harder to collect from an economy driven increasingly by small international transactions and bartering.

Sobered by the headlines, Cadoret prepares for a walk into town to pick up some food and to meet with his friends at the local cafe. He confers with his home assistant, a robot that works with the home communication system to attend to basic household chores. The robot was a good investment, Cadoret muses to himself so cheap to get good help these days, why not? The robot's computer processing power is equivalent to that of a human mind, yet is no more expensive than what a personal computer cost back in 2008. Cadoret instructs the robot to remind his wife Estelle of their party in the evening when she awakes and to tend to some household chores. The robot asks some questions and downloads further suggestions for the best way to prepare for the party from a social media site—for robots.

In the village Cadoret eases into a chair at a small table in front of a street-side cafe to await some close friends. As he waits for them he views some messages to him on the table's hologram display, replying to some and then publishing some thoughts in his personal social media space. He could have used his mobile media device to view and publish these messages, but because it communicates with the table's hologram display anyway he finds it to be easier to read and more convenient. He is intrigued by the new electronic brain implants available that enable people to communicate with people using images and sounds projected directly into the brain, but he finds it to be a little too advanced for his tastes. His daughter Manon, however, has asked for one as a birthday present. "*Il n'y a rein d'importance*," Cadoret argues with her sometimes, but Manon argues that it's very important to her, even if it's not to him. Cadoret does well at his job, but like many professionals the competition in the global labor market for his services enabled by social media has not left him with an over-lavish lifestyle.

Because his friends still haven't shown up Cadoret brings up some of his social-network friends on "*le holo*" to catch up a bit, noting from the icons on the hologram hovering around the table that a few people in his network are in privacy mode. The automatic translation capabilities of his communications service work pretty well to keep his friends in China communicating with his friends in the United States during their conversation, but sometimes the subtleties of languages leave something to be desired in the translation. As he chats with his holographic friends, his village friends arrive, whom he introduces to his "*holo*" friends. His remote friends who speak French are invited to stay on for the conversation, including a friend in Mali, who has a keen interest in many French things.

As their conversation turns to local politics, a new icon begins to glow on the hologram display, indicating that the village's mayor has something to say about this issue. Cadoret activates the recorded thoughts of the mayor from an earlier conversation, which prompts them to request a live holo meeting with him. The mayor obliges, and their expanded conversation causes new icons to glow on the hologram display; politicians from other villages nearby whose interests align with this topic are being made aware of the conversation through their social connection, though none of them join in this time. They conclude their brief chat with the mayor, go into a group privacy setting on the hologram display, and for a moment discuss with one another what they've heard.

Cadoret realizes that he needs to get to his shopping, so he says goodbye to his local and virtual friends and walks down the street. He passes a woman who smiles at him warmly, but then looks at him a little more distantly; she's just seen on her GPS-sensitive communications implant that he's married. Cadoret makes it a point to keep that information public on his communication profile. As the woman passes by the stores, her implant is alerting her with information about merchandise in the stores that may be of interest to her and to people who are in the store who are in her social network. She "waves" to one of her friends in one store who also has the implant and has her own implant communicate a note to her mobile communicator of some items to research later on.

The woman goes into a store selling local and foreign handmade clothing, chats via her implant with the person in Morocco who made a skirt that she likes, and then walks out the door with the skirt; her implant has completed the transaction for her, transferring funds both to the merchant and to the dressmaker automatically. Her friends with similar interests, made aware of the transaction through her social media service, receive information about the store and the dressmaker automatically. The people chosen for this matching are selected very carefully for matches based on a wide range of personal activities and interests. Advertising is now mostly focused on matching people's real interests to the people who really meet them as precisely as possible and drawing them into personal conversations. There are still many brand-name goods, but for most people, brands are the people, goods, and services that their friends endorse.

Meanwhile, Cadoret stops by the baker to pick up the bread to which he has subscribed and to pick up a few extra loaves for the evening's party. He pays for part of his subscription on a barter basis by helping the baker with a small redesign of his shop. Being less on the cutting edge of technology, he still relies on the retina scanner at the baker's counter to complete his transaction for him as he enjoys a chat with the baker. He remarks into his mobile device how wonderful the bread is; his wife, who has turned off her privacy mode finally, looks at it through the hologram and agrees. At the greengrocer, Cadoret picks up his subscription produce, and then peruses some of the special items that he needs to pick up for their dinner; his mobile device pulls up some suggestions on the produce automatically and helps him to pick the best.

He also notes on the mobile device that the prices at one of the few remaining super-stores down the road are lower, but not so low that it causes him concern. Social media has made it easier for local merchants to succeed by providing better service and more precise inventory for natural and hand-produced items that local people really want. Many mass-produced items are now delivered direct from the factories in which they are custom-built to order, with purchasers able to select between specific factories the way that they used to shop through mass retailers' Web pages. Some local merchants do well acting as consultants for manufacturers, providing floor samples from various manufacturers and taking a percentage of the direct sale.

Although technology is everywhere in Cadoret's life, in many ways it seems as if there is less technology in his life than there was in his youth. With always-present communications networks and most of the world's knowledge and entertainment stored in computing centers, it is only the devices that he has locally that give a hint of technology, and most of those are designed to operate based on speech and touch. It's fairly rare that he uses a device such as a keyboard, and when he does, it's usually a holographic representation of a keyboard with a bio-feedback mechanism to simulate the feel of touching it.

Although speech-based social media has reduced reading by many people—most things are shared by speech or videos—the written word remains important as a means to learn things quickly that speech and symbols alone cannot provide efficiently. In many instances, people just speak into their communications devices and have their words translated into text automatically. In a speech-driven environment, social media has become all the more important a tool to facilitate work and everyday life, enabling people to communicate in groups more naturally and to facilitate collaborative learning and entertainment experiences.

How much longer reading will last is anyone's guess; Cadoret wonders on the way home. He's been hearing more people talking about protein computing, the merging of software and genetic engineering. The early experiments look promising, but ultimately he is glad that he will probably not live to think about the implications of computing based in cellular structures. As it is, the zoos filling up with re-engineered species from past eras are entertainment enough for him. Cadoret opens the door to his home, kisses his wife Danielle, hands his groceries to the robot, and prepares to begin another day of design work with his global colleagues and clients before a pleasant evening.

One Hundred Years from Now: Content Nation Offers a Way Forward

Eloise Cadoret is busy with her robot and her children Edouard and Camille putting the finishing touches on their packing up boxes at their home in Provence. After the death of her Mother Manon she chose to stay in the house for a while, which seemed like a good idea at first. The children were upset after the departure of their father for a new relationship, so having a familiar place to live would be comforting for them, she thought. When she decided to take on her grandfather's profession several years earlier, architecture still seemed like a fairly good profession to pursue, especially because she was able to call upon some of her grandfather's contacts from his social media network that he had willed to Manon upon his death and then given by Manon to her.

Unfortunately for Eloise, the shifting of the global economy left many of the descendents of those contacts in dire financial straits. Eloise was left with only a handful of people to provide any sort of valuable additions to her portfolio of clients. She has worked hard to build up her own clientele in nations in which the business and natural climate is more stable, but it takes time, even with the convenience and international power of social media, to get the accounts that will help her to make a living.

At the same time, France is hardly recognizable in many ways as the country of her youth, and less encouraging than ever for her own business. Without the centralized industries of past years and with the decline of agriculture as weather patterns have grown more violent, even people in formerly sunny Provence are challenged to lead what would have been a comfortable life a century ago. France is still a nation, but barely so. It has no military of its own, it has little budget for public services, such as education and roads, and many of its formerly public facilities are now owned privately by companies on contract to the European Union.

Where local governments are still reasonably prosperous, social media has enabled them to collaborate more effectively to develop public services autonomously. Though the uncertain economic conditions have made local autonomy difficult to manage at times, the capital that flows into business owners in Provence internationally through microcapital has helped them to do better than some areas of Europe whose economies and weather patterns make them less desirable investments.

Much of the world has suffered greatly in the past 50 years from the changing economy and climate, leaving nearly half a billion dead or near starvation due to widespread crop failures and problems with transportation. With violent storms disrupting ocean and air shipping more frequently, the assumption that goods could flow universally and uniformly throughout the world is no longer a given. Then there are the wars. With many parts of the world left with weakened central governments, the warlords of central and eastern Asia are looking at opportunities further abroad. Social media enables people to collaborate more effectively against these threats at a local level, but with thinning economic resources, it's not always possible to counter these roving armies, which also make use of social media to coordinate their bands of warriors rapidly. There are still large high-tech armies to counter these warlords, but they are deployed mostly to secure the dwindling resources of major companies. Increasingly war and nationhood are becoming disconnected from one another.

For the time being, though, the wars are still quite far from Provence, as Cadoret knows already from her communications implant. She had felt squeamish about having the operation to have it inserted into her brain when she was young, but now she barely thinks about its presence. Since protein computing has progressed to the point where communications implants can be living tissue, her ability to communicate with the world through her implant seems as natural as opening her eyes. The world's computing storage is moving rapidly to protein computing as well, with large caves providing safe environments in which the world's collective memories can "grow" together.

The natural growth of computer storage was a necessity, because it became less expensive to create computing power from readily available organic materials rather than shipping inorganic materials all over the world for manufacturing. Modern networking has done away with much of the "wired" world of computer communications, enabling organic computer storage to be built wherever it is most convenient, with great redundancy. As long as the planet as a whole exists, human knowledge is likely to remain intact indefinitely, but protein computing is still in its very early phases, mostly providing a safer and more easily upgraded version of earlier forms of computing equipment.

As Eloise tires from the packing, she takes a moment to rest and to pay attention to her implant's messages. At first, she wishes she hadn't. As the images of her world news icons appear as if hovering before her eyes, she decides to glance at the general news. Yes, she's aware that there's a comet fragment headed toward the earth. Yes, she knows that it's targeted to hit the middle of the Australian desert very soon. She's heard about it in detail for some time and tracks conversations of the experts that the world has trusted through social media ratings. She adjusts the personal importance of the story and it disappears from her display.

Eloise is more concerned with the messages from her friends in Vietnam, which are glowing brightest. Nguyen Van Anh, her best friend from her university days, has published a message that she's concerned about how the comet fragments might affect her family and is also on the move inland to Laos. Eloise can see in her communicator that Anh is already on the road, and confers with her friends in Laos briefly for ideas as to what might be a good gift for her when she arrives. Eloise had been thinking of moving to Vietnam, but she contracted into a new project through her social network that will be building a hospital in Africa. Although many parts of Africa have seen great death and destruction, there is a core of fertile regions in which "superclans" are using social media to collaborate on many key public initiatives.

Social media has accelerated the ability of local clans in Africa to build bonds of trust across a wide area rapidly, enabling them to collaborate on many local and regional projects that used to take central governments or companies to initiate. The global networks available to them via social media have also allowed them to access technical knowledge and financial support from interested people around the world, who become more and more socially integrated with these distant people, making them in effect global members of one or more superclans. These superclans may be fluid and overlapping over time as the need for technical support, trading partners, and social relationships shift, but their ability to sustain commerce, security, and health on a collaborative basis in a rapidly changing environment is making them increasingly attractive alternatives to hierarchical governments and organizations to ensure the surviving and thriving of many people.

Over time, many people like Eloise come to visit the homelands of the superclans, already familiar to most of them by name and face and touch through their embedded social media communications and eager to participate in their social fabric more fully, and to take advantage of the physical benefits of their collaboration. Although there is not much money for the project, Eloise will be a part of an international group of engineers and designers who will benefit from working in a region where food is plentiful and cheap and there is a willingness to use bartering and other non-monetary forms of compensation to make everyday life comfortable and comforting. Eloise will also use her skills for making handicrafts and playing the guitar to provide entertainment to the superclan—and to others beyond the clan.

Leadership in local clans still tends to go to the elders of a particular family, but leadership in superclans is more flexible—especially as more people arrive from different nations. In general superclan leaders arise from the discussions and collaborations of social media, with leadership and the willingness of people to follow leaders becoming self-apparent on a fairly instantaneous basis. Leadership conflicts in superclans are not uncommon, but the complex interdependencies built up for common projects hold factions to a minimum. The ground rules for superclan participation are clear, as are the grounds for expulsion by the rapidly expressed consensus of the superclan, so long-term conflicts within a superclan are fairly rare. Most people come and go on a purely voluntary basis, learning the benefits of global collaboration rapidly.

The superclan culture is an amalgam of local traditions and languages with the traditions and languages of their far-flung partners. Automated translation services have made it easier for people from many cultures to participate in this common culture, but the need to communicate in a common tongue when communications services are not in use is beginning to create some interesting twists in languages around the world. Education using common-knowledge resources available on the global communications network makes people aware of other cultures more easily, but still teachers relate these to the specific cultures of their students. Eloise's children are already very familiar with Vietnamese and African culture and share images and experiences with other children who are a part of Eloise's superclan.

Though superclans are an interesting development, their success on a global basis is hardly universal. Social media still enables more-traditional hierarchical organizations to succeed, but the ability of superclans to form and re-form rapidly to adjust to changing resources is challenging many cultures to consider more bottom-up forms of government and management. Mass manufacturing is still strong for many basic goods and those that require advanced technologies, but shifting market requirements is accentuating mass-scale custom manufacturing more and more. This has enabled technology to advance very rapidly, though with a greater variety of products and solutions within widely agreed standards managed via social media.

The other challenge from superclans is on a more fundamental level: many superclan leaders are women, who thrive in the collaborative culture of superclans and who find the increasingly oral culture facilitated by embedded communications of great benefit. Men still play a very important role in superclans, but with territorial issues of less importance to superclans than the ability to collaborate among many groups, warlike skills are of more limited use for ensuring their success. Notably, the warlords of central Asia are less interested in the types of embedded communications used by Africa's superclans; their communicators are designed for more heavy filtering of communications that facilitate hierarchical command.

Eloise ponders this as she looks at her children, who play hologram games while she is resting and reviewing communications with her peers. They are so different from many of the other children in the village, she muses. Protein computing communications implants are still fairly controversial with many people; ethical, religious, and legal issues have arisen that have put some people with the implants at odds with many of their neighbors. She gets many smiles when she ventures into the village to shop, but they do not last as long as before.

She still communicates with local and distant merchants as always in person and via holograms, but she finds that she is developing a style of speaking and interests that are not always similar to many of her old friends who have not opted for protein communications implants. She still enjoys French culture and the people of Provence as much as ever, but increasingly she is not sure what it means to be French. With almost every waking moment she is aware of the world and her place in a new kind of social grouping through her "always on" social media.

On the horizon of technology is a new development that has many people even more up in arms: the ability to pass on protein communications through one's own genes. Experimental versions of this technology are enabling people to develop protein computing for the human mind that is not only programmable but capable of merging its structure into the evolutionary code of humans. Not only will global communications capabilities be born into humans; they will have the ability to pass on their programming to future generations. "So much better to have a simple injection than that horrid operation," Eloise thinks. But....what will it mean? A touch of her grandfather's conservative outlook is still in her.

Eloise Cadoret's moment of rest is interrupted by a deep rumbling in the distance. She looks outside and notices a bright, glowing ball of fire passing through the air miles above her village. The comet fragment is headed toward its impact zone on the other side of the earth. It looks larger than she had expected. She decides to pay attention to the news alerts that she had dimmed out earlier from her consciousness. Now she knows why the icons were glowing so intensely. The comet fragment entering the earth's atmosphere is larger than expected. Much larger.

One Thousand Years from Now:
A World Transformed

It is late spring in Provence, France. Much of the landscape appears as it always does at this time of year now: covered in snow atop ice more than 12 feet thick. The glaciers flowing down from the mountains of the Alps are still to the north, but advancing by several feet every year. Small pieces of the rubble from the home of Georges Cadoret appear briefly sometimes in the summer months, but his village disappeared long ago, no match for the changing climate conditions in the aftermath of the cataclysmic collision of a comet fragment 900 years ago.

When the comet struck in western Australia the impact triggered massive earthquakes and tsunamis around the earth and deluged the atmosphere with debris. Millions of people died within days of the catastrophic event and billions more within the year as the debris blocked out sunlight needed for crops to grow and clogged engines on airplanes, ships, and other key forms of transportation. In all, more than a third of the world's population died from the aftermath of the comet collision itself, and a third more from the loss of habitats, crops, and farm animals within five years.

A near cessation of much of the world's industrial activity after the blast combined with the shaded sunlight to trigger a major shift in the earth's climate. Though there had been signs of an approaching period of rapid global cooling for several years, the heat from industrial output had masked its arrival in many ways. Now the glaciation of the world is well under way, with mean global temperatures already lower than at any time in the past 12,000 years. As usable territory is constantly shifting and people are on the move much of the time, ownership of key assets has become less important than being able to collaborate using the assets that are available at the moment.

Humanity has been transformed in an instant from a self-confident civilization to increasingly isolated pockets of human beings struggling to find the answers to surviving and thriving in the aftermath of this radical shift in global climate. Food, once plentiful, became a rare commodity almost overnight, triggering massive famines, wars, and a return in many places to a hunting culture. Nine hundred years after the collision of the comet fragment the world's population is beginning to stabilize at about 300 million people. Knowledge of agriculture, medicines, health care, energy generation, and other advanced technologies preserved from earlier years through global social media have helped to mitigate much human suffering, but the radical changes in habitats have left many people to focus on natural solutions available locally to address many of their problems.

This number of people, though a fraction of the world's population a thousand years ago, actually turns out to be rather a miracle. For a number of years, there was concern that the human race would disappear altogether, a victim of both unforeseen circumstances and its own negativity in the face of them. Many people, using the most advanced forms of social media, were able to keep in touch with one another through this period of radical transition and to sustain key relationships. Global economies are more fragmented, but goods and services are beginning to flow again, though much of the earlier industrial output has been replaced by natural produce and high-technology services for social media. Increasingly, mobile lifestyles make consumer goods less of an option for many; there are only so many things that are worth carrying from place to place.

The highly redundant global knowledge repositories based on protein computing had their own casualties during the climate shift, but in their highly stable underground environments, many of these knowledge repositories were able to adapt far more effectively than earlier technologies and kept people around the world in touch with one another and their common communications and knowledge assets. The lower population of humankind has provided them very ample ability to grow new storage that keeps up with people's communication and research needs.

Nations, as they had been known once, have virtually disappeared from the earth. With large centralized governments largely ineffective at managing life in a climate that is still shifting rapidly, the adaptive and highly scalable relationships formed through social media provided a more sustainable blueprint for global and local cooperation that enabled people to build consensus rapidly on trade relationships, renewed efforts at food cultivation, and developing technologies for the changed environment. People in this new era are used to building up trusted networks globally the way that used to be the purview of politicians and captains of industry. Investment capital has begun to flow again internationally, accelerating the growth of global business relationships.

One of the key models for success in this era has proven to be the "super-clan" model that had begun to develop in Africa and other regions 900 years earlier. Many of the world's successful civilizations are now based on super-clans, enabling many people to collaborate both locally and on a global scale and to change leadership peacefully through the informed consensus of people in their common social media communications networks. Leadership passes fairly fluidly from one person to another and may be ceded to people with special talents rapidly in times of crisis. Key assets are owned by the superclans, but within the clans, ownership is not as important as participating in the activities that lead to mutual success. Wars are not unknown in this era, but the complex networks of relationships built up through social media have kept many conflicts at bay, making it easier to come up with new value propositions in existing relationships rather than risking economic and social isolation.

Most successful in this environment are those who had inheritable protein computer communications implants tuned to the world's networked protein-based knowledge resources literally growing in caves across the world. With no additional technology required to reach these knowledge repositories, people with protein communications in their genes—people now known as "naturals"—have been able to build up knowledge and the relationships at an early age that help them to survive most effectively. Though add-on technologies can enhance the power of the naturals to solve problems, their ability to use social media almost from their first conscious moments has proven quite advantageous.

The genetics of the naturals has also created a schism of sorts in human society. People with external or electronic forms of social media technology are mating with naturals more infrequently, even though the dominant trait of their technology means that most children are born as naturals in "mixed marriages." The naturals seem to be relying more and more on one another to solve many of the earth's most challenging issues for survival. The culture of naturals is also creating a divide of sorts, with naturals appreciating certain kinds of stories, humor, and collaborative practices and other people just not quite seeing things the same way.

There is occasional violence and controversy concerning their role in society, but in general the ability of the naturals to adapt very rapidly to local and global opportunities seems to allow them to anticipate many of these points of social friction and to move on. Some have decided to forego the friction and set up their own communities, which still interact with others but that allow them to develop their own cultures in peace. Although there is still intense competition for many natural resources, game hunting is beginning to flourish in some regions, including as their prey some formerly rare species that escaped from world zoos in the wake of the global cataclysm—along with some earlier species regenerated via genetic engineering. The world's ecology is still frail and shifting, but the diversity of the world's species is beginning to reassert itself again, if slowly. Regenerated herds of mammoths are grazing in many places where they had grazed more than 10,000 years ago.

In one of these all-naturals communities in Africa, a child is born on this particular late spring morning, a boy who looks rather peculiar to his parents when he is first placed in their hands by the midwife. His head is rather large, longer than most babies' heads and a little more elliptical, and he has a somewhat small mouth. Other than these somewhat odd traits, he seems like a perfectly normal baby, though, so his parents are delighted, as most any other parents would be. They are aware of loved ones on their social network looking in on the birth, ready to bestow their social links to the new child, and of the network's identity guardian inquiring about the new child's name. The mother smiles, and says to the guardian in a rough French accent: "*Il s'appelle Adam—Adam Cadoret.*"

Ten Thousand Years from Now: Another New Epoch

It is late spring in what used to be called the Provence region in France. At the edge of a grassland stands a small band of people, clad in remarkably familiar clothes and with genetically engineered robots carrying equipment for camping and cooking. The glaciers of the recent ice age have retreated far to the north, leaving behind a new landscape of plants and animals. Our hardy band of descendents are on the hunt, but the abundance of large game such as mammoths, which their own ancient ancestors had been chasing through the recent glacial period for many of their meals, has given way to a mix of bison, elks, and plants with grains that are becoming popular foods for these nomads.

This band of hunters is on the move in part because of the seasonality of some of their favorite food sources, but also because they like it. They are the offspring of hundreds of generations of people who have become expert at living off of natural resources and at creating an abundance of natural resources through advanced genetic engineering. Most materials used in creating manmade goods are grown from bacteria farms that are easily created and moved; an abundance of foods can be made at will from a wide variety of genetic-engineering techniques. Hunger and want is rare in this world, helping world populations to stabilize.

Although these people are able to sustain themselves using highly advanced technologies, they are part of a culture that has chosen to live in harmony with its surroundings whenever possible, living off the land when opportunities present themselves, but having the ability to create nutritious foods, clothing, and shelter in many ways. They have more permanent camps and buildings to take advantage of less portable food sources and technologies at times, but in general they prefer a mobile lifestyle that enables them to enjoy many parts of the world as they please with their favorite people. For today, this group of hunters will return to a light, round, portable structure that resembles a Mongolian yurt—equipped with the latest solar and fuel-cell power technologies, of course. Their portable food-preservation equipment will allow them to share their hunting and gathering with many other people who have subscribed to their efforts. Nothing will go to waste and they will all both enjoy their efforts and profit from them.

As the people start returning to their camp, they pause and start laughing with one another. Someone in what was once called India has told a funny joke on their social network. They utter some chuckling sounds, but otherwise are fairly silent people. They are neo-naturals—the distant descendants of Adam Cadoret, people who have succeeded in large part by communicating most of the time through the networks in their minds that connect with people around the world constantly. Like Adam, a quirk of evolution has accelerated their ability to communicate through their genetically embedded social networks without uttering speech. Many of their "conversations" seem to happen automatically on a global basis, with universal concepts passing from one person to another in a universal language that can be translated into the very localized dialects that are preferred by many tightly knit clans for private communications.

Through the social networks of the neo-naturals they are rarely alone in the sense that you or I would understand it. They are always aware of the world of neo-naturals and the world of neo-naturals is always aware of them. Privacy can still be enforced as needed and desired and people are free to build or block relationships as they please, but in most instances it is considered a breach of etiquette to be off the network. There is a deeply embedded code of altruism in their society, which views everyone as an integral part of a greater organism and everyone succeeding through this organism. Unlike in past civilizations, though, their ability to succeed without any one person or group of people owning communications with others has enabled this sense of altruism to build much more flexible bonds of allegiance. Leaders come and go for specific tasks very fluidly, sometimes providing global unity for days or years and other times enabling small groups like the hunting party to succeed.

Although the neo-naturals enjoy their own company and are succeeding in surviving and thriving without much stress, there is still quite a bit of tension with clans of other species of humans. As populations of neo-naturals grew and became more successful than others in developing natural resources and high technologies, there were wars for many years as jealousies and tensions over shifting supplies and markets grew, eventually calling racial differences into question. The ability of neo-naturals to organize and respond more rapidly to military threats allowed them to prevail, however, even though on a daily basis such tensions are rare among their own kind. With populations of neo-naturals now in the majority and other populations of human species managing most of their affairs in collaboration with the neo-naturals through social media, tensions have been much lower in recent centuries.

The climate shifts in recent years toward more stable conditions have accelerated permanent settlements among the neo-naturals, but they are reluctant to emphasize this as a lifestyle. Individuals own things and trade thrives through advanced transportation networks that make it almost trivial to move from one place on the globe to another and to human settlements on other planets, but the ease of transportation has also made it far easier for people to be with others in their global social network at will, making getting tied down to any particular location as much of a burden as an advantage. Neo-naturals are automatically aware of where people and resources are at almost any time, so the fear of letting go of any one location as a permanent advantage for survival rarely arises.

In many ways, the neo-naturals are little different from us. They enjoy music, a good laugh, they get angry and sometimes even jealous. Much of what has made people humans for tens of thousands of years is still very much a part of them, but their ability to live naturally inside a global social network that has universal knowledge as a given for people's progress has changed their perspective on life and its goals. Individual accomplishments are recognized quickly in neo-natural society and rewarded often on an instantaneous basis. For the most part, it's the consensus of many people that drives the value in their society.

The passing accomplishments of individuals are rewarded on a personal basis, but it's the recognition itself that serves as most of the reward. Through the seemingly endless organic storage and sharing of global knowledge, nobody's published thoughts will go to waste. Everything that has been published by someone will find its correct contextual value in time. There is no need for pyramids in this culture, for people will not be forgotten; their publishing and their virtual images live on. In a sense, social media has enabled everyone to enjoy a particular kind of immortality, making concerns about lifespan and death in general somewhat less troubling to many.

On this late-spring day, philosophical thoughts about life and death are very far from the hunting party in Provence. They are enjoying a moment in the sun, laughing among themselves and with distant friends, breathing in the spring air and remembering collectively something fun that they did as children. The neo-naturals stop for a moment, form a line, and begin dancing in a herky-jerky fashion, arms pumping up and down, legs moving up and down madly in place. In their collective consciousness they pull up an ancient video of people around the world doing the same being led by someone named Matt. Then they see their social network appearing all around them, joining in the dance, everyone joining arms, pumping legs and arms, laughing—all for the joy of it.

The world has become a nation of publishers, and everyone is indeed a citizen.

Is This Our Future?

The futuristic scenarios that I have laid out in this chapter are pure speculation, of course, though hopefully speculation that will provoke some thinking about just how radical an impact social media may have on our work, our lives, and our future over time. Our survival as a species is hardly guaranteed. Our technologies help us to overcome many daunting challenges to human survival, but ultimately we are living organisms that have inherited most of our characteristics from animal ancestors in our distant past. What do the innards of a primate have to do with many of the challenges and opportunities facing our society today? Often it's hard to make that connection. Our technologies have so far outstripped our capabilities as living beings that we can lose sight of our humanness altogether.

Social media is a tool that asks us to reconsider how our technologies have evolved from beings who used social relationships based on language as our primary advantage for surviving and thriving in a complex and challenging world. The tools of publishing that were developed to form more-complex societies have taken many thousands of years to evolve to the point where they are beginning to catch up with our natural abilities to communicate and to form valuable human relationships. In a sense we are only beginning to learn how to be truly human publishers. Our ability to influence, to endorse, to lead, and to extend our bonds of altruism to others through publishing in ways that enrich our lives has just begun.

The good news that I get from considering the future of a world that is being transformed through social media publishing is that perhaps there is far more hope for humankind than we may be led to believe sometimes. Science-fiction writers can create rather bleak visions of the future, with wars, sinister machines, and other imagined evils plaguing humanity as much or even more than they do today. As we can see from the scenarios in this chapter, though, a better future will not be a perfect future. Even with our future evolution as living beings, it's highly probable that we will remain as human as ever.

Yet, what if our humanness grows in ways that call on our long-suppressed traits that have been in our genes for thousands of years? What if, using our own publishing, people decide on a different kind of future for themselves? It may take some humility on our part to get to that kind of future, but if social media can lead us to a world in which everyone's ability to publish to the world and to learn from the world takes on its full power, perhaps there is good reason to hope for such a future.

CONTENT NATION FUTURE RULE #1: *The future belongs to Content Nation.*

11 Conclusion: The Evolving Conversation of Content Nation

If you are reading this book after its appearance in print, then the latest president of the United States of America has been elected already. As I wrap up writing this book the election is in full heat, with many familiar themes being emphasized by the candidates, and the polls of voters showing a close election ahead. Regardless of the ultimate outcome of this election, though, one of the most telling moments in the growing power of Content Nation happened when the campaign for Senator Barack Obama made its announcement of his choice for a vice presidential candidate not by television or radio or print journalists, but through email and instant messages.

At about 3 A.M. on the day of the announcement, hundreds of thousands of people were told about Obama's choice of Delaware's Senator Joe Biden, including journalists for major news organizations who wanted to make sure that they were able to put out their reports on the announcement as soon as possible. Of course, most of the people who were eager to hear this news had already received it. One of the most coveted scoops that a journalist could break as news was communicated to the public without the assistance of traditional publishers. Journalists have played many important roles in this election, but this announcement to the public without the press playing a key role is indicative of how far Content Nation has come as a global nation of publishers. People delivering their own messages to the world is now the most powerful means of communication.

Putting It All Together

If I were to choose one thing for you to take away from having read this book, it would be this: you cannot underestimate how much our lives change when anyone can publish to everyone in the world. In ways sometimes small and sometimes enormous, social media has the potential to change our work, our lives, and our future in ways that would have been almost unthinkable only a couple of decades ago. Human productivity can soar to unimagined new heights. Markets can work far more efficiently and effectively to meet the needs of people on a more personal basis. Entertainment becomes not a passive experience, but a participatory sport in which anyone can play with anyone else. Politics can move into the hands of the people whom politicians are meant to serve. Society can both reclaim its roots as a means to connect people to one another through bonds of true altruism and leverage the most advanced forms of human organization to achieve astounding global and local goals that challenge some of our most basic assumptions about what humans can achieve as individuals, civilizations, and every scale of organization in between.

Perhaps most exciting of all, social media offers us the opportunity to consider what it is to be human in ways that humankind has not been able to explore effectively for thousands of years. When the people with whom we build close bonds and upon whom we rely for success in life could be anywhere in the world from any walk of life, the potential for our future as a species of life on this planet takes on a new and startling form. Instead of the organism of centralized civilization holding the keys to our bonds of altruism through publishing, we have been handed back those keys to create our own new civilizations as we please. Many will choose to enhance very traditional forms of human existence through social media, enlarging the rim of the Big Sombrero culture and economy with many rapidly evolving and shifting points of highly valuable collaboration and production, which can scale to mass goods and services very efficiently.

In enabling major shifts in where value is produced in human society, we will not be throwing away the advantages and legacies of modern civilization. Instead, we will be leveraging them to support new forms of value, allowing mass production and mass culture to benefit us when and where it pleases us, but being able to produce more value independent of the highly centralized distribution and control mechanisms of traditional civilization. The culture of artificial scarcity, encouraged by highly centralized publishing and marketing mechanisms, will give way through social media to a culture more focused on identifying and exploiting the natural abundance of human insight and innovation rapidly and efficiently, enabling more people to collaborate on projects large and small that respond to the threats and opportunities in a changing world more effectively.

In the process of becoming a society focused on exploiting the abundance found in human abilities, we are likely to see political changes as well. It will become ever harder to communicate political themes and objectives that don't have authentic support from everyday people. If the era of television ushered in mass communications that enabled the selling of politicians like tubes of toothpaste, social media ushers in the era of politics in which most facts impacting politics and policies are known instantly and openly. Political victories go to politicians who know how to influence grass-roots political conversations most effectively—again. Like many things in social media, the transformation that can come in political circles is less about technologies than it is about the ability of those technologies to scale rapidly and effectively to any level of human organization to build effective bonds between people.

Though many of our fundamental relationships may not change because of social media—we will still have families, friends, colleagues, customers, and sellers—social media expands enormously the range of contexts in which we can form close and valuable relationships and to focus rapidly on the most valuable relationships. The ease, affordability, and incredible inventiveness of social media publishing platforms provide us with a wealth of models through which we can form and organize our relationships, making it easier for us to form new patterns of highly scalable communities knitted together through the altruistic bonds of publishing. We will still be human in all ways, but we will allow our humanness to transcend artificial separations and bonds in favor of bonds that are closer to our natural relationships with one another. With social media, our humanness may take on new patterns in our relationships, but the cloth of humanity will be made more whole than ever.

The future looks bright in so many ways in a world powered by social media, even if it cannot replace some of our fundamental human darknesses. Thinking of social media as a way to change the genetic code of civilizations encourages us to recognize that evolving who we are as humans is not something that need be frightening or troubling. Our world was designed for change and for adapting to change. Inconstancy is the only true constant in the natural world, reminding us that the stability that we seek often in our own lives is an illusion. Yet, in the overall patterns of this world in the middle of constant change we can discover that our willingness to be adaptive to change enables us to find constancy; our civilizations become like the wind, on the move at all times, but returning again and again to press things forward without the presumptions of permanency. Social media encourages us to release our civilizations from the limitations of hierarchical control and to enable highly adaptive and flexible forms of human communication and organization to scale our ability to respond to change in ways that neither dinosaurs nor early mammals could ever ever attain or imagine. With social media, the opportunities for humankind to survive and to thrive for tens of thousands of years and more never looked so good. Content Nation provides us with tools that will help humans to endure longer than the pyramids.

Continuing the Conversation: ContentNation.com and You

I hope that you have enjoyed this book and that it has stimulated ideas that you would like to share with other people. You can do this anywhere using the world's abundant social media publishing resources, of course, and I encourage you to do so. In exploring places to create and to experience social media, I encourage you to visit ContentNation.com, the Web site at which this book was developed. At ContentNation.com you can experience content posted by me and other social media enthusiasts and become a member of Content Nation to add your own content; you can also create articles, weblog entries, and forum topics, build pages that embed content from other sources, build feeds of content that can be integrated elsewhere, and much more. Members of ContentNation.com may be invited on occasion to meet at special events and to join forces to develop new publishing projects that will carry the concepts and the content of Content Nation to others around the world. Regular weblog entries and topics posted for discussion will stimulate your own ideas and help you to meet other people interested your particular focus.

This book is just the beginning of the story of Content Nation. You and other people who wish to influence the world through publishing are the next chapter in the story of Content Nation—a story about influential publishers whose legacies of creativity have brought us so many new ways to survive and to thrive that will endure for many years to come. The story of Content Nation remains a story about you, one of the millions of people around the world who has the power of global publishing at their disposal to change our work, our lives, and our future. How the story ends is up to you.

The world is a nation of publishers. Be a citizen.

Photo Credits

U nless noted here all images and graphics in this book are royalty-free artwork licensed from Jupiterimages Corporation.

5, John Robinson, FreeRepublic, LLC
21, World Wide Web Consortium
41, Isabelle Trocheris, David Giovannoni
45, Shore Communications Inc.
46, Shore Communications Inc.
47, Shore Communications Inc.
48, Shore Communications Inc.
51, Robert Scoble, Scobleizer.com
59, Facebook.com, Apple Inc., C.C. Chapman
62, Hole-in-the-Wall Education Ltd., NIIT
63, From page 9 of IBM Report, "The end of advertising as we know It," by IBM Institute for Business Value, Copyright 2007, IBM Corporation
65, Compete, Inc.
66, Vero Pepperrell
68, Prof. Jayanta Chatterjee , Prof. T. V. Prabhakar, Dr. Runa Sarkar
69, Chris Thomas, Newsvine, Inc.
73, TechCrunch
74, HuffingtonPost.com, Inc.
76, SINA Corporation
77, Digg Inc.
79, Compete, Inc.
80, Robin Good - Luigi Canali de Rossi
82, BakeSpace, Inc.
83, The New York Times Company
84, The Houston Chronicle
87, Garrett, R. K., & Danziger, J. N. (2007). IM=Interruption Management? Instant Messaging and Disruption in the Workplace. Journal of Computer-Mediated Communication, 13(1), article 2
90, Jigsaw Data Corporation

91, General Motors Corporation
92, Information Technology Toolbox, Inc. and Lewis R Cunningham
97, GasBuddy Organization Inc.
98, Internet Marketing Center
99, Craigslist, Inc.
100, Amazon.com, Karin M. Signer, P. Schneider
105, Greg and Kat Baker
107, Dell Inc.
112, EepyBird.com
114, Facebook.com, Sebastien Ponton, Hayley Shields
117, Coca Cola Corporation
118, Facebook.com, Andy Harrison
118, Facebook.com, Coca Cola Corporation
119, Jay Hepburn
122, Penny Herscher, FirstRain, Inc.
124, NBA Media Ventures, LLC
125, Peter Harris
126, Bath 747
127, IZEA
128, Class A Splog
140, Central Intelligence Agency
145, ECNext, Inc.
149, Oracle Corporation
151, Nature Publishing Group
152, ALM Properties, Inc.
153, ALM Properties, Inc.
154, Compete, Inc.
155, LinkedIn Corporation
157, Facebook
158, myLayover.com
167, Dean for America / Democracy for America

169, Ron Paul
171, Is Bush Wired
172, Michelle Malkin LLC
173, Kos Media, LLC
174, Wonkette: The D.C. Gossip
176, Partrick Open Space Alliance, Matthew Mandell
177, Bob Adams
178, Bob Adams
181, Bev Harris, Black Box Voting
183, ActBlue
184, Slatecard
185, Obama for America
187, Burnt Orange Report
188, Clinton Democrats
190, Burma Global Action Network (BGAN)
192, Google, Inc.
195, New Zealand Police
196, The Conservative Party, U.K.
198, John Culberson
203, Stephen Hanafin
205, Saurier Duval, The Museum of Modern Betas
207, W. Andrew Elder
209, Magnus Kolstad
211, Facebook
212, John Blossom, Facebook
214, Muxlim Inc.
216, Shelfari, Inc.
217, MyBlogLog
218, Google, Inc.
219, FriendFeed
221, Scott Monty
222, NowPublic
226, Delver Communications Ltd.

228, ICQ LLC
230, i'm Initiative
232, A Little Pregnant
234, Wikimedia Foundation
236, Wikia, Inc.
237, Yelp
243, Sustainability of irrigated agriculture in the San Joaquin Valley, California Gerrit Schoups, Jan W. Hopmans, Chuck A. Young, Jasper A. Vrugt, Wesley W. Wallender, Ken K. Tanji, and Sorab Panday Proc Natl Acad Sci U S A. 2005 October 25; 102(43): 15355 (Fig. 4). Published online 2005 October 17. doi: 10.1073/pnas.0507723102. Copyright 2005 National Academy of Sciences, U.S.A.
250, Philip Tellis
256, Wikimedia Foundation
261, Randall Bennett, Joystiq, Weblogs Inc.
263, Doug Shore
268, Lulu, Inc.
275, Dr. Silvia Helena Cardoso
283, Boubacar Traore, Last.fm Ltd.
284, Commuto.com
286, LocalHarvest, Inc.
288, MicroPlace, Inc.
290, Ford Models
292, David Meerman Scott
293, National Aeronautics and Space Administration, Twitter
297, LG15 Studios, Jessica Rose, Ramesh Flinders, Miles Beckett, Greg Goodfried
299, Glassdoor.com
300, Wikileaks
303, Matt Harding

Index